IRON MEN AND COPPER WIRES

A Centennial History of the
Southern California Edison Company

By
William A. Myers

TRANS-ANGLO BOOKS

This is not the first time that Trans-Anglo Books has focused on the Southern California Edison Company. Back in 1965 we published Hank Johnston's *The Railroad That Lighted Southern California*, a history of the San Joaquin and Eastern Railroad, which provided access to Edison's famous Big Creek Hydroelectric Project in the High Sierras.

That book necessarily looked at only one facet of the Edison Company's colorful history. We are pleased now, on the eve of Edison's centennial, to bring to you the full story, as told by William A. Myers. Myers will already be familiar to some of our readers, for he authored *Trolleys to the Surf*, the history of the Los Angeles Pacific Company, published in 1976 by Interurban Press, parent company of Trans-Anglo.

This book was many years in the making. We think it will make a rich contribution to California history and we hope you agree.

IRON MEN AND COPPER WIRES

First Printing: January 1984
Printed and bound in the United States of America

FRONT COVER AND TITLE PAGE PHOTO: *An Edison crew installs 220,000-volt insulator strings on a tower in the La Crescenta Valley during conversion of the Big Creek Transmission Line to this new higher voltage in 1922.*
EDISON COLLECTION.

BACK COVER PHOTO: *Workmen adjust the servomotor that controls a tracking heliostat (mirror) at Edison's Solar One Generating Station, July 1983.*
JOSEPH O. FADLER PHOTO.

Library of Congress Cataloging in Publication Data

Myers, William A., 1947–
   Iron men and copper wires.

   Includes index.
1. Southern California Edison Company—History.
2. Electric utilities—California, Southern—History.
I. Title.
HD9685.U7S662   1983   338.7'6136362   83-17857
ISBN 0-87046-068-4

Published by
TRANS-ANGLO BOOKS   Glendale, California 91205

**Dedicated to the Men and Women
of the Edison Family—
this is your story**

JOSEPH O. FADLER PHOTO. 3

Acknowledgements

A work of this magnitude is necessarily the product of the cooperation of many people. The author regrets that by reason of sheer number, not all can be thanked individually, but he wishes to express his heartfelt gratitude to those who gave so generously of their time, knowledge, and resources. Many are members of the Edison family, retired or active employees who were eager to share their heritage; others are descendents of Edison or predecessor company employees, interested in what their ancestors accomplished.

Special thanks are due some whose contributions were especially invaluable. Edison's Chairman of the Board, William R. Gould, enthusiastically supported this project from its start, and graciously consented to write an introduction. A. L. Gustafson of the Company's Secretary's Department located many old stock certificates to be used as illustrations, and explained the complexities of early financial procedures. James Thompson Spencer, of Edison's System Development Department, who has 35 years of service with the Company, provided invaluable information concerning the history of interconnections, Edison's "Aluminum Highways," system reliability, and the naming of facilities. Kathleen Shigley, now retired, uncovered much of interest about the California Electric Power Company and its history.

Although they are now deceased, it was the author's good fortune to have known, if all too briefly, the irrepressible "Billy-the Wind" Young, and both David and "Dee" Redinger, all of whom provided many hours of fascinating anecdotes and insights into the earliest days of both Calectric and Edison.

Twenty years ago, the late Andrew Hamilton began to draft a history of the Edison Company. Although the project was never completed, his research notes and typescript proved an invaluable resource to the author, who acknowledges that several chapter titles and much of the information in the chapter "Energy for Victory" were borrowed from this earlier work.

Larry Burgess, the historian and "human dynamo" of Redlands, located old newpaper articles that shed new light on the historical significance of the pioneer Mill Creek Plant. Richard Fellows, grandson of the founder of Fellows and Stewart shipbuilders and a long-time friend of the author, discovered important information about Edison's historic Colorado River survey boat, the *Marble*. Joe Fadler skillfully produced many fine photographic prints for this project from negatives badly damaged by time. Mr. Carl Ferguson of Visalia supplied otherwise unobtainable photographs and biographical data on his grandfather, Ben Maddox. Dr. Robert Miller of the Santa Barbara Historical Society discovered a previously unpublished photo of the interior of that city's pioneer power plant. Bill Moore, the retired Editor of the Redlands *Daily Facts*, took time away from his own book project to furnish data on Henry Sinclair and Henry Fisher, and to give needed encouragement to the author. David Streeter of the Pomona Public Library found several fine photographs of the historic "Pomona Plant." To the Los Angeles Department of Water and Power, and to the municipal utilities of Pasadena and Riverside, are due thanks for providing pictures and historical data without any rancor over ancient history.

Finally, acknowledgement must be made to six very special people, without them this book would never have seen the light of day. Mac Sebree, publisher of Interurban Press, had the courage to take on a project much different in scope and content from past publications. Mrs. Lillian Castro resolutely waded through the author's poor handwriting and ignored many interruptions to type the manuscript. Rose Pearson, Charlie Basham, Linda Brooks and Stan Cann each carefully proofread the manuscript despite being given little time to do so. Lastly, realizing that a "thank you" is insufficient, the author expresses gratitude to his beloved wife Lynn for her help with the manuscript and index, for patiently accepting missed social engagements, and for keeping the new baby quiet while Daddy agonized over a manuscript that was written at a seemingly glacial pace.

William A. Myers

Table of Contents

6

Officers of the Edison Electric Company, November, 1907. Standing, left to right: Benjamin F. Pearson, Operating Superintendent; Russell H. Ballard, Vice President; Ray Raymaker, Superintendent of Overhead; W. H. Percy, Treasurer; seated, left to right: W. H. Darnell, Superintendent of Underground; John B. Miller, President; Al Selig, General Manager.
Edison Collection.

"Good Service, Square Dealing, Courteous Treatment"

8   The history of any corporation or institution is a story of people with courage, dedication, daring and creativity. This is especially true of the Southern California Edison Company and its predecessors, whose story spans nearly a century of challenge and progress.

Back in 1886, Edison's first ancestral utilities supplied a rudimentary electric service to a few dozen customers. From these beginnings, far-sighted pioneers worked to create an abundance of energy to light the homes and streets, run the electric railroads, power the factories and businesses, and irrigate the fields and orchards of Southern and Central California. Thanks to their dedication, electricity has become an indispensible component of our modern lifestyle.

Today, the Southern California Edison Company has become one of the nation's largest investor-owned utilities, third in size in number of customers served. It provides service to a population exceeding nine million people living in a 50,000 square-mile area comprising all or part of 14 Central and Southern California counties. This area includes over 800 cities and communities as well as some of the world's most productive farmlands.

THE EDISON ELECTRIC COMPANY
LOS ANGELES, CALIFORNIA
JOHN B. MILLER, President

President's Office, Sept. 26, 1905.

To Officers and Employes:

The Edison Electric Company desires to have the confidence and respect of the Public, with which it deals.

Officers, Agents and other employes should, in every reasonable way, endeavor to increase that confidence and respect by doing everything in their power to make the name of The Edison Electric Company synonymous in the mind of the Public for good service, square dealing and courteous treatment.

The Public gains its impression of the Company through contact with its representatives, and they will, therefore, be held responsible in every instance for carrying out the well established policy of the Company — "GOOD SERVICE, SQUARE DEALING, COURTEOUS TREATMENT".

Yours truly,

John B. Miller
President

William R. Gould,
Chairman of the Board and
Chief Executive Officer.
EDISON COLLECTION.

At Edison, we are proud of our established tradition of innovation and expertise in many fields: engineering, finance, operation and human relations. This spirit of creativity, a reflection of the need to operate within the public trust, has ensured the maintenance of a highly reliable electric service while responding to changing economic and industrial conditions and the social needs of the community. This tradition includes dedication to the motto first stated back in 1905 by then Edison President John B. Miller: "Good Service, Square Dealing, Courteous Treatment."

For over a third of the years of its history, it has been my privilege to have worked with the men and women who have been a part of what they chose to call the Edison family. In my later years, it has been a unique honor to have been among their leaders. I am humbly grateful to have spent most of my working life with these dynamic people—for me, it has been an exciting journey through a time of high adventure.

William R. Gould

The Pioneer Plants

Highgrove plant's engineer G.O. Newman beside original D.C. generator, c. 1887.
EDISON COLLECTION.

In the decade of the 1880s, Southern California was just beginning to awaken. The temperate climate and good agricultural potential of the region had long been a lure for the adventurous, but the expense and difficulty of travel discouraged most people from making the long journey from the East even after the Southern Pacific built a rail line to Los Angeles in 1876. This remoteness changed dramatically when the Santa Fe completed a second transcontinental railroad into Los Angeles in 1885. A fierce rate war erupted between the two

railroad companies, which quickly made travel to Southern California attractive and affordable. To accommodate the swelling tide of settlers, the huge cattle ranches that long had dominated the region, one by one, were subdivided into new towns and small farms. Once ridiculed as "the Queen of the Cow Counties," tiny Los Angeles shrugged off this nickname as she became the commercial center of the growing Southland.

Prior to 1879, only one electric lighting technology was commonly in use in the United States. This somewhat rudimentary "electric arc" system made light by causing an electric spark to jump between two carbon rods. A primitive, inefficient direct-current generator created the low voltage electricity for this technology, the chief drawbacks of which were its expense to operate, the danger of fire from the open spark, and the glaring brilliance of the light produced. Arc-lighting's most important American promoter was Charles F. Brush. His patented system was used in the late 1870s to light individual buildings in many cities in the United States. It was soon learned that although the arc-light was not really suitable for indoor use, it could be used for street lighting.

A Brush plant holds the distinction of having been the first central generating station to manufacture and distribute electricity upon demand to a number of subscribers or customers, when the California Electric Light Company began operation in San Francisco in September 1879. This "central station" concept was to become the cornerstone of the electric utility industry.

Thomas Edison in his chemical laboratory at Menlo Park, New Jersey, about 1879. Many of the experiments that led to the discovery of a satisfactory filament for the incandescent light bulb were performed here.
EDISON COLLECTION.

As this flood of new residents poured into Southern California's communities during the 1880s, they demanded the same quality of life they had enjoyed in the East. In addition to reliable domestic water supplies, telephones, street railways and other amenities that utilized the amazing technological advances of the late Nineteenth Century, many people were interested in the novel new method of lighting public streets using a mysterious "fluid" known as electricity.

Before electric illumination could gain universal acceptance, however, the objections to the arc-light system had to be overcome. In October of 1879, Thomas Alva Edison, already known as "the Wizard of Menlo Park," perfected an incandescent electric light bulb. Edison's light revolutionized the fledgling industry because it was safer to operate, easier on the eyes, and far less expensive than arc-lights. This invention, along with Edison's development of an entire improved system of power generation and distribution, marked the true beginning of the electric utility industry.

Replica of Thomas Edison's first incandescent light bulb, made on his original equipment in 1929 at the time of the 50th anniversary of its invention.
EDISON COLLECTION.

On September 4, 1882, Thomas Edison threw a switch to inaugurate electric service from a central generating station on Pearl Street in New York City. This plant, with its "Edison System" of generation and lighting equipment, was the first important attempt at extensive and continuing bulk power distribution. Its immediate success sparked the beginning of electric service in many American cities.

At first, the exciting electrical developments on the East Coast and in Northern California made little impact upon Southern California. As the old ways of life in the Southland began to disappear under the growing tide of new settlement, however, newcomers began to think about installing "new-fangled" electric light systems. In 1882, pioneer land developer George Chaffey installed a short-lived experimental arc-light at his Etiwanda ranch. Its powerful beam of light could be seen as far away as Riverside. Chaffey's demonstration created considerable interest among some people in Los Angeles, who began to think of electric street lights for that community.

Charles H. Howland, representing the Brush manufacturing interests, proposed to illuminate Los Angeles' streets by means of arc-lights placed upon high masts to be erected

Thomas Edison standing beside a bi-polar generator of his design, about 1885.
KEYSTONE-MAST COLLECTION, UNIV. OF CALIF., RIVERSIDE.

The resistance-grid voltage regulator bank at the Pearl Street Plant, from a woodcut in Scientific American, 1882.
EDISON COLLECTION.

One of the original "Jumbo" dynamos installed at Thomas Edison's Pearl Street Plant in New York City in 1882. These were the most efficient generators then made.
EDISON COLLECTION.

around town. A franchise was obtained and the Los Angeles Electric Company was organized to complete the project. Masts, 150 feet high, were placed at seven strategic street corner locations. Upon each mast were installed three arc-lights, which were to be supplied with electricity from Brush "dynamos" (generators) in a powerhouse on the corner of Banning and Alameda Streets. At 7:30 in the evening of December 31, 1882, Mayor Toberman ceremoniously turned on Los Angeles' first electric lights.

Although the Los Angeles Electric Company was that city's pioneer electric utility, it eventually lost its dominant position to more aggressive competitors. In 1904 it was reorganized as the Los Angeles Gas and Electric Company. Eventually some of its properties were acquired by Southern California Edison, but it is not considered to be the progenitor of the Edison Company.

The earliest true ancestors of the Southern California Edison Company were all organized in 1886. The earliest of these predecessors, the partnership of Holt and Knupp, was created to light the streets of Visalia. The next oldest, The Santa Barbara Electric Light Company, was organized to bring electric light to the Mission City, while the last of the three was the effort of an individual entrepreneur to bring electricity to Riverside, Highgrove and Colton.

An early newspaper article reports that the first electric lights were seen in Visalia in 1879, as an exhibit in a circus which visited town that year. In March, 1885, Visalia's progressive newspaper, the *Tulare County Times*, offered to donate a steam engine which had run its presses to anyone interested in putting into service an electric lighting plant. These offers notwithstanding, it was not until the day before Christmas of that year that Visalians heard of the first serious plans for an electric system for their community.

F. S. Holt, one of the renowned Holt Brothers of Stockton who were then manufacturers of farm implements, and who would later develop the Caterpillar tractor, constructed the Visalia Iron

This old stereopticon view shows one of Los Angeles' original street light masts near the corner of Main and Commercial Streets.
AUTHOR'S COLLECTION.

Original power plant of the Los Angeles Electric Company stood at the corner of Banning and Alameda Streets.
COURTESY LOS ANGELES DEPT. OF WATER AND POWER.

and Agricultural Works at Locust and Center Streets in Visalia. During an interview printed in the local paper on December 24, 1885, Holt announced that "a system of electric lights will be established in connection with the iron works," and noted that "the consumption of a half a cord of oak a day would produce enough electricity to illuminate Visalia." This was at a time when the magnificent oak trees of the Southern San Joaquin Valley were being removed by farmers interested in increasing their tillable acreage.

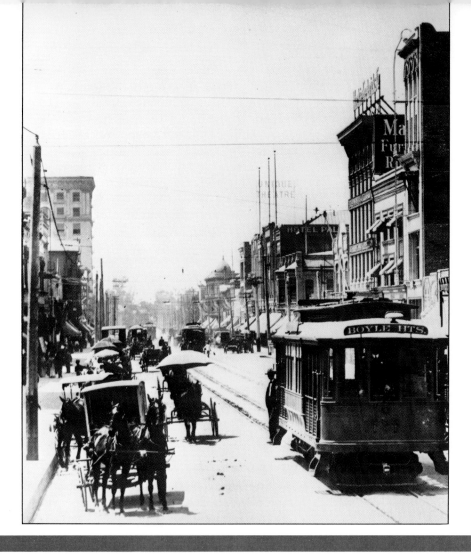

"The Works, which are located...in the rear of the new machine shops and foundry on Locust Street, are rapidly advancing toward completion, and it is now expected that the introduction of electric light will be one of the features of the celebration on the evening of the coming fourth—next Monday. A visit to the works by a *Delta* reporter on Monday disclosed a busy scene. Quite a large gang of men were employed on the building itself and in erecting the engine and other machinery....The engine and boiler are in position and nearly in readiness to run.... The dynamic machine which transmits [sic] the electric fluid, is capable of supplying 40 lights. Should more be required, as it is evident there will, another dynamo will be added...."

The system employed was that of the Western Electric Company of Chicago, then an independent manufacturer not yet owned by the Bell System. This was the first use of Western Electric arc-lighting equipment in California, which hitherto had been the exclusive province of the Brush Electric Light Company.

This view of North Downey Avenue in 1904 shows a district of Los Angeles served by the Los Angeles Gas and Electric Corporation. AUTHOR'S COLLECTION.

This pioneer enterprise truly began in May of 1886, when Visalian V. D. Knupp joined with Holt to form the partnership of Holt and Knupp. Orders were placed for the necessary equipment, which, as it arrived from the East, was installed in a brick building at the rear of the Locust Street iron works. In its July 1, 1886 issue, under the proud headline "The Electric Light: A Praiseworthy Undertaking by two Enterprising Citizens," Visalia's other newspaper, *The Weekly Delta*, described the new technology to its interested readers:

The Fourth of July, always a special holiday in that unabashedly patriotic era, took on special meaning to Visalians in 1886. As part of the evening's celebrations, Holt and Knupp's electric street lights were energized for the first time. The next issue of the *Tulare County Times* told of the day's events: the bands, parade of pioneers and soldiers, the oratory and poetry readings, the barbecue, the sporting events, fireworks, and, of course, the electric lights:

"Visalia looked even more beautiful in the evening than in the daytime. The city was flooded with brilliant light by the electric candles [arc-lights] which had been placed in position a day or two previous. The electric lights were a perfect success in every way, and the public verdict was unanimous in their favor. ... Judging from the general expression of satisfaction on the occasion of Visalia's first experience with electricity, there can scarcely be a doubt that the enterprising gentlemen to whom the city owes this attraction, will meet with deserved financial success."

A week later, another editorial reflected the popular enthusiasm by exhorting all businessmen to patronize the electric light works, for the good of Visalia. Alas, this excitement was short-lived. Although the plant was briefly operated to its full capacity, the service was extremely expensive. Despite Holt's earlier prediction, the wood-burning boilers at the powerhouse consumed over two cords of oak daily, which drove costs upward. By late August, this pioneer attempt at electric

Farmers came from miles around to see the Fourth of July parade and the new electric lights in Visalia in 1886.
LAKE COLLECTION.

service had ceased operation, its subscribers driven away by high costs and the unreliability of the system. Apparently, a fire caused by the arc-lamp in one subscriber's place of business was the coup de grace that forced the system's shutdown.

In October, 1886, V. D. Knupp bought out his partner and attempted to restart the service. Appparently service was rendered sporadically to those few customers who remained, but despite frequent calls to change to the safer incandescent lamp technology, Knupp's light works could not afford the conversion expense. Before long, mounting expenses forced Knupp to seek a complete reorganization of the business.

Early in 1887, Knupp joined with several new partners in raising funds for a gas plant to augment the electric works. In April, Knupp incorporated the Visalia Electric Light and Gas Company, capitalised at a mere $28,000, to take over his utility projects. The gas plant provided fuel for the boilers in the electric plant, and offered some lighting service as well. Use of the existing electric arc-lights continued. Financial problems remained, however. Knupp, eased out of the management of his utility company, left to organize Visalia's first telephone company. His partners in the Visalia Electric Light and Gas Company enjoyed no better success than had he, however.

By late in 1887, the electric lights had been entirely abandoned, and were replaced by flickering gas lights alone. This retrograde step is the only instance known to the author of the total abandonment of an electric lighting system among the predecessors of the Southern California Edison Company.

The curious history of Visalia's pioneer electric utility did not end with the cessation of arc-light service. In May, 1889, the company

solicited subscribers to a new incandescent electric light service to be provided from a completely modernised power plant. All during the latter part of the year the conversion took place, and on January 2, 1890, the first incandescent street lights were energized.

View south on State Street from Canyon Perdido, Santa Barbara, about 1890, showing one of the wooden arc-light poles at far right of photo.
EDISON COLLECTION.

This 1887 view of East De La Guerra Street shows the old Antonio Arrellanes adobe and an arc-light on a high wooden pole.
EDISON COLLECTION.

Financially drained by this effort, the company's owners sold out to a new group of investors, who reorganized under the name of the Visalia Gas, Light and Heat Company. Although gas lighting was discontinued by the new management, gas service for fuel purposes continued for some years more. The conversion to the safer, less expensive incandescent technology saved the fortunes of the Visalia Company, but just barely. By 1893, Visalia could boast of only 960 electric lights, and the still-high cost of service caused much complaint for the rest of the decade. More shall be heard of the Visalia Gas, Light and Heat Company in a later chapter.

Although the electric light plant in Visalia got off to a shaky start, that in Santa Barbara was quite successful, enjoying from its beginning great popular support. General Samuel W. Backus, who settled in the Mission City during the great population influx known as "The Boom of the Eighties," extolled the virtues of the electric lights he had seen in San Francisco. Out of his enthusiasm came The Santa Barbara Electric Light Company, which was incorporated on November 1, 1886, to bring electricity to that community.

Santa Barbara's newspapers swung their editorial weight solidly behind the project. The *Press* urged the City Council to execute a contract with the newly organized company for at least 10 street lights at a cost of $4 per light per week. It argued that "the electric light is a remarkable preventor of crime" and that "a well-lighted street will induce purchasers to come out in the evening."

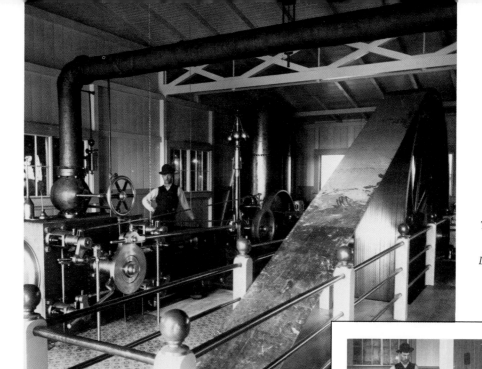

Two interior views of Santa Barbara's pioneer steam plant. Plant Engineer Tony De La Torre appears in each photo.
COURTESY SANTA BARBARA HISTORICAL SOCIETY.

the plant's promoters had to double the number of dynamos originally ordered so as to accommodate all those who wished to subscribe to the new service.

The *Independent* took a more immediate and practical point of view:

"Citizens who desire to show their public spirit and appreciation of the efforts of the organizers of the company are requested to subscribe the balance of the stock..."

During the following months, while the generating plant and distributing system were being built, excitement ran high. The public's interest was so great in fact, that at one point

On March 15, 1887, the system was ready. Two Thompson-Houston dynamos and their prime movers had been installed and tested. Two circuits had been strung through downtown Santa Barbara. One was to energize the powerful lamps mounted on 15 tall masts along State Street that would light that thoroughfare. The other circuit was to bring electric light to those homes, businesses and hotels that had subscribed to the service.

Promptly at 7 p.m. on March 15, the switch lever of Circuit No. 1 was turned and brilliant light flickered from each of the city's masts as well as the 150-foot iron tower at State and Victoria Streets. Then Circuit No. 2 came on and the lamps in the Post Office, the San Marcos Hotel, several residences and other buildings shone brightly. The crowd awaiting the historic occasion cheered loudly.

"Santa Barbara Brilliantly Illuminated"

At seven o'clock in the foggy evening of March 15, 1887, workmen at the Southern Pacific Railroad's construction camp at Rincon Point were startled by the sight of a brilliant glow that suddenly appeared over Santa Barbara, a dozen miles away. Some believed that the city gas works had exploded; all feared that the city must be on fire. More consternation ensued when, promptly at midnight, the eerie light winked out.

The mystery was revealed the next day when stagecoaches from Santa Barbara brought copies of the *Daily Press* carrying a story headlined:

ELECTRIC LIGHT: SANTA BARBARA BRILLIANTLY ILLUMINATED
"For the first time in its history the city of Santa Barbara was illuminated last night by the electric light. Promptly at 7 o'clock the lever at the Electric Light Works was turned and instantly a spark of light was seen on each of the thirteen city masts and on the high iron tower at State and Victoria Streets, and a moment later the whole city was lighted as if by pale moonlight ... The lamps burned with a clear, steady light and with little or no flickering.

"The unusual light attracted a large number of sight seers to State Street. The center of attraction was the Hawley mast, with its 8,000 candle power lights, which made the locality of the Arlington (Hotel) as bright as day. The influence of the mast is felt around four or five blocks. The scene as viewed from the wharf was very brilliant.

"At about 8 o'clock a dense fog drifted in from the sea and almost obscured the brilliancy of the lights, but the whole atmosphere appeared to be pervaded with a glowing light and walking was safe and comfortable in nearly all parts of the city ... At midnight, the electric works were shut down to be adjusted and made ready for the next night's work."

Thus, electric lights came to Santa Barbara, which was only the second Southern California town to get such service. No wonder, then, that those grizzled railroad workers were baffled, for few had ever seen that horizon-filling, white night-time glow that is such a familiar and comforting sight today.

The weekly *Independent* thrilled in print over the spectacle presented by the sight:

"The electric lights came out gloriously last night. The big mast at the corner of Victoria Street shone like an immense sapphire and flooded all the adjoining streets and gardens with a magnificent expanse of light."

Santa Barbara's original steam plant was replaced in 1901 by this handsome ediface, built on Castillo Street near the ocean.
EDISON COLLECTION.

Engineer De La Torre oiling a bearing on one of the Santa Barbara plant's Thomson-Houston dynamos.
EDISON COLLECTION.

In June 1901, the United Electric, Gas and Power Company purchased the Santa Barbara electric plant and system, which by now had grown far beyond its two original dynamos and power circuits. The old plant that had stood on the corner of Ortega and Santa Barbara Streets was replaced by a more modern steam plant at another site in town. This new plant was eventually destroyed in the great earthquake of 1925. Today, no trace remains of these early steam-plant ancestors of the Southern California Edison Company.

At the same time the Santa Barbara plant was established, Edison's third forerunner was quietly being organized in the little community of Highgrove, near Riverside. In marked contrast to the publicity and community enthusiasm which attended both the Visalia and the Santa Barbara projects, the Highgrove hydroelectric plant was born out of quiet negotiations between Charles R. Lloyd of San Francisco and the Riverside Water Company.

Near Highgrove, the water company's irrigation canal dropped 50 feet, and Lloyd proposed to use this fall to generate electricity. Negotiations continued until November 1886, when it was agreed that Lloyd could lease power privileges at the site for $250 per month.

Inasmuch as Lloyd had no company behind him in 1886 and 1887, he engaged Gustavus Olivio Newman, chief engineer of the Riverside Water Company, to design and build the Highgrove hydro plant. The Swedish-born Newman had immigrated as a youth and had much experience as a civil engineer, but in 1886 very few hydroelectric plants had yet been built—in fact, the Highgrove Plant is believed to have been the first commercial hydroelectric plant built in California.

The Highgrove Plant originally contained three water wheels and three direct current dynamos housed in a square wooden building with a cupola on top. Enough electricity was generated to operate 15 arc-lights each in Riverside and Colton. The exact date that service began is unknown, but the Riverside Water Company's account books show that Lloyd made his first payment for water use in October 1887. In 1888, Lloyd formalized his operations by incorporating the San Bernardino Electric Company, which modernized the

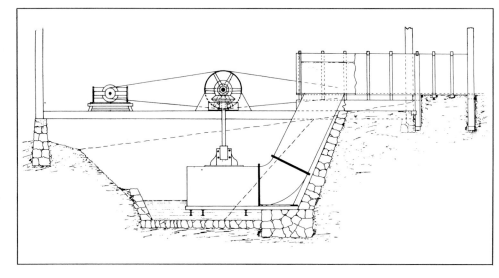

G.O. Newman's original drawing of Highgrove showing the complex gears and belts whereby the water turbine turned the generators.
EDISON COLLECTION.

Highgrove Plant in 1896. Ultimately this company was purchased by the Pacific Light and Power Company, which continued to operate the Highgrove Plant until it was destroyed by fire in March 1915.

20

Highgrove's builder Charles R. Lloyd paid the Riverside Water Company $250.00 a month "for the privilege of removing the electricity from the water" coming down a 50-foot drop from a nearby irrigation canal. Although the plant burned down in 1915, its foundations can still be seen today.
EDISON COLLECTION.

Whereas no traces remain of the pioneer steam plants in both Santa Barbara and Visalia, a substantial part of the Highgrove hydro plant survives today. Until recently, the big riveted steel penstock still carried canal water beneath Iowa Avenue in Highgrove, depositing it with a roar into the lower canal amidst the concrete foundations of the old plant. The area is still surrounded by a screen of eucalyptus trees planted by G.O. Newman when he was plant engineer in the late 1880s. Interestingly, until 1952, Southern California Edison continued to lease power privileges on the site of its first

In 1888, Charles R. Lloyd's San Bernardino Electric Company built a small hydro plant on Warm Creek where it crossed Mill Street in San Bernardino. When the water supply proved inadequate, steam equipment was installed in the same building. This plant was interconnected with the Highgrove plant. That same year saw a steam plant go into service in Pasadena, again primarily for arc-type street lighting.

In 1890, an energy war broke out in the City of Ventura between two long established utilities as each tried to capitalize on the popularity of electric lighting. The Santa Ana Water Company, which had provided the city's domestic water supply since 1870, organized a subsidiary, the Ventura Land and Power Company, to build a small hydroelectric plant on the Ventura River and to operate an electric lighting system. Not to be outdone, the Ventura Gas Company reorganized as the Ventura Gas and Electric Company and constructed its own power plant, using a gas engine as a prime mover. The gas company's plant was finished first and was energized on August 8, 1890. Apparently, it was more of a show of defiance, for the plant ran only for a few hours before shutting down forever. The

In 1902, Highgrove plant operator Guy Garner poses next to recently installed A.C. generator.
EDISON COLLECTION.

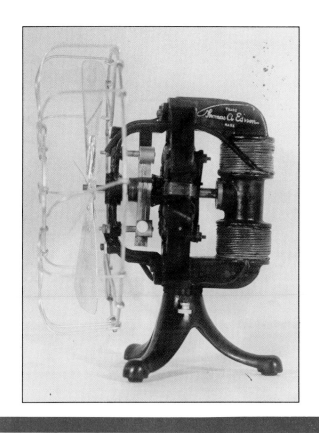

ancestral hydro plant from the Riverside Water Company for the same amount of $250 per month that had been negotiated so long before by Charles R. Lloyd.

Shortly after the establishment of the Visalia, Santa Barbara and Highgrove plants, several other pioneer electric utilities began service in various Southern and Central California communities. Eventually all of these systems would be consolidated into the Southern California Edison Company.

water company's plant was more successful. It began operation two weeks later, primarily for street lighting, and soon was providing service throughout the city of Ventura.

Primitive though these pioneer plants and their technologies seem today, they were warmly greeted by the communities they served. To most Californians, for whom memories of the privations of the frontier were still quite vivid, the brilliance of electric service was a comforting harbinger of civilization.

Although lighting was the first service provided by most power plants, other uses for electricity were introduced as the plants became more efficient and reliable. This D.C. fan is one early electric appliance.
EDISON COLLECTION.

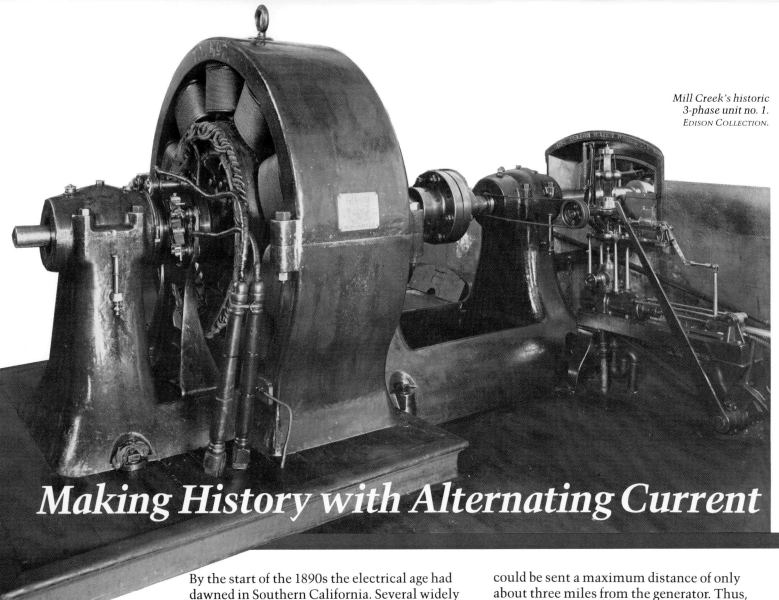

Making History with Alternating Current

By the start of the 1890s the electrical age had dawned in Southern California. Several widely separated communities already were receiving electric service, and others were clamoring for it. These pioneer power plants all at first used low-voltage direct current (D.C.) dynamos. Direct current, in which electrons flow in one direction from positive to negative poles as in a storage battery, could not be changed in voltage with the technology of that early era. Therefore the low generator voltage was also the transmission voltage. As a result, electricity

could be sent a maximum distance of only about three miles from the generator. Thus, these early plants could most economically serve urban areas with a concentrated population.

Fortunately, at this time, alternating current (A.C.) technology was emerging from American and European laboratories. Alternating current, in which the electron flow is reversed at split-second intervals, has the ability to be changed in voltage through use of the principle of inductive transformation. This meant that the output of alternating current generators could be raised to substantially higher voltages, enabling the energy to be transmitted great distances over wires of conventional diameters.

By 1890, a single-phase alternating current system developed by Nikola Tesla, William Stanley and others, was being marketed through the Westinghouse organization, and was beginning to find use in electric lighting installations. These A.C. generators produced a higher voltage that enabled service to be extended up to a distance of about five miles, substantially farther than with the older D.C. technology. An important component of these new, higher-voltage A.C. systems was the "converter," or transformer as it is known today, which reduced the high distribution voltage to the lower 120 volts that had already become the standard for safe interior wiring.

In 1890, alternating current generators were put into service in four of the pioneer power plants already in operation in Southern California—Santa Barbara, Highgrove, Visalia and Pasadena. In each case, the new machines were installed to increase the plant's capacity and to extend the zone in which service could be rendered. Additionally, a new electric plant went into operation in Santa Ana, where the A.C. machine was powered by a massive gas engine, the primitive single-cylinder progenitor of a modern propane-powered engine.

Far to the north of Los Angeles, in Mono County, an even more important A.C. plant went into service on August 18, 1892, when the Standard Consolidated Mining Company at Bodie began using a 120 horsepower synchronous alternating current motor to operate its mill. A small hydroelectric plant on Green Creek generated electricity that was sent the 12½ miles to Bodie at a pressure of 2500 volts. Although strictly speaking a private plant, it was nevertheless a commercial success, and drew much attention in the technical press.

Despite a growing awareness of the benefits of A.C. technology, it was still a long way from supplanting the well established D.C. system. Alternating current's cumbersome, inefficient sychronous motors precluded wide-spread power applications for the new technology, and its potential for truly long distance transmission was as yet untapped. By dealing with these weaknesses, two of the most important ancestral plants of the Southern California Edison Company played major roles in the commercial development of alternating current.

Dr. Cyrus Grandison Baldwin was appointed in 1890 to be the first president of the struggling little Pomona College. To relax from his administrative duties, Dr. Baldwin sometimes explored nearby San Antonio Canyon. As a result of his hikes he became interested in the idea of harnessing the fall of water around a ridge in the canyon known as the "Hogsback" to generate electricity to illuminate the streets of Pomona. Fired with enthusiasm, Baldwin presented the idea to the Pomona Board of Trade (Chamber of Commerce) and was promptly named chairman of a "Water Power Committee."

Dr. Cyrus Grandison Baldwin.
EDISON COLLECTION.

A.W. Decker at the San Antonio Canyon Plant.
EDISON COLLECTION.

Decker was a tuberculosis sufferer who had come to Southern California for its clean air and warm climate. He also was an engineer of extraordinary imagination and ability, and contributed much in his short lifetime. He held patents on a safety brake for elevators, improvements in electroplating, and an electric marking device for the manufacture of wooden rulers. In addition to his pioneer work in alternating current, he also designed the original electric system for the Mount Lowe Railway, the world's first mountain trolley line. It is a tragedy that Decker was little known in his own time and that his contributions are largely forgotten today.

Decker clearly saw that the Company's problem was not in designing a power plant to use the waters of San Antonio Creek. Rather it was how to transmit the resulting energy 14 miles to Pomona, the longest distance yet attempted for commercial electric service. Other engineers were skeptical of the possibility, but Decker knew of experiments in Germany, where high-voltage A.C. had been sent a long distance as part of a demonstration for the Frankfurt Exposition. Convinced that

Engineer Decker's handwritten notes were printed as a prospectus for the San Antonio Light and Power Company.
EDISON COLLECTION.

A. W. Decker in 1888, the year he settled in Southern California.
EDISON COLLECTION.

Baldwin knew nothing of electricity, but he visited the small hydro plant recently installed in Ventura and became convinced of the success of his idea. After some complications in securing water rights in the Canyon, Baldwin and other prominent Pomonans organized the San Antonio Light and Power Company in 1891. With a fortuitous stroke of genius, Mr. Almarian William Decker was engaged to be the company's engineer.

such an experiment could be made to be a commercial success, Decker specified installation of one 120-kilowatt single-phase A.C. generator with an output of 1100 volts, which would be increased to a then unheard-of 10,000 volts by using massive oil-filled "step-up" transformers. To arrive at this transmission line voltage, Decker reckoned that approximately 1000 volts of "pressure" would be needed for each mile of distance the energy would be transmitted, a rule-of-thumb that became convention for years afterward. Decker

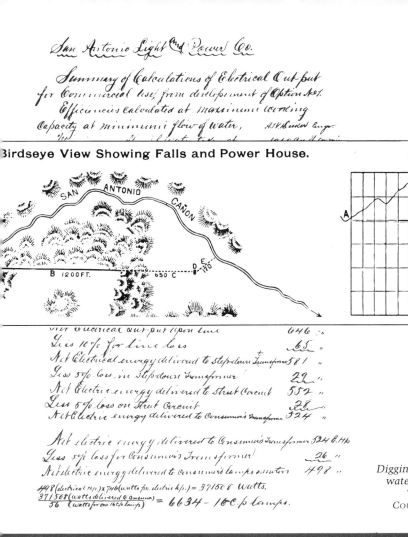

San Antonio Light and Power Co.

Summary of Calculations of Electrical Out-put for Commercial Use, from development of Option No. 1.

Efficiencies calculated at maximum working capacity at minimum flow of water,

Birdseye View Showing Falls and Power House.

SAN ANTONIO CAÑON
B 1200FT. 650 C

Profile Showing Levels.

3800F.
3500F.

Total electrical out-put upon line 646
Less 10% for line loss 65
Net Electrical energy delivered to Step-down Transformer 581
Less 5% loss in Step-down Transformer 29
Net Electric energy delivered to Street Circuit 552
Less 5% loss on Street Circuit 28
Net Electric energy delivered to Consumer's Transformer 524

Net electric energy delivered to Consumer's Transformer 524 E. Hp.
Less 5% loss for Consumer's Transformer 26
Net electric energy delivered to Consumer's lamps & motors 498

498 (Electrical Hp.) × 746 (watts per electric h.p.) = 371508 Watts.

371508 (watts delivered to Consumer) / 56 (watts for one 16 C.P. lamp) = 6634 − 16 C.P. lamps.

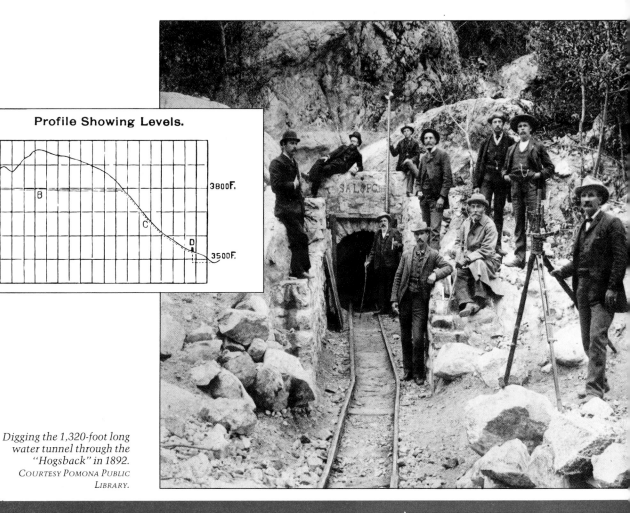

Digging the 1,320-foot long water tunnel through the "Hogsback" in 1892.
COURTESY POMONA PUBLIC LIBRARY.

---

developed by the Water-wheels into useful work.

Total efficiency of Electrical System 63%, i.e. — 63% of the power actually developed by the water-wheels, can be converted in electric energy and delivered to the Consumer as light.

Total efficiency of the entire System, delivered in electrical work 53%, i.e. — 53% of the theoretical power of the water-fall can be delivered to the Consumer as useful electrical work.

53% of 936 (theoretical Hp of waterfall) = 496 E.Hp. can be delivered

To Los Angeles 107 miles of Circuit, Cost of copper wire $67500.

San Bernardino	60	"	25500.
Pomona	30	"	6360.
Ontario	26	"	5512.

further proposed that at the other end of the transmission line, additional transformers would lower the line voltage to 1000 volts for safe distribution to customers.

It was Decker's incredible proposals to increase the line voltage above that of the generator output, to use oil-filled transformers and to use so high a voltage as 10,000 volts that caused contemporary engineers to scoff. When Dr. Baldwin delivered Decker's specifications to the Westinghouse Manufacturing Company, at

that time the nation's principal builder of A.C. equipment, the engineers of that company declared the plans impractical and refused to have anything to do with them. Still enthusiastic, Dr. Baldwin consulted with William Stanley, inventor of the modern inductive transformer. Stanley declared the plans feasible, whereupon Westinghouse agreed to construct the machinery.

to everyone's chagrin, not a drop came down into the plant's waterwheels! It was discovered the redwood boards that lined the long water tunnel leaked badly into the surrounding porous rock. Several weeks of delay had to be endured while the tunnel was relined with concrete. At last, on November 28, 1892, the plant was energized and electricity flowed at 10,000 volts over the 14 mile-long line to Pomona. A month later, on December 31st, a second line extending 29 miles to San Bernardino was placed into service. This established a world's record for commercial long-distance electric transmission.

The ideas of Almarian Decker were vindicated. His oil-filled transformers became standard in the industry, but the main reason why his San Antonio installation drew attention from around the world was his unique concept of step-up, step-down transformation of current for long-distance transmission of electricity. A technology had finally been developed that could enable electric service to be extended to any customer, no matter how remote he was from a generating station.

Interior of the Pomona Plant, showing switchboard at far left. The bank of transformers which increased the generator voltage can be seen in the left rear, while the generators themselves are in the right foreground.
COURTESY POMONA PUBLIC LIBRARY.

26 *This view of Second Street in Pomona taken about 1895 shows an arc-light hanging over the intersection. Energy for these lights came from the Pomona Plant in San Antonio Canyon.*
COURTESY POMONA PUBLIC LIBRARY.

After this controversy was settled, it took another year to construct the power plant. Most time-consuming was the digging of a 1300-foot-long tunnel through the Hogsback to carry the water diverted from San Antonio Creek to the power plant's penstocks. Eventually, however, the plant seemed ready. Dr. Baldwin, Engineer Decker, and many of the company's stockholders journeyed up the boulder-strewn canyon to see the plant go into operation. While all watched, a signal was given and water was turned into the tunnel, but

While A.C. history was being made in San Antonio Canyon, another important breakthrough was being developed 40 miles to the east in the citrus-growing community of Redlands. In October of 1892, Henry Harbison Sinclair and other Redlands capitalists incorporated the Redlands Electric Light and Power Company. They intended to produce hydroelectric energy at a plant to be built on Mill Creek, eight miles away, a distance that called for an alternating current installation. The problem was that the Union Ice Company,

Dynamo No. 2 at the Pomona Plant.
EDISON COLLECTION.

the new power company's most important potential customer, wished to install large electric motors in its ice manufacturing plant at Mentone.

No successful self-starting single-phase alternating current motor had yet been developed. Up to this time, at the handful of places where A.C. motors had been installed, including the Bodie plant mentioned earlier, the cumbersome synchronous motors required elaborate means to start and synchronize the motor, and required constant attendance. This clearly was not satisfactory compared to the ease whereby motors were operated on existing D.C. systems.

Impressed by the creativity of the San Antonio plant, that was then nearing completion, the Redlands men engaged Almarian Decker to design their plant as well. Once again, Decker's specifications were revolutionary. The very first sentence called for use of a three-phase alternating current system, an idea he had considered for the Pomona Plant, but which then had been rejected out of hand by Eastern manufacturers. This time, the newly organized General Electric Company was willing to bid on the job, and designed a new type "TY" 3-phase A.C. generator, a 250 kilowatt machine with an output of 2400 volts.

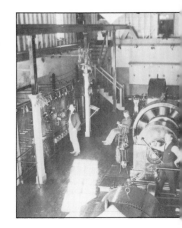

Three men were needed to operate the Mill Creek Plant in 1900. Here the day shift poses for their picture.
EMORY CHASE PHOTO.

27

Unit No. 1 at the Pomona Plant. The current collector rings of this single-phase A.C. machine are at left, and a big flywheel is at right.
COURTESY POMONA PUBLIC LIBRARY.

This new generator could operate motors without the need for constant attention. Better yet, these three-phase motors were self-synchronizing and could be started or stopped independently of the generator. Best of all, this new three-phase alternating current technology delivered a much smoother power torque to rotating machinery, and proved to be more energy efficient than the older single-phase A.C. systems.

Life at Mill Creek

At the dawn of the Twentieth Century, the operators at Mill Creek No. 1 hydro plant worked at one of the most remote places on the fledgling system of the Edison Electric Company. Although Redlands was only eight miles from the powerhouse, to get there involved a walk of two and-a-half hours, even longer if Mill Creek was swollen with storm runoff. The dubious delights of distant Los Angeles could be reached only after an hours-long ride on the local train from Redlands.

Around the powerhouse was a cluster of buildings: a bunkhouse for the unmarried men, cottages for married men and their families, a house for the plant superintendent, a machine shop and a barn. This small community was reasonably self-sufficient. It had to be, for there were times when the weekly supply wagon from Redlands couldn't get through.

The plant operators put in arduous 12-hour days. Before automatic governing devices were introduced, much of that time was spent standing in one position with his hands upon valves regulating water flow to the water wheels, eyes upon the voltage meter, alert to adjust to fluctuations in demand. Synchronizing generators to the system was still by trial and error. Repairs to equipment were made with what primitive tools were available, and it was fortunate when one of the crew had had prior experience as a blacksmith.

Perhaps because of the isolation and hard work, the people at Mill Creek were resourceful, close-knit and friendly. They enjoyed the outdoor life and shared hobbies. Two such young men were Emory Chase and William Cross, both operators at Mill Creek No. 1 from 1900 to 1903. During their off-duty hours they were avid amateur photographers, and have left us images of the innocence and sense of duty of that long-ago era.

Mill Creek's operating staff pose for a formal portrait by the Company photographer in 1913. Only a year later, most of this landscaping was swept away in a flood.
EDISON COLLECTION.

At their cabin up in Mill Creek Canyon, the wife and children of the headworks tender stare at the camera.
EDISON COLLECTION.

Off-duty high-jinks helped to relieve the weight of responsibility the plant operators daily carried.
WILLIAM CROSS PHOTO.

The children of Mill Creek's flume tender enjoy a ride on a gentle donkey.
EDISON COLLECTION.

Mill Creek's operating crew, the plant superintendent and his wife pose for an informal portrait.
WILLIAM CROSS PHOTO.

In December 1892, the history-making project got underway. A diversion dam was built in the gorge where Mill Creek came out of the San Bernardino Mountains, and a riveted steel penstock was laid to the plant site. The cement, lumber and machinery for the new powerhouse were laboriously dragged up the canyon from the end of the railroad at Mentone. Unfortunately, Engineer Decker was not able to supervise the project closely. His involvement with the construction of the Mount Lowe Railway, then being built near Pasadena, and his weakening health due to worsening tuberculosis, kept him away from Redlands. In Decker's absence, a young engineer named O.H. Ensign was brought in to oversee construction.

Sadly, Almarian Decker died on August 3, 1893, before the Mill Creek plant was completed, and so never saw the fruition of his far-reaching ideas. It was left to Engineer Ensign to complete the electric installation and to conduct the acceptance tests.

On September 7, 1893, the two original three-phase generators at Mill Creek first produced energy. At the power plant on that historic day was Dr. Louis Bell of General Electric, who had come West to solve the problem of how to synchronize the operation of these two units. He developed an acoustic device soon nicknamed "the growler" by the plant crew because of the noise it made.

Orange Street in Redlands, about 1890. Power poles are on the left side of the street, telephone poles on the right. An arc street light hangs over the middle of the street.
COURTESY MOORE HISTORICAL FOUNDATION.

Management and office staff of the Redlands Electric Light and Power Company stand in front of their office, about 1898.
EDISON COLLECTION.

Only primitive tools were available to help with plant repairs. Here Mill Creek's Unit No. 3 receives an overhaul.
EMORY CHASE PHOTO.

The people of Redlands enthusiastically welcomed the new power source. Within two and a half years an additional generator had to be installed at the Mill Creek plant to accommodate the growing demand. Interestingly, as early as 1894, motors were being installed to pump water to irrigate some of Redlands' many orange groves, the earliest known use of electricity in irrigation pumping service.

Thus, in a brief span of months in 1892 and 1893, electric technology and the fledgling electric utility industry were revolutionized by these two pioneer hydroelectric power plants built in Southern California. The San Antonio plant established the commercial feasibility of long-distance transmission. The Mill Creek plant introduced three-phase alternating current, which was destined to become the type of electricity generated virtually everywhere.

Sadly, the San Antonio plant did not survive to great age. It was plagued throughout its short operating lifetime by an inadequate supply of water. During 1898 and 1899, then the two driest years on record in Southern California, a temporary steam boiler and engine was installed to run one generator. It is therefore ironic that the plant was heavily damaged by a flood early in 1900. A year later, the Sierra hydro plant, a new facility of slightly larger capacity, was built a half mile below the old plant and utilized much of the existing water diversion system. It remains in service today.

Interior of the Producers packing house at Redlands, an early customer for Mill Creek's electricity.
Edison Collection.

The Mill Creek plant has been more fortunate. The original generators were used until 1934, when they were replaced with one larger unit. Thus modernized, the plant remains in service today as Southern California Edison's Mill Creek No. 1 plant. It has the distinction of being the oldest active poly-phase power plant in the United States. Appropriately, one of the two historic original generators has been preserved and is on display at the station.

Interior of the Mill Creek Hydro Plant in 1898. Due to drought conditions, Unit No. 2 has been belted to a steam engine placed just outside the west wall. In the right foreground are D.C. exciters and arc-light dynamos.
Edison Collection.

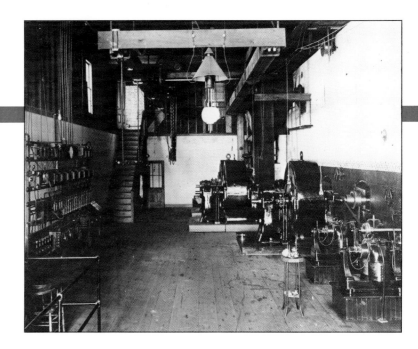

Birth of the Edison Name

By 1896, with a population approaching 100,000, the City of Los Angeles was well on its way to becoming a major metropolis. Several leading citizens were expressing concern that electric service had not kept pace with the city's expansion. The Los Angeles Electric Company, which had been operating an arc-lighting system on the city's thoroughfares since 1882, was unable to fulfill more than a small part of the burgeoning demand for residential and industrial electric service. The Company had replaced its original steam plant with a larger facility at Alameda and Palmetto Streets, had increased the number of street lighting masts to 35, and had introduced alternating current service, but to many, these improvements seemed inadequate. Indeed, Los Angeles' several streetcar companies, already as a group the largest consumers of electricity in the city, operated their own generating plants and in some areas offered electric service to those living alongside their trolley lines.

This view of Fourth Street looking east from Hill shows part of the downtown area served by Edison, whose main office was at 120 East Fourth Street. AUTHOR'S COLLECTION.

of today's Southern California Edison Company, the West Side Lighting Company paved the way for the introduction of the Edison name, and originated the skilled management team that would guide Edison's destiny for many years.

Peck and Wright first formed a partnership to conduct a lighting business as early as 1888, when they entered into a street lighting contract with the then-independent city of San Pedro. An expenditure of about $2,000 secured for the partners a small steam generating plant that was quickly placed into operation. Unfortunately, in 1892 the Federal Government decided against appropriating money to improve the harbor at San Pedro, which immediately threw the town into a recession. The town trustees cancelled their street lighting contract, leaving the little power plant with insufficient business. It was shut down, and later, in the absence of Peck, Wright sold the plant for scrap.

Upon his return, Peck persuaded Wright to repurchase the light plant and relocate it in Los Angeles, an area of much greater potential. For

This situation persuaded Elmer E. Peck, an electrical engineer; Walter S. Wright, an attorney; George H. Barker, a merchant; and William R. Staats, a financier, to organize, in 1896, the West Side Lighting Company in Los Angeles. Perhaps the most important ancestor

West Side Lighting Company's original power plant on Twenty Second Street, as it appeared some years after its abandonment. EDISON COLLECTION.

The Bonnie Brae Drug Store and Soda Fountain in Long Beach installed this Hotpoint range for short-order cooking, and advertised "Eat electrically cooked food and be happy!" EDISON COLLECTION.

over a year, Peck unsuccessfully tried to secure an operating franchise from the City of Los Angeles. He finally turned to the County Supervisors, who, in 1895, granted him a franchise to build and operate his plant outside the city limits to the Southwest, in what was then county territory. Late that year the power plant, consisting of an 80-horsepower Buckeye steam engine, a boiler and a Western Electric 30-light arc dynamo, was installed in a small frame building on Twenty-second Street just east of Vermont Avenue.

The Los Angeles City Hall as it appeared in 1896, when West Side Lighting was struggling to win a franchise.
TITLE INSURANCE COLLECTION.

Interior of Los Angeles No. 1 Steam Plant as it appeared in 1902, before its conversion to a substation.
EDISON COLLECTION.

Broadway shows the effects of Los Angeles' Conduit Ordinance. Although the lines of three power companies, five telephone companies and two telegraph companies run down the street, all are in underground conduits. Only the Los Angeles Railway's trolley wires can be seen overhead.
AUTHOR'S COLLECTION.

In late March, 1896, Wright discovered the existence of a Los Angeles franchise permitting the operation of a power system within the city. He bought the franchise for $100. There was, however, a provision in the franchise requiring installation of electric lights in the Los Angeles City Hall by April 15, 1896, or the franchise would become null and void. After purchasing the franchise, there remained only two weeks in which to fulfill the contract by building a

In December, 1895, just before the little steam plant was put into operation, Wright and Peck entered into an agreement with George H. Barker and William R. Staats to organize a new partnership, the Walter S. Wright Electric Company. Shortly thereafter, the plant began to generate electricity to supply a total connected load of eight arc-lights. Peck and his associates continued their efforts to secure a franchise from the City of Los Angeles, and in the meantime did not confine their business to the County territory, but extended their lines into the city by setting poles on private property.

three and one half-mile distribution line up to the City Hall. Those two weeks were feverish with activity. All eight employees of the small company pulled on overalls and helped to string wire. By using the existing poles of the Los Angeles Traction Company, and even sawhorses on the roofs of some downtown buildings, a power line was extended to the City Hall, then on Broadway in the block north of Third. At 4:55 p.m. on April 14, 1896, the day before the franchise would have expired, clusters of electric lights were burning in the City Hall tower.

Edison Electric Company crew paused a moment to "watch the birdie" during 1897 Los Angeles undergrounding project.
EDISON COLLECTION.

With their franchise secured, the association of Peck, Wright, Barker and Staats incorporated the West Side Lighting Company on June 5, 1896. George H. Barker, one of the famous Barker Brothers of furniture store fame, became the company's first president. As expected, the volume of business quickly outgrew the tiny plant on Twenty-second Street. Accordingly, the abandoned powerhouse and machinery of the defunct Second Street Cable Railway Company, at Second and Boyleston Streets, was purchased for $3600. The equipment in the Twenty-second Street plant was moved into the new facility, named Los Angeles No. 1 Station, which was converted from its former cable-winding function into an electric generating station having a capacity of 435 kilowatts.

In its first year of operation, the West Side Lighting Company extended its lines through the residential district west of Bunker Hill. All the while, however, ways were being studied to extend service into the downtown commercial district. Except for arc-lighting by the older Los Angeles Electric Company, the potential load for the area had scarcely yet been touched. The problem faced by the new power company was

Sam Darnell, West Side Lighting's first lineman, demonstrates his pole-climbing technique. At first, each lineman carried around all of his equipment in a wheelbarrow.
EDISON COLLECTION.

The last horse-and-buggy to be used by Edison's Meter Department.
EDISON COLLECTION.

how to bring its distribution lines into downtown. Already most downtown streets were shadowed by unsightly tangles of telephone, telegraph, arc-light, fire alarm, trolley and railway feeder wires. Late in 1896 the City Council passed an ordinance prohibiting, with few exceptions, further overhead line construction in a downtown area designated the "Conduit District." West Side Lighting's officials realized that the only way to extend service into this area would be to adopt an underground direct current conduit system.

They also recognized that the best system, already in use in many Eastern cities, was the "Edison three-wire" conduit technology, invented by Thomas Edison.

In the early years of the electric manufacturing industry, when the many competing technologies were protected by patents, it was customary for the various patent-holders, or their designated manufacturers, to franchise local companies for exclusive territorial operating rights to a given technology. In July of

35

Santa Barbara Gas Plant,
about 1905. This was the
largest of Edison's gas-
making plants.
EDISON COLLECTION.

Cooking with Edison Gas

To those who remember the energy wars between Edison and the Gas Company in the years after World War II, it may come as a surprise to know that, once upon a time, Edison was in the gas business. As John Miller pursued his philosophy of amalgamating small utilities, he acquired a number of local gas plants that came to be operated under the banner of the Edison Company.

Most of these plants had been built in the waning years of the Nineteenth Century when there was no natural gas service in Southern California. Each little gas plant manufactured its own, processing coal or oil in retorts to obtain a smelly, sooty artificial gas that was distributed to local customers through low-pressure pipe systems. By 1907, Edison operated a dozen of these isolated gas systems in Santa Barbara, Santa Monica, Ocean Park, San Pedro, Long Beach, Santa Ana, Whittier, Monrovia, Pomona, Colton, Redlands and Riverside. In these communities, the local Edison office displayed electric and gas appliances, and frequently had signs exhorting customers to "cook with gas." The largest Edison gas market was in Santa Barbara, which was served by the subsidiary Santa Barbara Gas and Electric Company, organized in 1909. The next largest group of gas customers was in

Long Beach, served by the Long Beach Consolidated Gas Company, formed by Edison in 1910. The smallest gas system was in Colton, which was a consistent money loser, and therein lies the reason why Edison surrendered its gas business.

Edison's principal product, electricity, was recognized to be cheaper and superior to the dirty, inefficient artificial gas, and because of the small number of gas customers overall, the expense of modernizing and interconnecting the systems was felt to be unjustified. In the belief that the gas business was destined to die anyway, Edison began disposing of its gas properties beginning with the Colton system in 1907. The last to be sold was the Santa Barbara system in 1919.

Ironically, Edison's gas plants were sold to either the Southern Counties Gas Company or the Southern California Gas Company, both of which began introducing natural gas service in 1913 in ultimately successful efforts to save their faltering business. Before long, Southern Counties and its parent, Southern California Gas, would develop into strong competitors to Edison, especially in the residential market where they encouraged their customers to "cook with gas."

Prominently displayed in Edison's Whittier Local Office are these ornate, nickel-plated gas stoves.

When this photo was taken in 1906, Whittier's gas system was operated by Edison.
EDISON COLLECTION.

The ditch and pipe crew of Edison's subsidiary, the Long Beach Consolidated Gas Company, pose for their picture on Cherry Avenue in 1913.
EDISON COLLECTION.

reasons of speculation, the original Los Angeles Edison Electric Company never owned or operated a power system and never obtained any operating franchises. Three years later, when the West Side Lighting Company desired to use Thomas Edison's patented system of underground distribution in Los Angeles, it was discovered that West Side was unable to use the technology because of the Los Angeles Edison Electric Company's prior and exclusive Southern California rights to it.

Shortly thereafter, West Side's President Barker took a train to San Francisco to confer with General Electric officials on the possibility of a merger between West Side and Los Angeles Edison. As a result of these talks on December 1, 1897, a new company was incorporated. The Edison Electric Company of Los Angeles took over all the properties and franchises of the West Side Lighting Company and the valuable equipment licenses of the Los Angeles Edison Electric Company. George Barker became president of the new Edison Electric Company and the rest of the former West Side management carried their jobs over to the new company as well.

The new Edison Electric Company of Los Angeles immediately set to work installing the Edison underground conduit system that would enable it to provide service to downtown Los Angeles. In the spring of 1898, a new substation, designated Los Angeles No. 2, was built in an alley behind East Fourth Street. Edison tubes were laid from there down all the streets in the "Conduit District," from Main to Broadway, and from Temple south to Seventh. This was the first Edison-type D.C. underground system to be installed in the Southwestern United States, and is the reason for the introduction of the Edison name into the corporate title of both Edison Electric and its successor, Southern California Edison.

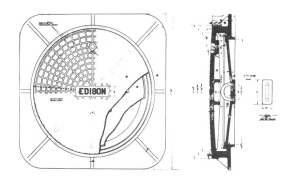

1894, for example, a group of financiers from San Francisco had organized the Los Angeles Edison Electric Company in order to obtain a license from Thomas Edison's General Electric Company to use the Edison name and Edison patents in the Los Angeles area. Created for

It should be pointed out that although the new company had the right to use Thomas Edison's name, to indicate that it was the local franchised user of his patented electrical equipment, the great inventor personally had no connection with the founding or operation of the Edison Electric Company of Los Angeles. Nor has there ever been any special business relationship between the various Edison companies that have operated in the United States—each has always been an independent, locally or regionally owned concern.

Light and Power Company, along with Henry Fisher, a prominent, and wealthy, Redlands resident, had organized the Southern California Power Company, acquired water rights on the upper Santa Ana River, and started construction of the station now known as Santa Ana River No. 1.

As this large power station neared completion in 1898, the Edison Company saw that its 3000 kilowatts of generating capacity would relieve their power supply problems. Sinclair and Fisher agreed that a merger was logical, so in June, 1898, the Southern California Power Company was purchased by the Edison Electric Company. There remained one major problem—how to bring the energy from the new plant into Los Angeles over a distance much longer than yet had been attempted for electrical transmission.

The problem became the concern of Orville H. Ensign, Southern California Power's Electrical Engineer who had come over to Edison in the same capacity after their merger. Ensign

38   Soon after service to downtown Los Angeles began, the Edison Electric Company found it was having difficulty making enough energy to meet the rapidly growing demand for electricity, despite the addition of more generators to its Second Street steam plant. At this crucial moment, the Edison management learned of a potential new source of generation, hydroelectric power from the Santa Ana River out near Redlands. Back in 1896, Henry Sinclair, president of the Redlands Electric

proposed to build an 83-mile long power line from the Santa Ana River No. 1 hydro plant to Edison's Los Angeles No. 1 station, to be energized at 33,000 volts. This would be by far the highest-voltage, longest-distance transmission line yet built in the country.

World-record setting Santa Ana River to Los Angeles 33,000-volt line as it originally appeared.
EDISON COLLECTION.

Carrying construction materials into Santa Ana Canyon during the rebuilding of the 33,000-volt lines from the Santa Ana River Hydro Plants after the flood of 1916.
EDISON COLLECTION.

The weakest area in high-voltage transmission design was believed to be insulators, which at that time were made of glass from designs adapted from use on telephone and telegraph lines. Ensign was convinced that insulators could successfully be designed to handle pressures as high as 40,000 volts in all weather conditions. On a trip to the Trenton, New Jersey, works of the Locke Insulator Company, the engineer used his pocket knife to whittle soft ceramic clay into a shape he envisioned. Thus was born the famous "Redlands" insulator with its distinctive "petticoat" design, the first glazed porcelain insulator specifically designed for high voltage electrical work.

The benefits of Ensign's insulator design work were realized by the industry even before the Santa Ana River Line went into service in February 1899. A few months earlier, a shorter, 40,000-volt line using the Redlands-type insulator, was energized in Telluride, Colorado. Before long, insulators patterned after Ensign's original design were being used on new high-voltage power lines placed into service throughout the West.

With a major source of energy thus assured, the Edison Electric Company began to seek new customers, both in Los Angeles and in surrounding communities. Where possible, the systems of existing local companies were purchased, such as those of the Pasadena Electric Light and Power Company in 1898 and the Santa Ana Gas and Electric Company in 1899, but in many instances new lines were built to bring electricity into areas that had not previously had service.

Mrs. Colby, in white, and her assistant came to Edison from General Electric in 1912 to demonstrate early electric cooking appliances.
EDISON COLLECTION.

The dynamic leader of the Edison Company's destiny for a third of a century, John Barnes Miller was also an avid pipe smoker. A small tobacconist's in Los Angeles prepared for him a special mixture called "JBM" with a picture of the Big Creek No. 1 Hydro Plant on the label.
EDISON COLLECTION.

In 1901, John Barnes Miller became president of the Edison Electric Company. Destined to exert great influence upon Southern California's electrical future, Miller had joined the West Side Lighting Company early in 1897, receiving the princely sum of $100 a month to be that company's General Manager. A year later, Miller had become Treasurer and a Director of the Edison Electric Company. He was one of the first utility executives to recognize the necessity of providing the public with the best possible service at the lowest cost, and his call for "Good Service, Square Dealing and Courteous Treatment" in customer relations became the motto of the company he led.

John Miller believed that the prosperity and future growth potential of Southern California depended upon an adequate supply of electricity, a commodity upon which the public was increasingly dependent. Financing for new facilities was a pressing concern throughout the industry at the turn of the century, a time when electric utility stocks and bonds were considered highly risky speculations. Miller felt this drawback could be overcome if the inefficient, financially weak local power companies could be welded together into one large, stable regional system with a large base of mortgageable property. Therefore, upon assuming the presidency of the Edison

Not long after the Appliance Department was established in 1910, these salesmen posed for their portrait with the tools of their trade.
EDISON COLLECTION.

Before World War One, Edison customer services included free replacement of burned-out light bulbs by the delivery boys of the Lamp Department. This service was important in the days prior to the widespread use of the modern standard screw base light bulb.
EDISON COLLECTION.

Company, Miller began negotiating mergers with other utilities, and soon gained a reputation as "the Great Amalgamator." As a measure of the confidence in which President Miller's philosophy was held, in September 1902, a group of Eastern banking concerns gave unprecedented but welcome backing to the recapitalization of Edison Electric as a $10 million corporation. The Edison Electric Company was on its way to becoming a major utility enterprise.

Over the next few years, Edison purchased utility properties in a number of Southland communities. Among the most unusual were the streetcar system and a public bath house in Santa Barbara, acquired with the purchase of that city's gas and electric company.

This display in Edison's Fourth Street office showed the new Edison-Mazda lamps then being introduced. These were the first bulbs to achieve modern levels of brightness and efficiency.
EDISON COLLECTION.

EDISON MAZDA LAMPS

Convenient and Quick

Trolleys to the Bath House

When Edison purchased the utilities in Santa Barbara in 1903, it inherited two unusual operations, a street railway and a salt water plunge or bath house. "Los Banos Del Mar," as the bath house was called, was located on the beach at the foot of Castillo Street adjacent to the Edison power plant. In the early days when Santa Barbara was isolated from the rest of the Edison system, it had its own steam power plant. Warm condenser cooling water from the plant was piped next door to the bath house where it was used to heat the swimming pool's water. At that time it was one of the few heated plunges in Southern California, and the bath house was popular with residents and visitors alike.

In the plaza in front of the Bath House terminated the "Beach" line of the Santa Barbara Consolidated Electric Railway. From there trolley cars could be taken to Oak Park, to the Mission and the State Normal School, or out Haley Street to Milpas. Incorporated in 1895 to electrify the city's mule car lines, the Consolidated Electric Railway conducted its business with little four-wheel wooden narrow-gauge cars until 1913, when the momentous decision was made to convert the entire system to standard gauge.

A new company was formed, the Santa Barbara and Suburban Railway, the tracks were widened and new cars purchased. When the original bath house burned down in 1913, it was replaced by an even more magnificent building.

Yet, in spite of these improvements, the automobile began enticing passengers away from the trolleys and revenues began to drop. The trolleys carried on in the face of mounting deficits, earthquake damage and demands from the city to pay for paving the streets upon which they ran. Finally, the Santa Barbara and Suburban Railway ceased running on June 30, 1929, and trolleys disappeared from the Mission City. "Los Banos Del Mar" carried on alone, its pool no longer heated because the power plant had been demolished, but eventually it too succumbed to changing times and bathing habits.

Old narrow-gauge trolley No. 8 stands by the old car barn on Quarantina Street about 1906.
EDISON COLLECTION.

42

A concert in the bandshell on the second floor of the Bath House has drawn a large crowd. Some arrived on Santa Barbara Consolidated Railway Car No. 8, parked at the end of the line at left.
EDISON COLLECTION.

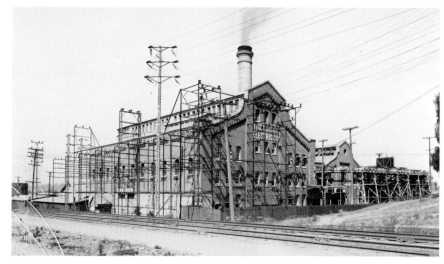

Even more important than the acquisition of these new properties were the new electric plants built to supply them. An important tenet of John Miller's consolidation plans was the replacement of antiquated, inefficient local power plants with an interconnected network of modern facilities. The economies resulting from such modernization were passed on to the customer in the form of rate reductions. New hydroelectric plants, preferred because of their low cost of operation, were built on Lytle Creek near Rialto, on the Santa Ana River below the existing plant, and on Mill Creek east of Redlands. Los Angeles No. 3, a large 8,000-kilowatt steam station built in 1904 on Alhambra Avenue near the Los Angeles River, was the first in Southern California to utilize the new, highly efficient steam turbine technology. L.A. No. 3 also served as a switching center for Edison's growing transmission network. Its massive brick structure and 150-foot tall concrete stack still stand as memorials to another era, although its generators were scrapped over 60 years ago.

By far the most ambitious power development yet undertaken by Edison Electric, however, was the building of the first of a series of three projected hydro plants on the Kern River. Begun in 1902, it took five years to build "K.R.1," as the plant was nicknamed, but when completed, its four 5,000 kilowatt generators more than doubled Edison's generating capacity. Kern River No. 1 was squeezed into precipitous, rocky Kern Canyon miles from any settlement on a site surveyed by F. C. Finkle, Edison Electric's Chief Hydraulic Engineer.

44

The five years required to complete the plant was a long time by earlier standards, when power sites had been more accessible and generators smaller. For the Kern River project, a road had to be blasted from the canyon walls, and heavy wagons of provisions and building material were laboriously hauled by plodding strings of horses over 20 miles to the plant site from the nearest railroad. Indeed, the San Joaquin Valley town of Edison owes its name and its beginnings to this railroad siding, appropriately but laconically named "Edison."

Just before Christmas of 1906, "K.R.1" leaped into the nation's headlines when a cave-in occurred in a tunnel being excavated for the plant's penstock pressure pipeline. Six men were buried beneath falling rock, earth and timbers, and all were presumed dead. Three days later, however, one of the rescue crew "mucking out" the tunnel felt a faint tapping on one of the railroad rails running down the shaft. Rescue operations were stepped up while newspapers around the world carried progress reports.

Concreting in the penstock pipe leading to Kern River No. 1 Hydro Plant, 1906. During the excavation of this tunnel, not far from this spot, occurred the cave-in which trapped miner Hicks.
EDISON COLLECTION.

High up on the south wall of Kern Canyon, a hoisting works was placed to lower penstock pipe into the tunnel leading to the powerhouse.
EDISON COLLECTION.

Because of the danger of further collapse, rescue workers drove a new tunnel 110 feet through the mountainside to where the trapped miner lay. He was Lindsey B. Hicks, who had managed to squirm under a muck car when the tunnel had collapsed. For agonizing days he lay entombed in darkness beneath the rail car, but when the rescuers got closer, a pipe was pushed through the rubble to him. Through it he drank warm milk, talked with comrades, and listened to phonograph records.

A team of mules strains to haul one of the heavy generator stators up to K.R.1, 1906.
EDISON COLLECTION.

After 16 days, Miner Hicks was rescued alive. A horse and rider rushed to Bakersfield, where the news was telegraphed to the world. After a short stay in the hospital, Hicks returned to work. A theatrical agent signed him to describe his experience, but after disappointing crowds, the tour was cancelled. Tragically, Hicks is said to have been killed some years later when he stepped in front of a train.

An Auto Trip to the Kern River in 1914

In a time when rapid, trouble-free travel by automobile is viewed by most as a basic necessity, it is difficult to imagine a time when even a short auto trip was time-consuming, and long trips, undertaken only when absolutely necessary, could involve real hardship. Consider an inspection trip made early in 1914 from Los Angeles to the Kern River No. 1 hydro plant by a party of Edison officials. The group of adventurous travellers on this 150-mile journey included driver and photographer G. Haven Bishop, Chief Electrical Engineer Jim Lighthipe, Superintendent of Transmission George Stockbridge, General Superintendent Benjamin "Uncle Ben" Pearson and his son, engineer H. W. Dennis, Chief of Construction "Ray" Raymaker, Distribution Superintendent Sam Darnell and mechanic Edmunds from the Edison Garage.

This band left Los Angeles bright and early in the morning. Bishop drove a Pope-Hartford touring car, while Edmunds drove a National. Because this was a year before the fearsome old Grapevine Highway was opened through Castaic along Edison's Kern River transmission line patrol road, the big touring cars had to travel roundabout via Saugus, Acton, Palmdale, Bailey's, Tejon and Bakersfield. About two hours out of Los Angeles, as the caravan passed Mint Canyon near Acton, the Pope-Hartford broke part of its suspension. While some made coffee over a campfire, Jim Lighthipe went rabbit hunting, and others played cribbage, Edmunds and Raymaker drove the National back to Edison's Saugus Substation to telephone for help.

At 4:00 p.m., a relief car from the Edison Garage in Los Angeles arrived at Mint Canyon with repair parts, and Edmunds took only an hour to fix the Pope-Hartford's suspension. At 5 p.m. the band left the relief auto behind and resumed their journey, but got only as far as Acton before halting because of fog and darkness. The Edison group stayed that night at a small hostel that catered to the crews of the nearby Southern Pacific Railroad.

The next morning the caravan proceeded to Palmdale, where gasoline was found for the two autos. The long grind across the desert from Palmdale to Bailey's was marred by a further failure on the Pope-Hartford, when a stud holding the universal shaft sheared off. While Edmunds went to work with a piece of gas pipe and some bailing wire, the rest of the party went ahead at a slow pace; those riding in the National car alternating with those who hiked in front of it to avoid the dust. Edmunds eventually caught up to them in the repaired Pope-Hartford, but it was very late that night, their second out on the road, when they arrived at a hotel in Bakersfield.

The next morning Lighthipe and Stockbridge decided they had had enough and returned to Los Angeles on the train, Stockbridge leaving with the comment that he had not really expected that they would ever have made it that far! The rest continued on to the powerhouse, arriving after lunch. Though they had reached the Kern plant, the band's adventures were not yet over. As cloudbursts broke upon the mountains, Raymaker, Bishop and Edmunds took the two autos away from the plant out of Kern Canyon and onto the plains below, a precaution that paid off when floods in the afternoon washed out the road up the canyon to the plant. Grumbling somewhat, the rest of the weary band had to walk two miles out of the canyon to where the autos were waiting. On the way back to Bakersfield, the Pope-Hartford broke its differential when it got stuck in Cottonwood Creek, so the party abandoned it and crowded into the National to return to Bakersfield. The next morning, they heard that the road near Tejon had washed out so they all came home on the train, which was far more comfortable anyway. The two automobiles were rescued and returned to the Los Angeles Garage several weeks later.

To bring K.R.1's electricity into Southern California, James A. Lighthipe, an electrical engineer with General Electric who later came to Edison as Chief Electrical Engineer, designed a 118-mile long, 75,000 volt transmission line. This was the highest-voltage line in the nation at that time, but what really drew attention was that it was the first electric line ever to be supported entirely on steel towers. These towers were manufactured by the Wind Engine Company, a maker of windmills. Up to this time, although individual steel towers had been used for special applications such as river crossings, wooden poles were used almost exclusively on power lines. Edison soon learned that, far from causing service interruptions due to grounding problems, steel towers actually improved reliability due to their ability to better withstand storm damage.

Throughout the first decade of the Twentieth Century, President Miller continued his improvements, amalgamations and mergers until the Edison Electric Company's system

Linemen at work on one of the historic Kern River 75,000-volt transmission line towers, replacing the original pin-type insulators with new suspension type, 1916.
EDISON COLLECTION.

James A. Lighthipe, Edison's Chief Electrical Engineer from 1908 to 1924.
EDISON COLLECTION.

served many communities from Santa Barbara to Redlands. It had grown from a small Los Angeles company to one serving over 600,000 people in five counties. To reflect this expansion, Miller and the company's directors decided to change the company's name. On July 6, 1909, it was reincorporated as the Southern California Edison Company, capitalized at $30 million and still under the able management of John B. Miller.

47

Mules were used to bring supplies to the locations where towers were being erected for the Kern River 75,000-volt line. The trail hacked out by Edison for this project was later rebuilt as the original Grapevine Highway over Tejon Pass.
EDISON COLLECTION.

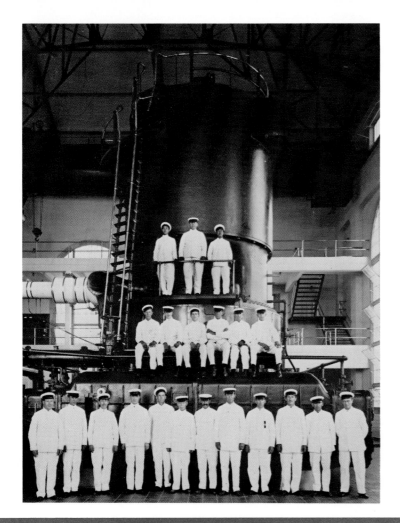

Dredger "City of Redlands" at work clearing Cerritos Slough, 1908. Timber framework in right background is shipway for Craig Shipyard.
EDISON COLLECTION.

The new company immediately sold a bond issue, the proceeds of which were used to put in hand a major construction program to upgrade its transmission and generating systems. Despite the completion of Kern River No. 1 only two years earlier, the demand for electricity had grown so quickly that Edison had leased the Los Angeles Pacific Railway's Vineyard Steam Plant to provide extra capacity. Thus, in 1909 it was decided to build a great new steam station to provide reserve capacity and emergency power for the entire Edison system, and also to enable the abandonment of the few small, obsolete steam plants remaining on the system.

Edison's Engineering Department, 1905. Man in bow-tie, third from left, is Peter H. Ducker.
EDISON COLLECTION.

48

An early move towards aesthetic designs were mission-style substations. This example was Edison's original Beverly Hills Substation.
EDISON COLLECTION.

The site chosen for the new plant was on a barren mud flat called Rattlesnake Island—today's Terminal Island—adjacent to Cerritos Channel in Long Beach Harbor. It was in 1906 that a group of men first planned to convert the Cerritos Slough's salt marshes into a harbor for Long Beach. Unlike the massive government effort in nearby San Pedro, this harbor building project was to be done with private capital and necessarily limited funds from the City of Long Beach.

A young mechanical engineer working for Edison, Peter H. Ducker, designed and built an electrically operated dredger, the first ever to operate on the Pacific Coast. Named "City of Redlands" because it was financed by Redlands capitalist Henry Fisher, this dredger was launched on January 23, 1908 and cleared the channels to form Long Beach's harbor. When construction began on Edison's Long Beach Steam Plant in 1910, the "City of Redlands" assisted in the laying of condenser cooling water conduits into Cerritos Channel.

The new station featured three gigantic vertical steam turbines: Unit No. 1, installed in 1911; Unit No. 2, added in 1913; and Unit No. 3, placed in service in 1914. They aggregated 47,500 kilowatts, a tremendous amount for power plants of that era. Each of the turbines, which weighed hundreds of tons, bore a big brass plaque that carried the stern notice, "not licensed for use with aerial craft." A far cry from the highly automated steam plants of today, Long Beach required 155 men to run it, including janitors whose sole job was to polish the plant's brasswork and scrub clean the terra-cotta tile floors.

Two never-ending tasks were keeping Cerritos Channel free from sand that could clog Long Beach's cooling water system and shovelling sea shells and marine growths out of the big seawater conduits. The "City of Redlands" was responsible for clearing the sand, but one day's storm could undo a week's worth of dredging. To clean out the cooling water tunnels, the entire plant staff and local high school boys hired for the job were issued shovels and wheelbarrows. These cleanings began at

midnight and often continued well into the next day, and not infrequently resulted in the filling of three railroad hopper cars with the shells and muck.

Long Beach burned fuel oil, not the refined product of today, but a heavy, viscous residual oil not much better than road tar. The lines carrying the oil fuel from the plant's storage tank to the boiler house were at first laid directly on top of the marshy soil of Terminal Island. In winter, and early on cold, foggy mornings, the oil inside the pipes became sluggish and would not flow. When this happened, gangs of workmen were sent out to comb the nearby ocean beach for driftwood, which was then piled every few feet along the pipeline and set on fire. This would warm the pipe enough so that the oil would flow to the boilers.

In addition to the construction of Long Beach Steam Plant, Edison crews built a new network of 66,000-volt steel tower transmission lines to interconnect the system, replacing the earlier 33,000 volt wood pole lines. Although it was no longer an important generating plant, L.A. No.

3 was still the central switching station for the Edison transmission system. From it, 66,000 volt lines extended to Colton on the east, Santa Ana on the southeast, Long Beach Steam Plant on the south, Santa Monica on the west, and Pasadena on the northeast. The 75,000-volt line to the Kern River was reconstructed, retaining the existing steel towers but replacing the old pin style insulators with the same suspension type insulator strings that had been developed by Jim Lighthipe for use on the new 66,000-volt lines.

This shows how assembled steel towers were raised by gin-poles in the days before large mechanical cranes. Here, one of the steel towers for Edison's new 66,000-volt transmission network is being raised.
EDISON COLLECTION.

Miss Vera Ebert, Edison's first "Cooking Expert", or Home Economist, conducts a demonstration at the Redlands office in 1916.
EDISON COLLECTION.

During Electrical Prosperity Week in 1915, the Company fitted out an electric wagon with this display of electric appliances.
EDISON COLLECTION.

E.H. Mulligan, Edison's District Agent (local manager) in Pasadena, stands proudly beside his new electric auto.
EDISON COLLECTION.

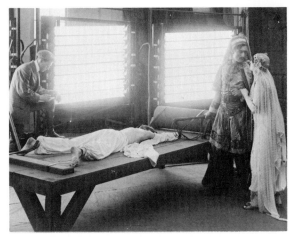

Along with these improvements came others that drew attention in the industry. By 1914, all company transportation, except in remote areas, had been converted to the use of electric or gasoline-powered vehicles. Through direct sales to the public, Edison was increasing the residential use of such electric appliances as irons, toasters, ranges, percolators, vacuum cleaners, washing machines and many other items familiar today. Edison's New Business Department encouraged electric irrigation pumping, oil pumping and had helped the burgeoning motion picture industry by developing "artificial daylight" floodlighting as

As moviemaking switched to indoor studios, "artificial daylight" floodlighting was developed.
EDISON COLLECTION.

movie making switched from outdoor to indoor locations. Electric streetlighting, long a mainstay of the industry, was rapidly supplanting arc-lighting with powerful and more efficient incandescent bulbs. Many communities demonstrated civic pride by installing decorative "electroliers," as new street light posts were called. The light bulb itself was still a marvel, for in 1916 the completion of the Santa Monica Pleasure Pier drew big crowds to see its dazzling display of electric lights.

Activities of electric companies came to be more closely watched as utility systems tended to become territorially franchised monopolies. In exchange for permitting these consolidations, the public demanded and got, closer regulation of rates. The City of Los Angeles' Board of Public Utilities had regulated Edison rates in that city since 1902, and several other municipalities also exercised some form of regulation, but systematic and effective supervision of Edison and California's other public utilities began on March 23, 1912, following passage of the state's sweeping Public Utilities Act of 1911. Besides regulating rates, the State Railroad Commission—which was re-designated the California Public Utilities Commission in 1946—assumed wide powers over corporate finance, quality of service, consolidations and franchising. Edison and most other utilities welcomed the uniformity and impartiality of state regulation in contrast to the frequently bitter, punitive and politically motivated municipal regulation that had prevailed before.

Responding to a growing awareness by both consumers and utility managements that competition between companies for the same customers only pushed rates upwards by

In 1915, the Sun Drug Company in downtown Los Angeles drew much interest with its animated electric sign for Eastside Beer, which showed a girl diving into water.
EDISON COLLECTION.

The famous Ocean Park Pier was one of Southern California's many popular seaside resorts. Elaborate lighting such as this helped to attract more night-time patrons.
EDISON COLLECTION.

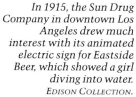

Long before radio or television, in the election of 1912, Edison provided a unique service. When the company received the official results, station operators all over the system blinked the lights to a pre-arranged code. Here, substation operator E.P. Chase gives two blinks signifying Woodrow Wilson's election.
EMORY CHASE COLLECTION.

forcing expensive and wasteful duplication of facilities, the Railroad Commission established geographic "spheres of influence." This formalized the boundaries between utility systems and made it difficult for new utilities to invade the service area of an existing company without real justification. Unfortunately, this protection did not extend to the expansion efforts in subsequent years of municipal and other government-owned electric utilities, which were not regulated by the State Commission.

By the middle of the second decade of this century, the Southern California Edison Company had become one of the nation's premier utilities, with an aggressive and creative marketing program, a modern physical plant, rates among the lowest in the nation, and an established reputation for the creativity of its employees.

51

Pacific Electric's "Old Mission Trolley Trip" excursion at San Gabriel Mission, about 1918. COURTESY HUNTINGTON LIBRARY.

Power for the Big Red Cars

At the same time the Edison Company was expanding throughout Southern California, another power enterprise was growing under the skillful guidance of one of the giants of California history—Henry Edwards Huntington. Tall, broad-shouldered and blue-eyed, with a military moustache that turned white with the years, Huntington dominated the economic life of the Southland for a generation. Beginning in 1898, he invested in trolley lines, interurban electric railways, landholdings, electric, water and gas utilities

and numerous other industrial and commercial enterprises. Ultimately, the income from these businesses was used to finance Huntington's enduring legacy to Southern California, his magnificent Library and Art Gallery in San Marino.

Huntington first became interested in electric utilities in 1902, when he joined with William G. Kerckhoff and Allan C. Balch to create the Pacific Light and Power Company, primarily to assure adequate electric power for his various trolley enterprises. Balch and Kerckhoff, however, had been active with electrical developments for some years already. In the 1890s, they, too, had been intrigued by the possibility of improving the quality of electric service to Los Angeles, just as were Peck and Wright of the West Side Lighting Company. In 1897, Kerckhoff and Balch incorporated the San Gabriel Electric Company to construct a hydroelectric plant near Azusa at the mouth of San Gabriel Canyon and transmit the energy into Los Angeles.

Although the Azusa Plant did not pioneer some new technology as had the earlier Redlands or San Antonio projects, it was, along with Edison's Santa Ana River No. 1 Plant, one of the first two hydroelectric stations to be built in Southern California on a modern commercial basis. The San Gabriel Electric Company encountered the same difficulties in its bid to penetrate the Los Angeles market as did West Side Lighting, both in trying to get a franchise from the City Council and in having to place its downtown distribution system underground. Eventually, all these problems were overcome and electric service began on June 30, 1898.

Interior of the Azusa Plant, showing the unusual two-phase A.C. generators.
EDISON COLLECTION.

Henry Huntington in 1904, when he was known as the "Trolley King".
COURTESY HUNTINGTON LIBRARY.

As originally constructed, the Azusa Plant contained four two-phase, 300 kilowatt Westinghouse generators. These machines produced electricity that was transmitted to Los Angeles, a distance of 23 miles, at 16,000 volts pressure. A brick building at Third and Los Angeles Streets downtown served as a substation, receiving station and reserve steam plant. From it extended single-phase and two-phase 2,400-volt lines for light and power service, and 220-volt three-wire direct current lines for lighting service in the downtown area.

To conform to the "Conduit Ordinance," these lines were placed underground in "conduits" made of creosoted two-by-twelve inch Oregon pine planks grooved to take the electric cables and spiked together "sandwich-fashion."

Despite the comparatively crude technology with which it started in business, the San Gabriel Electric Company quickly became an important utility. In 1900, when the Sierra Power Company was reorganized out of the old San Antonio Light and Power Company, and its

Birthplace of the PL&P system was the Azusa Hydro Plant, built in 1898.
EDISON COLLECTION.

53

This small mission-style building was PL&P's office and substation in then-rural Hollywood. Pepper tree-lined dirt road is today's bustling Sunset Boulevard.
EDISON COLLECTION.

new "Sierra" hydro plant was built below the flood-ravaged ruins of the historic Pomona Plant, Balch and Kerckhoff contracted for some of the new plant's output, which was carried over a new power line from San Antonio Canyon to Azusa. Early in 1902, San Gabriel Electric purchased the distribution system of the East Side Lighting Company in Boyle Heights and East Los Angeles. Of decisive importance for the future of the company,

however, was the signing of a contract with the Los Angeles Railway to provide off-peak energy to help power its many trolley cars. In this connection, Henry Huntington, President of both L.A. Railway and the fledgling Pacific Electric Railway, suggested to Kerckhoff and Balch that their San Gabriel company might be reorganized to assume complete responsibility to generate the power needed by his growing street railway empire.

Tailrace of the Sierra Hydro Plant, built in 1901 after the nearby Pomona Plant was destroyed in a flood.
COURTESY POMONA PUBLIC LIBRARY.

From his suggestion came the Pacific Light and Power Company, which commenced operating the system of the San Gabriel Electric Company on April 1, 1902. From then until their merger in 1917, the history of PL&P, as the new enterprise was quickly nicknamed, somewhat paralleled that of the Edison Company. Both were large, successful amalgamations of many smaller companies that had sprung up around the turn of the century. Often during these early years of growth, Edison and PL&P were energetic rivals, reflecting the philosophies of their respective leaders.

The new direction of PL&P was obvious from the start, for Henry Huntington, as trustee for L.A. Railway, owned 51 percent of its stock, and the bulk of its generation went to operate the yellow cars of the Los Angeles Railway, the Red Cars of the Pacific Electric and the communities served by those trolley lines. In the first year of PL&P's existence, energy sales amounted to 1.1 million kilowatt-hours. The following year it rose to 2.8 million kilowatt-hours, a pattern of growth that would be repeated for a quarter century as the network of electric railways spread throughout Southern California.

Looking south on Spring Street from Fifth, about 1905, shows the trolley cars of the Los Angeles Railway to be the predominant form of wheeled transport on the street.
VERNON SAPPERS COLLECTION, COURTESY RICHARD J. FELLOWS.

To meet the growing demand for power, PL&P began to acquire existing power companies that controlled resources from which large amounts of electricity might be developed. Aside from the Sierra Power Company, purchased outright in 1902, the first major acquisition was the Kern River Company, which, since 1897, had been constructing in rather desultory fashion a hydroelectric plant on the Kern River ll miles below old Kernville.

A Los Angeles civil engineer named Hawgood had conceived of generating electricity on the Kern River as early as 1895, but not until 1897 did his Kern River Company begin development work to hold his water rights. Because investors could not be found for the project, probably because of the proposed power plant's distance from any sizeable market, the company languished until 1902 when it was bought by PL&P. Immediately

55

Rush hour, 1910-style, shows L.A. Railway and Pacific Electric trolleys lined up for three blocks on Seventh Street.
COURTESY HUNTINGTON LIBRARY.

"Comfort, Speed and Safety"

"Comfort, Speed and Safety" was the proud motto of the Pacific Electric Railway, once upon a time the world's largest interurban trolley system. From Canoga Park to Balboa, from Santa Monica to Redlands, over 7,000 "Big Red Cars" daily sped to all corners of Southern California on the gleaming rails of this once-mighty rapid transit network. Created by Henry Huntington in 1901, the Pacific Electric built hundreds of miles of trolley lines from Los Angeles into surrounding communities in the first decade of the Twentieth Century. Sold to the Southern Pacific in 1910, the system continued to grow by new construction and merger until, by 1924, the Pacific Electric operated over 1100 miles of railway in four Southland counties.

Southern Californians had a half-century love affair with the Red Cars, which, more than just transportation, were members of the family. The thousands of daily interurban and local trains carried commuters to work and back home to the suburbs. They took housewives to market, children to school, young couples on dates, families on outings. The Pacific Electric offered many excursions for tourists and residents alike, such as the "Balloon Route" to Venice and Redondo Beach or the world-famous Mount Lowe trolley trip. So impressed were many visitors by the Southern California they viewed from the windows of the trolleys that they remained to become residents.

Pacific Electric trains brought newspapers to the doorstep daily, and enabled a far quicker delivery of local mail than can be done today. They carried fresh local produce to market, brought fish up from San Pedro and bananas from ships in Long Beach Harbor. Most of the Southland's produce and manufactured goods began their journey to market behind the silent, pollution-free electric locomotives of the P.E.

Many of the Red Trains were fast, like the famed "Catalina Flyer," which rushed vacationers down to the Great White Steamship in Wilmington at speeds in excess of 90 miles an hour! Some were glamorous, like the popular "County Fair Specials" that went to the Pomona fairgrounds, or the "Angel City Limited" that hurried in from San

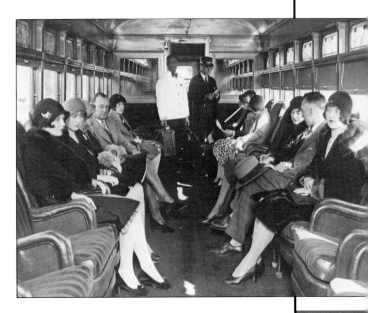

Bernardino. Others were just maids of all work, carrying commuters or local traffic. All did their jobs well, providing reliable transportation upon which most Southlanders depended.

The Pacific Electric operated until the end of World War Two, but over the next six years most of the system was converted to bus operation. The last former Pacific Electric trains, then being run by the Los Angeles Metropolitan Transit Authority, ceased operation on April 8, 1961.

Box motors unload freight and produce at Pacific Electric's Eighth Street Yard adjacent to Los Angeles' produce market. AUTHOR'S COLLECTION.

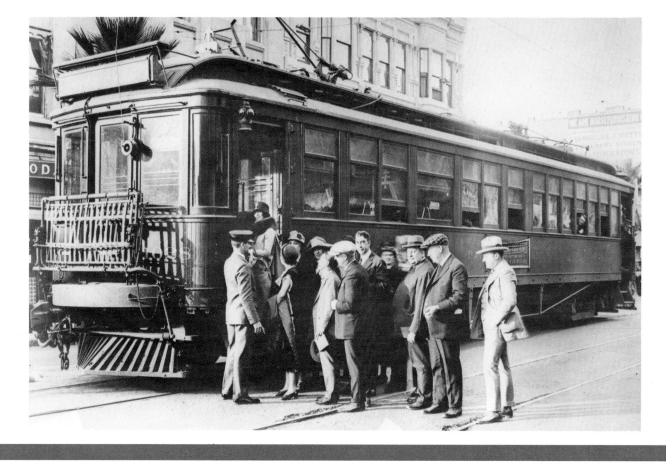

The parlour cars attached to Pacific Electric's Catalina Steamer Trains featured comfortable plush seats. These were the fastest trains on the system.
AUTHOR'S COLLECTION.

Passengers re-board their private car after visiting Riverside's Mission Inn, one of the sights on P.E.'s "Orange Empire Excursion".
AUTHOR'S COLLECTION.

The Borel Hydro Plant as it appeared in 1909, with its original generators, later replaced.
EDISON COLLECTION.

work was begun to rush the plant to completion, spurred by the need to develop energy for the many new Pacific Electric trolley lines Huntington was building at that time.

Water was diverted from the river near old Kernville and carried by canal and flume to the powerhouse, named "Borel", in honor of Antoine Borel, a San Francisco financier and associate of Huntington. The plant's 10,000 kilowatts were transmitted at 55,000 volts over a 127-mile long power line to Los Angeles. The receiving station, Kern Substation, became the hub of PL&P's original transmission system. Sixteen thousand volt lines from the Azusa and Sierra plants were routed into it, as was a line from the Mentone or Santa Ana River No. 3 hydro plant when it was built in 1904.

When Borel hydro plant went into operation in 1904, it was the most remote power plant serving Southern California. As with other hydro plants on both the Edison and PL&P systems, a village of homes grew around Borel to accommodate the operators and their families. One early photograph shows the resident station crew proudly posed for their portrait, each wearing a collegiate-style sweater emblazoned with a block-letter "B" for their "alma mater," Borel.

Among the small properties PL&P acquired in its early years was a little trolley line on Euclid Avenue in Upland and Ontario, which came as part of the 1904 deal whereby PL&P obtained water rights for power development on San Antonio Creek. The Ontario and San Antonio Heights Railway began life in 1888 as an animal-powered line. Mules hauled the rail car

Picturesque Borel Hydro Plant on the Kern River was PL&P's most remote generating facility until Big Creek was built.
EDISON COLLECTION.

58

Hauling turbine scroll case to Borel in 1912, during reconstruction of water turbines.
EDISON COLLECTION.

to the top of the street in Upland and rode down in a special platform behind the car as it coasted back to Ontario. When it was decided to electrify the line in 1898, the railway company built a picturesque hydroelectric plant near the mouth of San Antonio Canyon. Because it was made out of field stone, locals soon dubbed the plant "Stone Castle." The trolley tracks were extended over to the new building, which doubled as a car barn, and a park was laid out around it. The railway was operated by PL&P until 1912, when it was sold to Pacific Electric. The Stone Castle continued to generate power for PL&P until it was struck by lightning and burned in 1916. Its stone walls still stand today, engulfed in a growth of wild blackberries.

In July 1905, Henry Huntington purchased the Redondo Townsite Company as the prelude to a new development project for that sleepy seaside resort. Huntington believed that Redondo could be developed into a port for Southern California's lumber trade, and that the town itself could become an important suburb of Los Angeles. He bought the local trolley company and upgraded service to Los Angeles, while the townsite company built a plunge and fun-zone on the beach to promote tourism. Most importantly, he saw in Redondo a fine site for a new steam station for his power enterprise, because of its proximity to ocean water for cooling and to oil wells for fuel supply.

The firm of Charles C. Moore and Company of San Francisco built the Redondo Plant over a span of two years. In September, 1907, exacting acceptance tests were conducted upon the

plant's massive double-angle, tandem compound reciprocating engines, a design that was similar to other units previously installed in New York to power the subway system, but which was considered by most engineers to be obsolete in the face of steam turbine technology. To the surprise of many, Redondo's three huge engines, each driving a 5,000-kilowatt generator, were found to comprise the most efficient steam plant in the United States, squeezing a record 253 kilowatt-hours from each barrel of fuel oil. This achievement

The curious mule cars of the Ontario and San Antonio Heights Railroad had a platform at the rear so that the mules could ride down the long Euclid Avenue hill back to the line's starting place in Ontario.
AUTHOR'S COLLECTION.

Blackened ruins of the Stone Castle Hydro Plant after the fire of 1916.
AUTHOR'S COLLECTION.

Pacific Light and Power's old Redondo Steam Plant was a wonder of its day. It gained renown as the most efficient steam plant in the nation, despite its use of old-fashioned double-angle, tandem compound reciprocating steam engines.
EDISON COLLECTION.

Redondo Steam Plant, 1912.
EDISON COLLECTION.

received considerable attention in the technical press of that time, but it was the last hurrah for old-fashioned stationary steam engines. Just three years later, when more capacity was needed at Redondo, two 12,000 kilowatt turbo-generators were installed. This new capacity enabled the retirement of the remaining small steam plants scattered about the PL&P system, including Pacific Electric's own power plant on Central Avenue in Los Angeles, which the power company had operated under lease for several years.

Like most early-day steam plants, Redondo had its troubles. Twice the big oil-filled Kelman circuit breakers exploded and blew out the walls of the switch gallery, making it necessary to call in fire companies for miles around. Because the plant lay on low, swampy ground only a few yards from the beach, it experienced frequent trouble with high tides and flooding, and its crew boasted of working in the only powerhouse in the world where engineers had to wear rubber boots. Redondo was built on the coast to enable ocean water to be brought into the condensers, devices that took exhaust steam from the engines and turbines and condensed it back into water to be reused in the boilers. This condensing action caused a vacuum in the engines, which improved their efficiency. In many of the reports filed in the early months of the station's operation, there appears the notation "frequent loss of vacuum due to seaweed clogging the sea lines."

Although much of the electricity produced at Redondo and the older hydro plants went to power Huntington's vast system of trolley lines, a growing amount of the energy output went to homes and businesses in the PL&P

When running at full output on cool mornings, the exhaust steam from the Redondo Plant made a spectacular plume that could be seen for miles. EDISON COLLECTION.

service area. Indeed, in many towns over the previous few years, electric service and trolley service had begun concurrently, as crews from the different Huntington-owned companies worked side-by-side to bring about the inauguration of those services. By 1910, the demand for electricity in this interlocked network of railways and communities was again outstripping the supply. As noted above, new generators were added at Redondo, but that was recognized to be only a short-term measure. Energy from Redondo, despite that

plant's efficiency, cost four cents a kilowatt-hour to produce, while hydroelectric power could be generated for under *one-tenth of one cent per kilowatt-hour*. Clearly, Pacific Light and Power would find it beneficial to invest in new water power facilities.

This realization persuaded Huntington, Kerckhoff and Balch to undertake the Big Creek Project, the largest hydroelectric

development yet begun in the country. The construction history of this project is treated in detail in a subsequent chapter, but suffice it to say here that its magnitude required substantial new financing. In 1910, Huntington and his associates incorporated a new company, Pacific Light and Power Corporation, capitalized at $40 million, which then sold bonds in an equal amount to raise money for the construction effort.

61

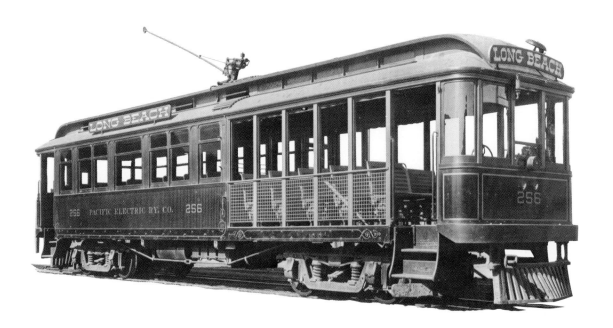

The Big Red Cars made Southern California famous for its excellent rapid transit system. These big wooden cars were the mainstay of P.E. service for forty years.
COURTESY RICHARD J. FELLOWS.

At this time, Huntington, who was approaching his sixtieth birthday, sold his half interest in the Pacific Electric Railway to the Southern Pacific Company in exchange for their minority interest in his Los Angeles Railway. This streamlined Huntington's complex railway empire, enabling him to concentrate on serving the profitable Los Angeles marketplace, while the region-wide Pacific Electric received the benefit of the vast financial resources of the Southern Pacific. Shrewdly, however, Huntington ensured that his Pacific Light and Power Corporation retained the valuable contracts to provide energy to the now-independent Pacific Electric as well as to the still Huntington-owned L.A. Railway. Thus, with both financing and a market assured, and with the formerly complex tangle of intertwined business interests now much simplified, Huntington and the new Pacific Light and Power Corporation could get on with the task of building Big Creek.

It may come as a surprise to learn that Henry Huntington, that great master of electrical properties, was also the founder of the Southern California Gas Company. In 1908, he purchased control of the City Gas Company and the Domestic Gas Company, both small companies vigorously expanding their gas systems in Los Angeles in the face of fierce opposition from the entrenched Los Angeles Gas and Electric Corporation. Two years later, Huntington incorporated the Southern California Gas Company as a wholly owned subsidiary of Pacific Light and Power, specifically to own and operate any gas properties PL&P might obtain incidentally to its acquisition of electric systems.

At first, Southern California Gas operated only the Los Angeles systems inherited from City Gas and Domestic Gas, but in 1911, not long after Huntington purchased the San Bernardino Gas and Electric Company, which had developed from Charles Lloyd's original Highgrove hydroelectric plant built years earlier, the gas system in San Bernardino was turned over to the new gas company. At the same time, Edison's Riverside gas system was purchased, and Southern California Gas was on its way to becoming a regional utility.

By 1912, however, Huntington was having second thoughts about his gas properties. After two years of operation the Southern California Gas Company was losing money and was deeply in debt to its parent corporation, PL&P,

siphoning away funds that were needed for the Big Creek Project. Deeply committed both financially and philosophically to the major construction effort at Big Creek, and believing, as did Edison's management at the same time, that the future of energy lay with electricity, he decided to part with the gas company.

Huntington and his long-time associates Kerckhoff and Balch were then engaged in separating their various utility commitments, which included the San Joaquin Light and Power Corporation and Fresno's water and trolley systems as well as PL&P. The results of this amicable separation were to have far-reaching effects upon the utility development of Central and Southern California. By the early summer of 1913, when all the maneuvering ended, Huntington retained full control of Los Angeles Railway and gained complete ownership of Pacific Light and Power—including the Big Creek Project then under construction—and substantial, but as yet undeveloped, water rights on the South Fork of the San Joaquin River. In exchange, Kerckhoff and Balch obtained full control of the San Joaquin Light and Power Corporation,

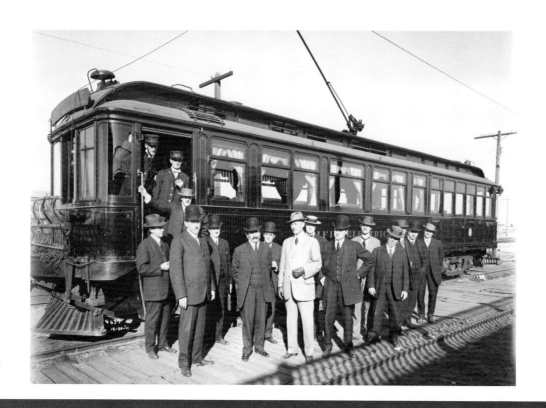

including operating plants and water rights on the North Fork of the San Joaquin, and ownership of the Southern California Gas Company. Although it is doubtful if anyone realized it at the time, the way had been prepared for the future division of the San Joaquin Valley into the service areas of two unrelated electric companies, and for the separation of the gas business from the electric business in Southern California, each of which ultimately would come to rest in the hands of two independent and fiercely competitive utilities.

In 1913, however, all this was in the distant future. Huntington at last had full control of PL&P, with no nervous partners to complain as he poured more millions into the Big Creek project, which he saw as the key to Southern California's future prosperity, believing it would free the region from expensive steam-generated electricity and the uncertainties of supply from small local hydroelectric plants.

Businessmen, too, used the Red Cars. Here, a group of Edison officials pose beside the sumptuous parlour car "El Peregrino" at Seaside Station, following a visit to the Long Beach Steam Plant, under construction nearby.
EDISON COLLECTION.

The complexities of his vast power and railway enterprises did not preclude Huntington from taking an interest in the business potential of other areas. One such example was his acquisition of control of the Ventura County Power Company in 1914.

Ventura County Power grew out of the Ventura Land and Power Company of 1890, whose electric plant in Ventura, built in the face of bitter opposition from the local gas company as mentioned in an earlier chapter, was one of the earliest electric lighting facilities to go into operation in Southern California. Reorganized in 1901 as the Ventura Water, Light and Power Company, it operated the electric, gas and domestic water systems in the City of Ventura and owned lands along the San Buenaventura River.

One of the directors of the company was William R. Staats of Pasadena, the financier who had been one of the founders of the West Side Lighting Company in Los Angeles and who was at that time a director of the Edison Company.

One curiosity of the electric system in Ventura was the original power plant itself, which was built adjacent to the water-powered flour mill of L.J. Rose, one of the company's founders. The hydroelectric plant used the mill's water system to operate its dynamos during the evening hours, when the flour mill was not in use. When, in the late 1890s, a succession of winters with little rain threatened to dry up the

A wagonload of new insulators is being taken from Ventura County Power's warehouse in Ventura to the site of the construction of the 33,000-volt line to Castaic.
Edison Collection.

Ventura County Power Company's headquarters office in Ventura, about 1910.
Edison Collection.

hydro plant's water supply, a small steam boiler and engine were installed to keep the plant running. This plant, with its unusual combination of prime movers, remained in service until 1906.

In October 1906, the Ventura County Power Company was incorporated and acquired the utility systems in Ventura, Oxnard and Santa Paula. Even at this comparatively late date, these small systems in Ventura County still provided lighting service only from dusk to midnight. Local socialites who anticipated giving a party that might go beyond midnight had to make a special arrangement in advance with the power plant engineer in order to secure an extra hour or two of electric light service. While appropriate for pioneering days when electric lights were a novelty, by 1906 these brief hours of operation were rightly considered to be poor service. Further, absence of continuous power service precluded manufacturing plants from installing electric motors with their resulting economies. The Ventura County Power Company was organized to do something about this situation.

It will be recalled that in 1907 Edison had placed into service its Kern River 75,000-volt transmission line. This power line climbed over the mountain barrier through Tejon Pass on a routing later followed by the Grapevine Highway, today's Interstate 5. Switching stations were located at Tejon, Castaic and San Fernando, from each of which some local business was served. No sooner had the substation at Castaic been built than the Ventura County Power Company decided to build a 33,000-volt power line from it to Saticoy, with branches to Oxnard and Ventura.

Building Ventura County Power Company's Castaic-Saticoy 33,000-volt line, 1907.
EDISON COLLECTION.

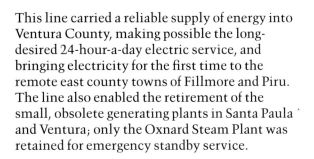

The picturesque Santa Paula Substation of the Ventura County Power Company. Prior to 1906, a gas-engine generator had been housed in this building.
EDISON COLLECTION.

This line carried a reliable supply of energy into Ventura County, making possible the long-desired 24-hour-a-day electric service, and bringing electricity for the first time to the remote east county towns of Fillmore and Piru. The line also enabled the retirement of the small, obsolete generating plants in Santa Paula and Ventura; only the Oxnard Steam Plant was retained for emergency standby service.

Ventura County Power Company was also in the gas business in Ventura, Oxnard, Hueneme and Santa Paula, and held the distinction of providing the first natural gas service in Southern California. In 1904, natural gas was obtained from wells on company-owned and leased lands near Ventura and piped to the gas plants in Ventura and Oxnard, where it was blended with artificial gas manufactured from oil. While not as good as straight natural gas, this so-called "blended gas" was far superior to the manufactured product alone. The Ventura Company also owned domestic water systems in Ventura and Oxnard, the latter being sold to the city in 1912.

Plant Engineer Milton Nicholson stands by the Corliss engine at the Oxnard Steam Plant, about 1910.
EDISON COLLECTION.

The Oxnard Steam Plant as it appeared in 1921, just before its abandonment.
EDISON COLLECTION.

The B Street Pumping Plant in Oxnard as it appeared in 1912, was part of the domestic water supply system owned by the Ventura County Power Company.
EDISON COLLECTION.

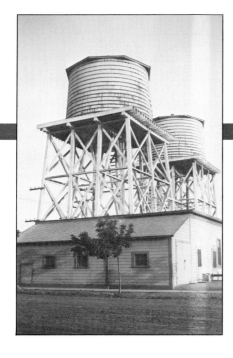

The utility system just described carried on for a number of years, but trouble was looming on the horizon. The 33,000 volt power line from Castaic, upon which the electric service of the Ventura Company depended, was only a single line, vulnerable to damage and interruption. If the power line did fail, the Oxnard Steam Plant did not have the capacity to carry the whole system by itself, and some customers had to do without. A power system such as this, without redundant transmission and with inadequate reserves, will sooner or later get into difficulties.

Into this discontent strode Henry Huntington. His Big Creek plants had just come into service and he was anxious to find new outlets for their energy. Pacific Light and Power had a substation in San Fernando to provide energy to the Pacific Electric, one of whose rail lines terminated there. Huntington saw that a power line could be extended from San Fernando westward through Chatsworth and the Simi Valley, ultimately to connect with the Ventura County system. With the desperation of drowning men, the owners of the Ventura County Power Company seized at Huntington's offer.

Over the next several months, negotiations were conducted that resulted in Huntington purchasing stock control of the Ventura Company, although it retained its separate corporate identity. Then, PL&P Vice President George C. Ward, who represented Huntington in the negotiations, announced that a new power line would be built from San Fernando, and that the Ventura water system would be offered for sale to the city. These moves succeeded in calming the criticism that had been leveled at the previous management.

Ventura County Power's Armageddon came in January 1914, when unusually heavy rains caused the worst flooding in recent memory all over Southern California. The vital 33,000-volt line was washed out in several locations between Castaic and Saticoy, and Ventura was without light or power for two days and nights. This outage, following others that had plagued the system previously, brought immediate and prolonged criticism from the community, even to the point where some people called for construction of a city-owned plant.

As promised, a new 16,000-volt line was constructed from PL&P's San Fernando substation through Chatsworth, Santa Susana, Moorpark and the Simi Valley—all of which areas thus received their first electric service—and was tied into the existing system at Saticoy. The 33,000-volt line was reconstructed for 16,000-volt operation, but the connection to Edison at Castaic was retained for emergencies. This loop line arrangement, with power available from either of two sources, greatly improved the quality of electric service enjoyed by Ventura County residents.

Although Ventura County was of minor interest to him compared to the other areas in which he was involved, Henry Huntington's improvements there illustrate the personal commitment he felt towards the development and improvement of all of Southern California. His two great trolley companies, Los Angeles Railway and Pacific Electric Railway, were in large measure responsible for the pattern of growth that made Southern California a community of suburbs, a pattern that was acceptable as long as the electric trolley was the mode of transportation, but which was turned ugly by the internal combustion engine. Of

Magnate Henry Huntington at age 70, when he was a director of the Southern California Edison Company.
COURTESY HUNTINGTON LIBRARY.

equal importance and benefit was Huntington's Pacific Light and Power Corporation, whose power lines followed those of the trolleys to bring electricity to a wide area of the Southland. The crowning achievement of Henry Huntington was his far-sighted Big Creek Hydroelectric Project. Originally built to power the Big Red trolley cars, Big Creek, with its promise fulfilled of abundant, low-cost electrical energy, would power the homes, transportation and commerce of the entire region for decades into the future.

A Pacific Electric excursion train leaves the Hollywood Subway enroute to the Western beaches, about 1925.
AUTHOR'S COLLECTION.

First delivery of electric power to the booming mining camps of Tonopah and Goldfield was in October, 1905. The following Fourth of July, miners and citizens enthusiastically celebrated the arrival of the electric age with a horse drawn float, shown here in front of the power company's Tonopah office.
EDISON COLLECTION.

Sagebrush and Tower Lines

What was in many ways the most colorful of all Southern California Edison's predecessor companies owed its beginning to a burro. Early in 1900, Jim Butler, an erstwhile Nevada farmer, packed his burro and went prospecting in the desolate deserts and mountains of Southern Nevada. One night the animal was turned loose to forage, and the next morning, while Butler was engaged in recapturing the burro near the summit of a hill, his eyes were attracted by the glint of mineral in a nearby ledge of rock. With his prospector's hammer, he chipped off a few samples, which, he eventually learned, were rich in silver ore. The outcrop was the only surface trace of the famous Mizpah Ledge that subsequently produced millions of dollars worth of silver and resulted in the opening of Tonopah, one of the greatest silver camps in the history of the nation. Two years later, just 26 miles away from Tonopah, the fabulously rich gold deposits of Goldfield were discovered.

Despite their remote, waterless locations, both the Tonopah and Goldfield discoveries soon brought rushes of miners, prospectors and entrepreneurs, all determined to "strike it rich." By 1904, both towns were wide open camps filled with the frenzied speculation, opportunism and lawlessness that was typical of the mining history of the American West. Among the fortune seekers who arrived that summer were two men from Colorado; Loren Curtis, an hydraulic engineer, and Charles Hobbs, a former official of the Denver and Rio Grande Railway. "Grubstaked" by investors back in Denver, Curtis and Hobbs had come for the purpose of locating mining claims, but found the territory pre-empted by those who had arrived previously. Discouraged about not finding paying mining claims, the two men were nonetheless impressed by the fact that development of the fabulous riches of the two camps could not continue without provision of some cheaper power than steam engines whose fuel and water both had to be brought long distances at great cost.

Both men believed that hydroelectric power might be generated upon one of the many streams on the eastern slope of the Sierras and brought to the mines in Nevada. A reconnaisance of the area revealed that Bishop Creek was an ideal watercourse upon which to site, if necessary, several power plants. Hobbs and Curtis returned to Denver and presented their ideas to a group of capitalists, including prominent mine owner Frank J. Campbell and U. S. Senator Lawrence C. Phipps. These men pledged an initial $300,000 to the enterprise and, aware that at least two rival hydroelectric projects threatened to beat them to the mining

69

camps, they reached the daring decision to start construction work immediately without waiting on the assurance of power contracts from the mines.

The Nevada Power, Mining and Milling Company was organized in·Denver on December 31, 1904, and actual construction work on Bishop Creek was begun the following day. There followed nine months of difficult but fast-paced construction. A site was chosen on Bishop Creek for the first hydroelectric plant, today called Bishop Plant Four, which

Freighting supplies over the White Mountains during the winter of 1904-05, during the building of the line from Bishop to Tonopah.
EDISON COLLECTION.

Tonopah, which would make it the third longest power line then in service. The biggest challenge was posed by the country through which the line was to run, for it would traverse at a maximum elevation of 10,500 feet, the treacherous White Mountains, notorious for 20 foot snow falls in winter, and then would cross a waterless desert, where summer temperatures exceeded 120° F.

Named Plant Four although it was the first hydro plant built on Bishop Creek, the facility had gotten ivy-covered walls by the time this picture was taken in 1923.
EDISON COLLECTION.

originally was to have only one 750-kilowatt generator. Before long, however, it was seen that the Nevada load would overtax that one unit, so a second generator was installed by the time the transmission line to Nevada was completed.

That transmission line was in many ways the most difficult part of the project. It was proposed to be energized at 55,000 volts, then the second highest voltage in use in the nation, and was to extend 113 miles from Bishop to

Notwithstanding that it was then the dead of winter, a hardy group of surveyors left the town of Bishop for the White Mountains to survey a route for the power line to Tonopah. Almost literally on the heels of the survey crew, a construction outfit followed to erect the line of wooden poles. Slogging through the precipitous mountains encumbered by early spring snows, the crews set poles, fitted insulators and strung copper wire.

Back in the Owens Valley at Laws, the railroad station nearest to Bishop, train after train on the Southern Pacific's narrow gauge Owens Valley line brought carloads of supplies for powerhouse and transmission line. Ponderous generator parts were laboriously freighted up to the plant site, urged by long strings of mules. Pack trains and buckboard wagons carried material along an ever-lengthening road to where the power line was going up.

By the time the summer of 1905 had arrived, the transmission line crews were out of the mountains and onto the desert slopes below. In the blistering heat of July and August, the work went forward, although workers had to wear

Silver Peak Substation, a major switching point for lines going to the various Nevada mining camps, was a remote place in 1918.
EDISON COLLECTION.

thick leather gloves just to pick up tools without burning their hands and had to wear bandanas over their noses to filter out some of the choking alkalai dust churned up by the incessant supply wagons. Water had to be freighted out to the construction camps on the desert in large wooden barrels, at a cost to the company of over a dollar per barrel, at a time when a lineman made only four dollars a day.

Building the wooden-stave flow line to Plant No. 2 on Bishop Creek, 1908.
EDISON COLLECTION.

Long strings of mules hauled ponderous generators from the narrow gauge railroad station near Laws to the Bishop Creek power plants miles away in the foothills.
EDISON COLLECTION.

Tex Rickard's famous Northern Saloon, a hub of Goldfield's sporting activities during the boom days.
WILLIAM J. YOUNG COLLECTION.

Billy Young on the eve of his retirement in 1953.
WILLIAM J. YOUNG COLLECTION.

72

"Billy-The-Wind"

William J. Young became a legend in his own time. In 1906, he arrived in Goldfield, which at that time, was the height of its great boom. There were many temptations for a young man earning the fabulous wage of four dollars a day. The largest, wealthiest and most exciting gambling dens and saloons were found there, of which the most famous was Tex Rickard's "The Northern." These establishments never closed their doors, and each kept up to 12 bartenders busy at all times as well as 50 "housemen" to look after the gaming tables. In 1906, Rickard promoted the Nelson-Gans lightweight world championship title fight, which lasted 30 rounds in Goldfield's broiling sun, and during which over $1 million in side-bets is believed to have changed hands. If these diversions weren't to one's liking, there were always stock promoters and outright con men eager to sell usually worthless mining stocks.

Ignoring these enticements, Billy Young became enamoured of automobiles. His first job in Goldfield was with the Western Gas Engine Company, where he learned to drive and repair the sleek "Horseless Carriage." At a time when it took a skilled specialist to keep an auto running, Billy developed a reputation for his proficiency as a driver and mechanic.

In May of 1910, Billy was hired to chauffeur officials of the Nevada-California Power Company. So impressed were they by Billy's proficiency, that he was put on the payroll to drive officers and carry the Company's mail. When the Southern Sierras Power Company was organized in 1911, some important legal documents had to be taken from the Company's office in Goldfield to the County Courthouse in Riverside. Most would have made this trip by train, as such a journey by auto over the unpaved desert roads would have taken from four to six days. Undaunted, Billy Young volunteered to get the documents there

by auto within 24 hours, and did so, earning for himself the lasting nickname of "Billy-the-Wind."

For a number of years he carried mail up and down the system. Lonely operators at remote facilities would hopefully scan the horizon for that pillar of dust that always meant "Billy-the-Wind" was coming. He was also an avid amateur photographer who, because of his travels, was frequently at the site of historic events and able to record them for posterity.

Repairing a blown cylinder head gasket in Cajon Pass, about 1918. EDISON COLLECTION.

His skill as a machinist also was of great value to the Company. He was frequently called upon to repair machinery or devise special tools in order to keep aging facilities in operation. Billy Young retired in 1953 as Supervisor of Hydro Plant Maintenance, responsible for the plants on the Eastern Slope of the Sierras, many of which he had helped to build.

From the beginning the power enterprise was successful, but in 1907 that success was marred by tragedy. Frank J. Campbell, who had been President of the Nevada Power, Mining and Milling Company since its inception, was also owner of the famous Vindicator Mine at Cripple Creek, Colorado. During a bitter miners' strike at Cripple Creek in 1904, 13 non-union employees of the Vindicator Mine were killed in a bombing incident. Campbell's unrelenting hounding of the men responsible for this murder ultimately broke the power of the Western Federation of Miners, whose leader was implicated in the bombing. Bitterness over Campbell's anti-union stance was carried to Nevada by former union miners from Cripple Creek who drifted to Tonopah and Goldfield and attempted, during the Spring of 1907, to unionize all activities in those camps, including dance hall girls and newsboys. One day Campbell was walking down Goldfield's Main Street returning to his hotel, when he was set upon by several men and beaten severely around the head. Although not killed outright, he was injured so badly that he resigned from the company and later died as a result of his wounds.

Why the Company mails were late that day.
WILLIAM J. YOUNG COLLECTION.

Finally, however, all was ready. The Bishop Creek Plant had been installed and tested and the long power line completed. On September 19, 1905, the first hydroelectric energy was delivered to Goldfield, and two days later, power went on in Tonopah. Both towns turned out to celebrate the event with a bawdy gusto that was long remembered, for the arrival of low-cost power at the camps meant more mining work could proceed, resulting in a boom economy and jobs for all.

Another Coloradan, Delos A. Chappell, was elected to succeed Campbell. Under Chappell's able guidance the company expanded its horizons. In 1907, it was reorganized as the Nevada-California Power Company, and a $5-million bond issue was sold to finance construction of additional power plants on Bishop Creek, a second power line to Tonopah, and line extensions north to Round Mountain and Manhattan in Central Nevada, and south to Rhyolite, just east of Death Valley.

During Tonopah's bustling boom days, even some of the dance halls in the red light district featured electrically lighted signs.
WILLIAM J. YOUNG COLLECTION.

1910 that James S. Cain, Bodie's and Mono County's most influential citizen, organized the Pacific Power Company to provide electric service to Bodie and certain nearby mining camps just over the border in Nevada.

Construction immediately began on a hydroelectric plant on Mill Creek, which drains into Mono Lake, at a site on the flank of Copper Mountain near where a small copper

Bodie in its waning days as a mining town, about 1912. WILLIAM J. YOUNG COLLECTION.

Nestled in a high mountain valley in Mono County north of Bishop lies the town of Bodie, which is today a remarkably well preserved "ghost town." In 1910, although already in decline, Bodie was still an important mining community of several hundred inhabitants. It will be recalled from an earlier chapter that in 1892 the Standard Consolidated Mining Company at Bodie installed a pioneer alternating current plant to run their mill. There was no general service to the community from this facility, however, and it was not until

smelter had earlier stood. The Jordan Plant, as it was called, was a poured concrete structure typical of Western power plant construction practice of that time. The plant was completed and put into operation in January 1911, and by means of a transmission line 124 miles long, Pacific Power Company began to furnish electric power to such famous old mining towns as Aurora, Lucky Boy, Rawhide, Fairview, Wonder and Nevada Hills. To the citizens of Bodie, who for years had endured each winter the isolation, darkness, bitter cold

The Jordan Hydro Plant operator on duty, 1911. He is sitting with attention on the switchboard meters, and with a hand on the exciter needle-valve control, ready to respond to quick changes in demand. EDISON COLLECTION.

Bodie after a typical winter snowfall.
EDISON COLLECTION.

the way of any danger, and a new plant was built and placed into service by year's end. This plant is today Edison's Lundy hydro plant.

As a result of this disaster, the worst ever to befall any facility belonging to Edison or a predecessor company, and because of the general decline in mining activities after 1910, the Pacific Power Company began to lose money, and in 1915 defaulted on its bonds. In a complex series of legal and financial moves, including the drama of a public auction of the company's assets on the front steps of its office in Bodie, the old management organized a new company, Pacific Power Corporation, to take over the former company's business and properties. Surprisingly, financing was even found to begin construction of a new hydroelectric plant on Rush Creek, and to obtain water rights for another on Lee Vining Creek.

One of six very early model Caterpillar tractors used to haul materials to the Rush Creek plant site from the Benton railroad station, 56 miles away.
EDISON COLLECTION.

and high snowfall that resulted from the town's remote, windswept high mountain location, the arrival of electric service brought a measure of cheer and relief to an otherwise dreary time of year.

Tragically, however, less than two months after going into operation, the Jordan Plant was destroyed by a huge avalanche that swept down Copper Mountain on the night of March 8 and 9, 1911, as a result of a tremendous snowfall from an unusually severe winter storm. Of the half-dozen or so people who lived at the plant, only one woman was rescued alive. Charles O. Poole, at that time Chief Engineer of both Pacific Power Company and the Nevada-California Power Company, found a new site for a replacement power house that was out of

Sale of properties of bankrupt Pacific Power Company in front of the Bodie office, August 30, 1915.
EDISON COLLECTION.

Avalanche at Jordan

Paul Greenleaf, a junior operator at the Jordan hydro plant near Bodie, and later Southern Sierras' Construction Superintendent, had gone up to Nevada to read the meters at the Lucky Boy Mine, and so was away from the powerhouse when it was destroyed by an avalanche. His apparent misfortune at being chosen for the unpopular meter reading duty proved to be lucky, for all the other operators at the plant perished. Greenleaf wrote an interesting report of the 1911 disaster that was reprinted in the *Sierras Service Bulletin* in June 1937:

"We had very little snow up until the night of February 20. It started to snow that night and snowed continuously, with practically no interruption until the morning of March 8 (1911)....I got back to Bodie (from Lucky Boy) at 10 o'clock on March 9. As we had several slight interruptions, I had been in direct communication with the power house up until about 11 o'clock. At that time I went to bed at the substation, along side of the transformers. At five minutes of 12 the power went off. I repeatedly tried to get in communication with the power house over the telephone and when I could not raise anyone, at 4 o'clock the next morning, started on snowshoes (skis) for the power house.

"The storm was very severe at this time and I lost my way....I ran across the marker for the mail road and found I was back within 3 miles of Bodie. I then returned to Bodie and got a Swede named Ericson who had a reputation of being the best (cross country skier) in the county. We started back toward the powerhouse at about 11 o'clock....We were so exhausted when we got nearly to the powerhouse site that we decided to go to the Fred Mattley Ranch first to get warmed up and something to eat before we tried to go over to the power house....

Searching the ruins of the Jordan plant for survivors of the avalanche, 1911.
WILLIAM J. YOUNG
COLLECTION.

"Mr. Mattley told me that the slide had taken the power house out. He and I took the telephone out of his house and carried it on our back over to where the slide had occurred. We cleared the ends of the 'phone line up out of the slide, then connected his 'phone and tried to call Bodie, but found the line dead. We then went all over the snow where the powerhouse had been, calling names of the fellows who were there and could not get any response. We were so exhausted that we went back to Mattley's ranch and did not return to the powerhouse site until the next morning.

"Mr. Ericson wanted to go back to Bodie so I made arrangements with him to patrol our 'phone line as he went back, to see if he could clear it. About 9 o'clock the morning of the 11th I heard Mr. J. S. Cain talking to Lucky Boy on the 'phone. I broke in on his conversation and told him just what had happened....

"During the morning of the 11th, as the weather had cleared, a number of local ranchers and our Engineer, Mr. Burke, came over to the slide and we all started to dig to rescue anybody that we might possibly find. The powerhouse, two cottages, the little barn and old mill building, the old smelter building and our storeroom were completely demolished, and the snow was from 14 to 20 feet deep over where these buildings had stood. We started digging pits to see what we could

find. We found the generator of the powerhouse still on its foundation and recovered Mr. Peacock's body first. Second, we found the Mason's cottage and dug down and found Mr. and Mrs. Mason at about noon on the 12th. Mr. Mason was dead in the same bed as Mrs. Mason and their dog, who were still alive. It took us about four hours, cutting the timbers and digging in and moving debris to release her so that we could get her out. She was conscious all this time during the rescue work.

"We took a pair of skis and made a temporary sled and put her on it and took her over to the Conway Ranch. We kept Mrs. Mason there several days, but the circulation in her right leg below the knee would not return. As we were unable to get a doctor out there to attend to her, we remodeled the sled, put a mattress on it, wrapped her well up in blankets, manned the sled with 12 men on skis and pulled it by hand the 18 miles to Bodie. Eventually she was taken to a hospital in San Francisco, where she lost her leg but otherwise recovered.

"After Mrs. Mason's rescue had been made we started the next morning looking for the rest of the bodies. (After all were found,) we made a little plot of ground over back of Mattley's for burying. We built bonfires on the ground to thaw it out, after we had dug down through the snow, so that we could dig the graves and bury our six men...."

For several years prior to this, the owners of the Nevada-California Power Company had been associated with Jim Cain in the affairs of Pacific Power. As early as 1913 Nevada-California Power had built a transmission line north from Bishop through Casa Diablo and Mammoth to Lee Vining and the Lundy hydro plant to interconnect the two systems. Over the next few years more and more of the output of the Lundy and Rush Creek plants went southward over this line as Pacific Power's load declined. A merger between the two became increasingly attractive, and in 1917 it was consummated.

The financial problems of the Pacific Power Company were a warning of the consequences of too great a dependency upon the mining industry as a market for power. As early as 1907 there was a falling off in the business of the Nevada-California Power Company due to a nation-wide business recession that resulted in a cut-back in mine development work. By 1909 it was clear to the company's management that

of today's Sierra Pacific Power Company. Serious consideration was given to extending service to the great San Joaquin Valley to the west, but the intervening Sierra Nevada range with its high, snowbound passes and severe winter weather meant that transmission lines would be subject to frequent interruption. To all, it seemed apparent that only to the south could new markets be found, in the rapidly growing Southern California region.

78 *Thunderstorm over Bishop, 1906.*

many of the mines in Central Nevada were nearing exhaustion, and with the depletion of the mines, the Nevada demand would fall off as the population dependent upon mining operations decreased.

Clearly, more stable markets had to be found, but where? To the east beyond Tonopah was only empty desert. To the north, the small population around Carson City and Reno was already adequately served by the existing Truckee General Electric Company, forerunner

There were obstacles, of course. First, in order to enter the settled area south of the San Bernardino Mountains, it would be necessary to build a power line longer than any then in use, across desert territory then sparsely populated and with very little power demand of its own. Second, once such a line was built, the company would have to compete with Edison and Pacific Light and Power, both well established and already serving virtually all customers in that field that in their judgement could feasibly be reached.

Chief Engineer Charles O. Poole looking at the dam at the intake to Plant Four on Bishop Creek, 1905.

Chief Engineer Charles O. Poole travelled around the country looking at other long distance power lines. Upon his return, he conducted an experiment to demonstrate that electricity could be sent over 200 miles without an objectionable line loss. On the Fourth of July, 1911, a day upon which traditionally there was a very low demand for electric service, the two transmission lines from Bishop Creek to Tonopah and Goldfield were briefly taken out of service. Using temporary jumper connections, the lines were so arranged that power sent out from Bishop Creek on one line would circle via Silver Peak,

Making a splice in the aluminum and steel cable during construction of the tower line over Cajon Pass in May of 1912.
EDISON COLLECTION.

Goldfield, Tonopah and Alkalai substations and return on the other line to the starting point. This circuit was 220 miles long and provided a favorable comparison to the proposed southern transmission line. The demonstration was a success, proving that a very long power line could be successfully and economically operated, even without synchronous condensers to control reactive energy on the line. This was a revelation to power engineers around the nation who had not believed such a design workable.

Engineer Poole had another surprise up his sleeve. Aluminum cable with a steel strand core—today's familiar ACSR, "aluminum cable, steel reinforced"—had recently been developed as an economical alternative to copper wires, and was being used in the Pacific Northwest on short power lines. Poole suggested that the new line to Southern California use this cable because of its lower cost and superior mechanical strength.

With these engineering questions dealt with, in June 1911, President Chappell and his partners incorporated the Southern Sierras Power Company as a subsidiary of the older Nevada-California Power Company. During 1911 and 1912 this new company undertook the construction of the facilities necessary to extend power service into Southern California. Key to this was of course the so called "Tower Line." This 238-mile long line, then the world's longest power line, left Bishop and ran southwards through the Owens Valley and the

Bernardino. During 1911, local franchises were secured to conduct business in San Bernardino, both city and county, and in Riverside, Kern and Inyo Counties. Early in the next year, several 33,000-volt power lines were constructed from San Bernardino out towards Perris, Hemet and Elsinore, Rialto and Bloomington, East and West Riverside, and distant Corona, all of which communities looked forward to their first, or improved electric service.

Southern Sierras' big Alco truck hauling a load of poles out to Elsinore, 1913.
EDISON COLLECTION.

Lowering the turbine spindle into its housing, during construction of the San Bernardino Steam Plant, 1912.
EDISON COLLECTION.

Construction of the line into the Perris Valley is typical of the conditions of that day. Survey crews first located the line south from San Bernardino to Colton, across the Santa Ana River, parallel to Iowa Avenue in Highgrove, up the Box Springs Grade and south to Perris along Perris Boulevard. Despite these grand names, all the roads mentioned were then just dirt country lanes. The survey completed, construction crews went to work, but because of weather and the varying terrain, progress was slow. All work was still done by hand or performed with the aid of mule power, so as a result only from three to seven poles a day could be set. So remote was much of the area that supply camps followed the men as they built the line, and materials and supplies were hauled down daily from San Bernardino.

The Southern Sierras Power Company's local office in Perris, about 1918.
EDISON COLLECTION.

sagebrush dotted rocky wastelands of the Eastern California desert, across the shimmering sands of the dreaded Mojave Sink, and over precipitous Cajon Pass into the lush San Bernardino Valley. The supply and patrol road built alongside was later reconstructed by the State of California as U.S. Highway 395.

An additional hydro plant was built on Bishop Creek, making a total of five facilities on that stream, and an auxiliary steam plant and distributing substation were built at San

The Alco truck again, now carrying employees and their families in Fourth of July parade in Riverside, about 1915.
EDISON COLLECTION.

On June 3, 1912, just under a year from the date it was incorporated, the Southern Sierras Power Company began service to Rialto and Bloomington, and 11 days later the line to Riverside and Perris was energized. The circuit protection switches for this line were of the air-break type, not the more traditional oil circuit breaker, and being both sensitive and automatic in operation, they would sometimes kick open for the slightest interference on the

Raising a power pole using gin-poles and lots of muscle, during construction of the line to Perris, 1912.

power line. Their operation on short circuits at night was occasionally spectacular, as sometimes the flaming arc would refuse to break for a considerable time, causing brilliant flashes to be visible for many miles. At one time an operator at Edison's Colton Substation called his opposite number at Southern Sierras' San Bernardino station to report that he had seen an immense ball of fire shoot far into the nighttime sky from a breaker on Southern Sierras' Riverside line three miles away.

The towns of Hemet and San Jacinto were eager to get their connections to the new Southern Sierras system. Both had their own private power plants, but this energy was available only to a few commercial and residential customers, and only for a few hours in the evening of each day. When the new service was begun in mid-year, the communities could at last enjoy electricity 24 hours of each day. Southern Sierras' office in Hemet posted a sign which proclaimed "Let Electricity Be Your Watch Dog, Burglars Will Not Raid Where There Is Light."

At the time the Nevada-California Power Company was investigating the feasibility of extending service to Southern California, another aspect of the utility business came under their consideration. Telephones are an essential tool in the operation of a power system, both for day-to-day power dispatching and to deal with emergency situations.

81

endanger power system operations, it was decided to turn over the company phone system to a subsidiary company to be managed by men experienced in telephone operations. At this time, the local telephone utility in the Owens Valley, the Inyo Telephone Company, was facing a financial crisis. It had become necessary to completely reconstruct its toll line from Bishop to Lone Pine, because the original line had been placed on inferior poles which had rotted, yet Inyo Telephone did not have the resources to pay for this replacement.

With the completion of the southern extension imminent, in March 1912 the management of the Power Company concluded a deal whereby they purchased Inyo Telephone, turned over to

Main exchange and office of the Interstate Telegraph Company in Bishop, about 1923.
EDISON COLLECTION.

An early sales booth for Southern Sierras, probably about 1913.
EDISON COLLECTION.

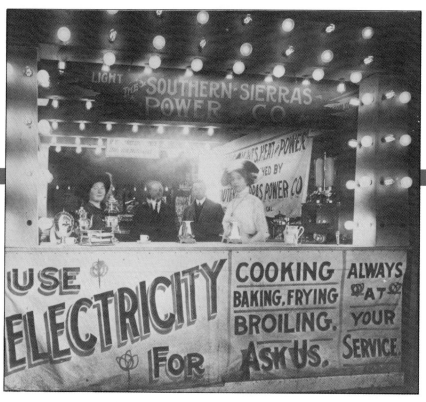

Unfortunately, at that time the Power Company's phone line to Nevada was so poor that satisfactory conversations could rarely be held between the Nevada substations and Bishop by persons who were not skilled in the use of noisy circuits.

Faced with the prospect of having to operate a much longer communications line to Southern California in conjunction with the Southern Sierras extension project, yet not wishing to prolong telephone service so poor that it might it all of the power company phone lines to be reconstructed and operated for both commercial and company traffic, and guaranteed a bond issue to pay for all improvements, repairs and extensions. Inyo's management and employees remained to operate this enlarged telephone network, the name of which was changed to Interstate Telegraph Company to reflect the fact that it also did business in Nevada.

By 1914, Interstate had taken on the dimensions it would have for the next 40 years. Its service extended from Bridgeport in Mono County, California, and from Tonopah and Goldfield in Nevada, southward parallel to the lines of the Power Companies to Victorville and San Bernardino. As had been anticipated when it was organized, this small but important subsidiary operated a quality local and long distance telephone service for the public and for the operation of the power system.

Because its management had first started in the power business to serve the mines of Nevada, the Southern Sierras Power Company was not

adverse to searching out stable mining operations in the Mojave Desert to which electric service could be brought. So, although there were comparatively few customers to be found in the area between Bishop and the Cajon Pass, in its first few years of operation taps were taken off the Tower Line to serve Inyokern, the chemical plants at Searles Lake, the Randsburg gold mining district, the cement mills at Victorville and Oro Grande, and the Santa Fe Railway's shops at Barstow.

The Yellow Astor Mine, near Randsburg, was a Southern Sierras customer until shut down by World War Two.
EDISON COLLECTION.

Patroling the Victorville-Barstow 33,000-volt line in 1922.
COURTESY ART MULLINS.

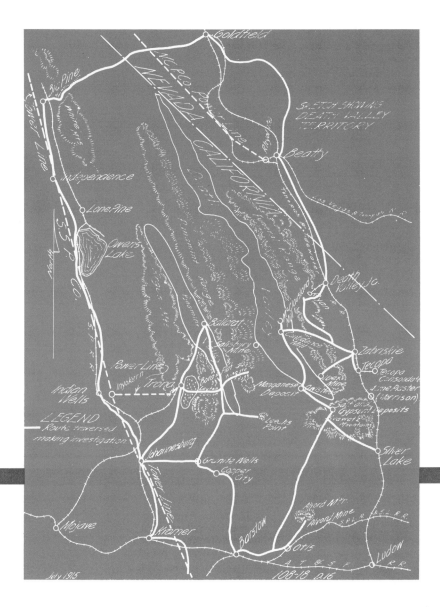

In keeping with this policy, in 1915 staff engineer H.N.Siegfried was dispatched to the area surrounding Death Valley to find other possible loads. Thanks to atrocious road conditions, it took Siegfried and his party, travelling in two automobiles, some 15 days to make the loop journey from Riverside to Death Valley Junction, Rhyolite and Goldfield, returning via Big Pine and Victorville. He discouragingly identified only three mining enterprises large and stable enough to justify a

H. N. Siegfried and driver during a survey for new business, about 1915.
Edison Collection.

power line, and they too distant to be economically served. Nevertheless, his report is a fascinating account of the real hardships involved in automobile travel in the days prior to World War One.

Despite disappointments like the Siegfried Report, by 1915 it was apparent to the management of the Southern Sierras Power Company that their gamble to penetrate the Southern California marketplace would be successful. After only two and a half years of

Route of H. N. Siegfried's 1915 journey through Eastern California to find new business for the Southern Sierras Power Company.
Edison Collection.

service, the southern load already nearly equalled that in Nevada, and gave every promise of continuing to grow at a rapid rate. It was for this reason that the managers of the Nevada-California Power Company and the Southern Sierras Power Company undertook another corporate restructuring in midyear of 1915. They saw that substantial new funding would be required to accommodate the growth anticipated on the power system, but the bonding capacity of the existing companies had been reached.

Delos Chappell and his partners considered merging Nevada-California Power, Southern Sierras Power, Pacific Power, Interstate Telegraph and their other properties into one new unified company. They were concerned, however, that the interstate nature of their business, plus the fact that it was engaged in power, telephone and telegraph, water, and non-utility operations simultaneously, coupled with the unsettled nature of state and federal utilities regulation at that time, would make it difficult for such a unified system to operate. It was decided, therefore, in keeping with common financial practice of that time, to

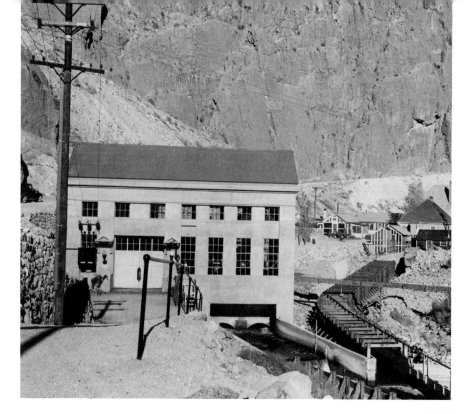

Adams auxilliary hydro plant in the Owens River Gorge, which used the old generator and turbine removed from the abandoned Holtville hydro plant. This plant was sold to the City of Los Angeles in 1934.
EDISON COLLECTION.

Accordingly, the Nevada-California Electric Corporation was organized and began business as a non-operating holding company on July 1, 1915. Although all the subsidiary companies, or "Allied Companies" as they were called, had a common management, including Interstate Telegraph and the non-utility properties, each

with a substantial and irreversible drop in business as mining in Nevada began its long decline. Five years later, they had undertaken a successful penetration of the Southern California marketplace by acquiring a growing load in a new service territory without conflict with the existing utilities in the area. To be

form instead a holding company. Unlike many such companies floated in that era, however, this was done not for reasons of financial manipulation, but simply to create a unified management structure within a controlling corporation whose much larger bonding capacity could be used to fund improvements and extensions as needed upon any of the underlying companies.

continued to conduct business under its own name. Nevada-California Power, for example, continued to operate the electric lines in Nevada and Mono County, while Southern Sierras ran the southern part of the system.

With this last restructuring and refinancing successfully completed, the management of Southern Sierras and its allied companies had every reason to view the future with confidence. Back in 1910 they had been faced

sure, at first business was light, for their lines had been built far in advance of population growth and commercial development, in itself a courageous gamble on a scale without precedent in the electric utility industry at that time. Nonetheless, the builders' faith was justified, for in the decades to come, Southern Sierras Power, although it served no major urban centers, would by its electric service bring the comforts of civilization into Southeastern California's rural districts and remote desert regions.

Flumes down the Kaweah

Walking the flume to Kaweah No. 1 hydro plant.
EDISON COLLECTION.

In July 1891, the Secretary of the Visalia Gas, Light and Heat Company, which succeeded to the bankrupt Visalia Electric Light and Gas Company in 1890 and had been providing electric service to that San Joaquin Valley town for just a year, published a notice in the *Visalia Daily Times* that, commencing August 1st, the electric light works of the company would close down nightly at 1 A.M. Responding to a *Times* reporter, the Secretary stated that this cutback in service was an attempt to get the electric business on a paying basis, and in order

to do so it would be necessary to increase the number of lights in use and to shorten the hours of service. If this could not be done, the reporter was told, then the electric plant would go out of business.

In commenting upon this state of affairs, Ben M. Maddox, the outspoken editor of the *Times*, called attention to the possibility of using the waters of the Kaweah River to generate much less expensive electricity.

"That power could be brought here," Maddox pointed out, "on wires and used for a multiplicity of purposes. Our streets could then be lighted and residence and business houses illuminated at greatly reduced prices. In the day time the same power could be used to run electric fans in houses where electric lights were used, and machinery of all sorts would be driven cheaply and satisfactorily.

"If the electric light companies of Visalia and Tulare do not care to utilize water power that is so accessible for the purposes above mentioned, there ought to be some way for the people of the two cities to do it."

Maddox' words were prophetic but premature, for the longest power line then in use was less than 12 miles long, and the historic "Pomona Plant" with its 29-mile long transmission line to San Bernardino, was still a year and-a-half in the future. Visalia lay some 35 miles west of the best power plant site on the Kaweah, a seemingly unbridgable gap in 1891. But the crusading editor would not give up, and his newspaper kept hammering at the proposition of harnessing the Kaweah.

His reasons were valid. Tulare County had gone through stages of cattle raising and dry-farming of wheat. In 1891, a new phase began when Captain A. J. Hutchinson at Lindsay set up a six-horsepower gasoline engine to pump water to irrigate crops of oranges, lemons, olives and grapes. Hutchinson's experiment proved that the dry San Joaquin Valley was rich and fertile, needing only water to make it blossom and produce. Despite hot summer temperatures, a water table lay close to the surface, and Maddox was quick to point out that with an electric

Ben Maddox saw that winter snowstorms in the nearby Sierras could benefit Visalia by creating a reservoir of snow which, as it melted, could generate electric power for the Valley town.
LAKE COLLECTION.

Ben M. Maddox, visionary newspaper editor and power pioneer.
COURTESY CARL M. FERGUSON.

Pumping plant and orchard near Exeter, 1914.
EDISON COLLECTION.

supply from the Kaweah that would be both cheap and abundant, electric pumps could draw this water up to irrigate virtually any crop desired.

It was not too long before Maddox began to interest others in his idea. One was William H. "Billy" Hammond, County Clerk and brother of John Hays Hammond, the famous California mining engineer who had made a fortune in the gold fields of South Africa. The other was Albert G. Wishon, a Missouri-born real estate agent and businessman then living in Tulare, who was in later years to rise to the presidency of San Joaquin Light and Power Corporation. In 1895, Hammond and Wishon made an engineering study of the Kaweah's flow and organized the Kaweah Power and Water Company with the backing of men from Los Angeles and Pasadena, for capital could not be raised locally in Tulare County.

In 1904, the year the second Kaweah Power Plant went into service, Visalia still displayed many traces of its rural heritage.
EDISON COLLECTION.

Wishon proposed to build a small hydro plant at Lime Kiln Point on the Kaweah River near Lemon Cove. After going through the powerhouse, the water was to be carried in a ditch to irrigate orange groves at Exeter. The hydroelectric power produced was to be used primarily for irrigation pumping, although the partners hoped to send some to Visalia. Work actually began on the project early in 1895, with Wishon as general superintendent, bookkeeper and camp boss over a work force of about 200 men.

This pumping plant near Exeter was typical of the hundreds built to utilize the cheap power generated on the Kaweah. Note the transformers on the raised wooden platform at right, a construction method unique to the Mt. Whitney system.
EDISON COLLECTION.

89

A few months later Wishon visited the Mill Creek Plant near Redlands, which had then been in successful operation for nearly two years, and was impressed by the three-phase installation with its self-starting motors. He also visited the plant of the San Joaquin Electric Company under construction 38 miles east of Fresno, whose power line would be the world's longest when it was completed later that year. These excursions convinced him that he and Hammond had planned too small. The partners proposed to their financial backers that work be

Flume for Kaweah No. 2 hydro plant, under construction, 1904.
EDISON COLLECTION.

search for a suitable "high-head" plant site depleted their resources, and once again they had to look for financial backing, with no result.

As a last resort, in 1898, Hammond resolved to visit his famous engineer brother in London in the hope of securing his endorsement of their project. Wishon had just earned a $4,600 commission from a real estate deal. He gave his partner $1,500, which was used to outfit him and secure passage to Europe. Maddox prepared an elaborate prospectus, and off Hammond went. When he arrived in London he cabled home for another $500 as he had found that the correct attire for a London businessman consisted of tailed morning coat, gloves, spats, a top hat and walking stick.

Thus accoutred, Hammond went to visit his brother. On his first evening in London, Bill had dinner with brother "Jack" and a business associate, Leopold Hirsch. The next day, when serious discussion of the Kaweah project came up, John Hammond agreed to put up half the funds needed and Hirsch the balance. It turned out to be as easy as that.

stopped at Lemon Cove in favor of a site further upstream where a higher fall of water could generate a much larger amount of electricity. Unfortunately, the backers, frightened by

Wishon's change of mind, withdrew their support entirely and this first project to generate power on the Kaweah died stillborn.

In the meantime, Hammond and Wishon had also become associated in the management of the Visalia City Water Company. They hoped that, with the income from this enterprise, plus that from Wishon's real estate business, they could undertake the Kaweah development themselves. The still enthusiastic Ben Maddox joined their partnership. To their chagrin, the

Hammond returned to Visalia in September, 1898, with $200,000 in letters of credit. At a suggestion from Hirsch, it was decided to avoid the delays inherent in constantly having to cable London to obtain approvals from a Board of Directors by authorizing all work to be done in the name of "the Partnership of W. H. Hammond and A. G. Wishon acting as the Mount Whitney Power Company, not incorporated." To assist the partnership, Robert McF. Doble, a prominent western hydraulic engineer and brother of the man who had improved the Pelton waterwheel, was engaged to design the power plant and hydraulic system.

Doble's plans called for a plant having a static head of nearly 1300 feet, to be supplied by water carried in a wooden flume extending up the East Fork of the Kaweah. This was the highest head plant yet built in the country, requiring steel penstock pipe of the very maximum tensile strength that then could be manufactured. Furthermore, because of the remoteness of the terrain in which it would be built, the flume down the Kaweah itself represented a difficult construction job.

A local lumber mill was purchased and veteran mill operator A. D. Comstock was hired to turn out the redwood timbers and planks that would be needed for the thirty thousand foot long flume. The finished wood was hauled by wagon up to a point near the diversion where the flume was to begin, and was lowered down to the river. Construction progressed in sections, and as each thousand-foot length was completed, the water temporarily was turned

Tarring the new Kaweah No. 1 flume in 1947. This metal structure replaced the original redwood box, which was nearly 50 years old.
EDISON COLLECTION.

into it to enable more lumber to be flumed down to a point near where the construction work was going on. At a convenient place, the water was diverted out and the lumber was carried the rest of the way to the work site upon dollies running down the flat bottom of the flume, which was built first, in advance of the sides. This was the most convenient way to build the flume, which over much of its length, ran alongside sheer and rocky faces of the mountainside that were difficult of access. The head carpenter on the job rode a bicycle back

and forth along the flume to check progress at the various locations where work was being done, despite the danger that a slip could have resulted in a fatal fall.

The flume itself was made entirely of redwood. The box was three feet wide and two feet deep, built of 1x12 inch planks battened with 1x4's and caulked with spun oakum. This was supported on a framework and underpinning mostly made of 4x4 inch timbers, a foundation which gave trouble and had to be replaced

The original Lindsay Substation in June of 1899, a few days before service began from the Kaweah hydro plant.
EDISON COLLECTION.

91

Electric chick brooders increased output at the Hauser Ranch in Fontana.
EDISON COLLECTION.

William Verburg of Gardena adjusts the radio in his cow barn, about 1939.
EDISON COLLECTION.

Rural Electrification

Bringing electricity to Rural America was long a problem for some power companies. The great distances involved and the expense of facilities that would bring in little revenue kept many urban-based utilities from providing service to outlying rural districts. To Edison and its predecessors, however, rural electrification was always an important part of their business. As described in this chapter, the Mount Whitney Power Company thrived almost exclusively on rural business, for the largest town on its system, Visalia, had only about two thousand residents at the turn of the century. Another Edison predecessor, the Redlands Electric Light and Power Company, pioneered the use of three-phase motors for irrigation water pumping, a load that grew to great importance on the Edison system until the displacement of agriculture by suburbs in the years following World War Two.

In the 1930s, at a time when many of the nation's utilities were being criticized for their slowness in extending rural service, Edison was hailed for its creative rural electrification programs designed to reduce the traditional drudgery of farm life. Farm families could enjoy conveniences such as radios, hot water heaters, dishwashers and refrigerators, just as did their city cousins.

Many important labor-saving devices were offered just to farmers, however. Poultrymen took advantage of efficient new electric brooders, hatchers and "egg candles." Nurserymen utilized special new electric lights to nurture seedlings. Citrus packing houses, which long had used electric motors for conveyor belts, now added new labelling, wrapping and waxing machines. Butter churns, milking machines and sterilizing devices were used by dairy farmers, many of whom also, during that "Golden Age of Radio," installed radios in the cow barns because music dramatically increased milk production.

through the years. The redwood box itself proved very durable and lasted until replaced by the present metal flume built in the late 1940's. The entire wooden structure was put together with old square nails, as it was believed that wire nails, which had then just recently been introduced, would not adequately hold in redwood.

Construction work began in October 1898, and although it was hoped to have the plant ready by the following April, delays postponed completion for two months. Service began to Lindsay Substation on June 26, 1899, where the first load appropriately was a pump motor. Three days later, the circuit to Visalia was energized. An ecstatic Ben Maddox issued a triumphant special edition of the *Daily Times* with the headline "Now Ready for Business. Living Wires Bring Power From The Kaweah To Lindsay and Visalia," beneath which flowery prose described the project and its proprietors, and the benefits that would accrue to the region now that low-cost electric power had arrived.

Electric milking machines in use at the DeVierra Dairy in Artesia, about 1938.
EDISON COLLECTION.

From the beginning, the company's main business was to supply power for irrigation pumping. To this end, many annual flat-rate contracts were made with the farmers and ranchers of the area as quickly as they could be persuaded that electric motors really worked.

Tustin plant of the Mutual Citrus Association installed new waxing and wrapping machines in 1938.
EDISON COLLECTION.

In Visalia, flat-rate lighting schedules were offered at a rate much below that of the Visalia Gas, Light and Heat Company. The *Times* published the following rate schedule in June of 1899:

"Residence Lights (bulbs of 16 candlepower):

2 lights per month—$1.00

3 lights per month—$1.20

4 lights per month—$1.55

5 lights per month—$1.80

6 lights per month—$2.05

Additional lights above 6, $0.25 additional per month each;

Power loads, $50.00 per horsepower per annum."

The Mount Whitney Power Company was formally incorporated on December 22, 1899. Three months later, the partnership of Hammond and Wishon turned over to the company the physical plant that had been built under their direction, in exchange for 20 percent of the stock of the new corporation.

Mt. Whitney Power's Lindsay Substation as it appeared in 1904 after reconstruction in brick.
EDISON COLLECTION.

The other 80 percent was held by John Hays Hammond, who bought out Hirsch's interest. Ben Maddox was elected a director of the Company.

The Mount Whitney Company's creators, (l-r): William H. Hammond, Ben M. Maddox, and Albert G. Wishon relax at the Kaweah Powerhouse in July of 1902. Just two months later, Wishon had left the partnership.
COURTESY CARL M. FERGUSON.

During 1900, the enthusiasm of the original partners was amply vindicated as the Mount Whitney Power Company signed up new business far and wide. The Visalia Gas, Light and Heat Company sold out to the new concern, and operation of its obsolete old steam plant was abandoned, although in 1906 it was entirely reconstructed to provide a backup to the hydro plants. Notwithstanding these successes, there was trouble on the horizon.

Interior of the Kaweah Hydro Plant in 1904. Here too, operator is poised near needle valve control wheel to adjust to variations in load demand.
EDISON COLLECTION.

Albert G. Wishon, in later years as President of the San Joaquin Light and Power Corporation, Mount Whitney's arch-rival.
COURTESY PACIFIC GAS AND ELECTRIC COMPANY.

Albert G. Wishon envisioned a great expansion of the services of the Mount Whitney Company in order to bring the benefits of low-cost hydroelectric energy to farms and towns throughout the San Joaquin Valley. All during 1901 and 1902 he urged John Hammond, the principle owner of the company, to invest large sums in additional power developments on the San Joaquin, Kings, Kaweah, Tule and Kern Rivers, and increasingly Wishon chafed at Hammond's refusal to do so. John Hammond, although an American by birth, lived year 'round in London by preference, and while pleased with his investment and appreciative of the benefits it was providing to the region, considered the power business distinctly secondary to his mining interests. In short, he told Wishon in September 1902, "If you don't like it, resign." Thus were the talents of this far-sighted man lost to the Mount Whitney Company and its successor, Southern California Edison. Wishon moved to Fresno where he joined John S. Eastwood—of whom we shall hear more later—and subsequently William G. Kerckhoff and Henry Huntington—about both of whom we have already heard a great deal—in the expansion of the little San

Joaquin Power Company into the valley-wide San Joaquin Light and Power Corporation. Today, Wishon is memorialized by Pacific Gas and Electric Company's A. G. Wishon Powerhouse built on the San Joaquin River below Edison's Big Creek Powerhouse No. 4.

While the departure of Wishon had no immediate effect upon the fortunes of the Mount Whitney Power Company, his bitterness toward John Hays Hammond was to have long-term consequences. During the first

company, which became known as Mount Whitney Power and Electric Company following a 1909 refinancing, successfully warded off competition from the rival Tulare County Power Company, which bankrupted itself trying to compete, with steam generation alone, against Mount Whitney's hydro generation.

Repairing damage to the ditch carrying water to the Tule hydro plant, 1914.
EDISON COLLECTION.

decade of the 1900's, the Mount Whitney Company expanded its service through most of Tulare County and even into small portions of neighboring Kings and Kern Counties. Two more hydro plants were built on the Kaweah: Plant Two in 1905 and Plant Three in 1913; while the Tule River hydro plant of the Globe Light and Power Company was purchased and completed in 1909. Transmission lines stretched out to serve Exeter, Tulare, Porterville, Delano and dozens of small farming communities in between. The

Despite these successes, the Mount Whitney Power and Electric Company failed to become the major electric utility in the southern San Joaquin Valley because A. G. Wishon had a long memory. Understandably still smarting from his enforced resignation, Wishon, as General Manager of the San Joaquin Power Company, aggressively pushed that Fresno-based utility's lines southward to encircle the Mount Whitney Company, effectively blocking its

Flume and ditch carrying water to Edison's Tule River hydro plant.
EDISON COLLECTION.

A team of surveyors checks the final alignment of the headworks of Kaweah No. 3 hydro plant in May 1914.
EDISON COLLECTION.

An electric-powered mixer prepares concrete to line the ditch which will carry water to Kaweah No. 3 hydro plant, 1913.
EDISON COLLECTION.

further growth. Wishon's two greatest coups came in 1910, when the San Joaquin Company purchased Bakersfield's electric utility system, and in 1914, when the Fresno Company built a hydro plant on the Tule River in the heart of the Mount Whitney Company's home ground. That was just about the last gasp, however. By 1914, the State Railroad Commission, flexing its new authority over utilities, was frowning

upon corporate expansion grounded within personality conflicts. In the future, they would approve expansion or merger only when it was in the clear interest of the customers affected.

As 1916 dawned, the Mount Whitney Power and Electric Company was facing a crisis. Although fenced out of the greater San Joaquin Valley marketplace, it had developed business within Tulare County beyond the wildest expectations even of Ben Maddox. In the past decade-and-a-half, agriculture, and those

communities in the area that depended primarily upon the success of farming ventures, had grown spectacularly, thanks, in large measure, to the rise in irrigated farms made possible by inexpensive electricity. Now this very success was raising the spectre of insufficient power supply as the region's demand exceeded the output of the Kaweah Plants. Both the steam station in Visalia, enlarged to 10,000 kilowatts by 1914, and the

small steam plant at Tulare acquired in 1915 from the Tulare County Power Company, had to be run more frequently in order to fill the demand, and this was proving expensive. An aging John Hays Hammond, still the majority stockholder, was no longer interested in spending large sums on improving the company, and began looking for a purchaser, anyone but A. G. Wishon.

Mount Whitney's Visalia Steam Plant as it looked in 1913, just before it was expanded.
EDISON COLLECTION.

Henry Huntington's Pacific Light and Power Corporation had completed, not long before, the Big Creek Project's initial development and was sending that power south to Los Angeles over a line that went right through the Mount Whitney Company's service area. Huntington had, in partnership with W. G. Kerckhoff, rescued the San Joaquin Power Company from bankruptcy in 1902. Later, he had sold out his interests to Kerckhoff in order to help finance the Big Creek Project, but now Huntington was looking for a San Joaquin Valley outlet for some of that hydroelectric energy. In June of 1916 Henry Huntington purchased John Hammond's controlling interest in the Mount Whitney Power and Electric Company.

In keeping with Huntington's long-standing philosophy, the company continued to conduct business under its own name. Ben Maddox, who had been Mount Whitney's General Manager since 1902, and a vice-president since Billy Hammond's death in 1908, continued in those positions in day-to-day charge of the Company. The most significant change, which went unnoticed by most, was the purchase of a large piece of land near Richgrove, at the south end of the Mount Whitney system, where the

A residential street in Visalia, with typical "California Bungalow" homes and new ornamental streetlights installed by the Mount Whitney Company in 1918.
EDISON COLLECTION.

A pumping plant near Lindsay, 1913.
EDISON COLLECTION.

echo of the old rivalry with A. G. Wishon. For many years H. G. Lacey had operated a power system in Hanford, purchasing its energy from the San Joaquin Light and Power Corporation via a long transmission line from Fresno. In 1919, Lacey's son offered to sell his small system to the San Joaquin Company. Wishon thought the price far too high, and said so in no uncertain terms, whereupon Lacey went over to Visalia to see Ben Maddox, who closed a deal on the spot to buy it for the Mount Whitney Company.

Big Creek transmission line crossed the Southern Pacific Railroad. Several years later, Vestal Substation arose on the site to provide an interconnection to ensure adequate electric service to meet the growing energy demands within Tulare County.

The Company's purchase by Huntington, and its consequent affiliation with a large regional power system, meant that changes would become inevitable. Before the old days were to disappear entirely, however, there was one last

When Henry Huntington sold his electric power interests to Southern California Edison in 1917, transfer of control of the Mount Whitney Power and Electric Company was included. Edison discontinued the use of the subsidiary company in 1920, and the Edison name began to appear on facilities in Tulare County. One important name remained the same, however, for Ben Maddox continued to be in charge of operations as Edison's San Joaquin Division Manager, a post he retained until his death in 1933.

The Hardest Working Water in the World

The imposing Sierra Nevada mountain range has dominated the history of California since the days of the Gold Rush. To its rocky canyons, wooded uplands and stark ridges have come many kinds of people, but aside from the great naturalist John Muir, few have had a more important impact upon the mountains than engineer and outdoorsman John S. Eastwood. Unlike Muir, who wished to preserve the Sierra untouched, Eastwood reflected the philosophy of his era and saw in the great range a wealth of resources that could benefit the people of California.

John Eastwood loved the mountains and was so knowledgeable about forestry that it is said he could correctly identify a tree in the dark just by the feel of its bark. As early as 1884, he made a reconnaisance survey for a logging railroad to run from Fresno to Pine Ridge, near today's Shaver Lake. Apparently, that was his first introduction to the San Joaquin River region to which he would devote so much time over the next thirty years. It was at that time, or soon after, that he conceived of the possibility of capturing energy from the area's streams with their precipitous drops of many hundreds of feet.

By 1894, Eastwood believed that hydroelectric developments such as he envisioned were becoming technically feasible. During that year, he investigated the San Joaquin River, and in April, 1895, he organized the San Joaquin Electric Company to bring hydro power to Fresno. Overcoming problems with equipment and ignorant subcontractors, and harrassment from the long-established Fresno Gas and Electric Company, Eastwood managed to complete his historic Crane Valley, or San Joaquin No. 1, hydro plant in a year's time. The electricity was sent to Fresno over the longest power line then in use, 38 miles long. It was seeing this facility under construction that gave A. G. Wishon and W. H. Hammond their inspiration to tackle a similar project on the Kaweah River.

Unfortunately, the San Joaquin Electric Company was driven into bankruptcy in 1899 by a combination of continuing bitter opposition from the existing Fresno utility and a succession of dry years that curtailed power deliveries. Eastwood was forced to surrender

In 1922, workmen carved out the "Million Dollar Mile" section of the road from Powerhouse No. 8 to Powerhouse No. 3, through the precipitous gorge of the San Joaquin River. EDISON COLLECTION.

John S. Eastwood was involved with early power projects throughout Central California. In addition to his dramatic exploration of Big Creek, Eastwood organized the San Joaquin Power Company to bring Fresno its first hydro-electric power. Civil engineers remember Eastwood for his invention of the thin shell multiple arch concrete dam, widely used in remote areas. COURTESY MRS. JEAN BROWNING.

summits, searching for the best combination of water flow and geography to locate a chain of hydroelectric plants of unprecedented size. Afraid of losing these new water rights, he kept them secret and separate from his faltering San Joaquin Electric Company. In 1900, after the

control of his company to a group of bondholders who, in turn, sold the property to W. G. Kerckhoff and Allan C. Balch of Los Angeles. Reorganized by them as the San Joaquin Power Company in 1902, the utility was later known as San Joaquin Light and Power Corporation, and was purchased by Pacific Gas and Electric Company in 1930.

Despite this setback, John Eastwood was not through. Between 1896 and 1899, he conducted more surveys from foothills to distant

failure of that company, he undertook a survey of the area now known as Mammoth Pool and organized the Mammoth Power Company to hold those water rights. Again, in 1902, Eastwood went up into the mountains to explore the area between today's Shaver and Huntington Lakes. This was an exploration saga unique in the annals of early power development. With only a string of horses and pack mules to carry his equipment, the indomitable Eastwood alone explored the rocky gorges and watersheds of the region.

The large volume of water this river carried even in late summer persuaded John Eastwood to name it Big Creek. EDISON COLLECTION.

filing water claims. He located a powerhouse site near the junction of Big Creek and Pitman Creek, where Edison's Big Creek No. 1 plant now stands. He walked over Kaiser Pass running levels to show that additional water could be diverted from the upper San Joaquin River near Florence Lake into Big Creek's watershed. He also envisioned the storage of that water and natural runoff in a large reservoir in Big Creek Basin, today's Huntington Lake, and the use of that water through three plants having then unprecedented "static heads" (vertical fall of water from reservoir to water wheel) of approximately 2100 feet, 1900 feet and 1500 feet respectively.

This latest series of surveys roused Eastwood's enthusiasm to a fevered pitch. In October, 1902, from a campsite at Big Creek, he wrote to William G. Kerckhoff about his findings:

> "It gives me great pleasure to inform you that I have completed the surveys for a tunnel line to the junction of Pitman and Big Creeks, and I can place before you the most remarkable power project yet presented."

Big Creek No. 2 plant, photographed in 1917 just before construction of additional units began. EDISON COLLECTION.

Late that summer, after miles of surveys all carefully entered into his diary, Eastwood discovered a boulder-strewn gorge that fell thousands of feet into the San Joaquin River. Naming this precipitous watercourse "Big Creek" because of the amount of water it contained even in late summer, Eastwood spent weeks exploring it and its tributaries, and

John Eastwood knew that he was an engineer, not a financier. Big Creek was his brainchild, but it required men of exceptional organizational talent to raise the money for it to become reality. He turned to Kerckhoff for help with no animosity over the failure of the original San Joaquin Electric Company venture, because Kerckhoff had arrived to pick up the pieces only after Eastwood had been eased out by others. Sadly for the engineer, however, his new project was too big for the

reorganized concern, which was still weak from the bankruptcy of its predecessor. Kerckhoff told Eastwood that he would discuss the project with his new business partner in Los Angeles, Henry Huntington, with whom he had organized the Pacific Light and Power Company.

Not unexpectedly, Huntington was interested in Eastwood's proposals to the extent of putting Eastwood on the PL&P payroll. Sent back to the

Big Creek area with a survey party, Eastwood spent the next three years preparing designs for the project, submitting his report in 1905. Huntington realized that the Big Creek Project held great value for the future. Unfortunately, early in the decade most of his attention, and financial efforts, were being expended on the tremendous growth of the Pacific Electric Railway system in Southern California, leaving little time or money for the power business except as necessity dictated.

For five more years Eastwood waited, still on retainer, buoyed by the knowledge that Southern California's explosive growth would soon create a demand for power that could be filled by his project. During this time, he developed a new type of reinforced concrete multiple-arch dam, a highly economical design that minimized the amount of material required, consequently reducing transportation costs. Ideal for construction in remote areas, eventually it was used to impound three reservoirs on today's Edison system—Florence Lake, Gem Lake and Agnew Lake.

This 1922 map shows the proposed ultimate development of the Big Creek Project to a size even larger than that first envisioned by John Eastwood. Still later plans added more powerhouses on the South Fork of the San Joaquin, but none were built before the depression ended work. Today, the Balsam Meadows Plant is near the site of old Powerhouse No. 5.
EDISON COLLECTION.

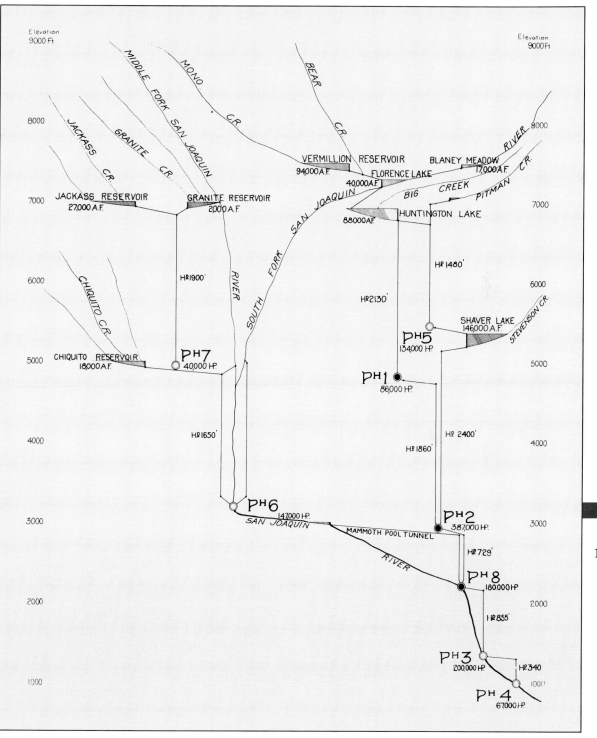

103

104   Early in 1910, Henry Huntington decided that the time had arrived to commence the Big Creek Project. He had already purchased from Eastwood the necessary water rights in exchange for stock in the reorganized Pacific Light and Power Corporation, whose securities were sold to pay for the tremendous construction expenses. Tragically, Eastwood himself was to play no role in the effort, for in November 1910 it was decided to hire Stone and Webster Engineering Corporation to manage this project, whose complexity was to rival that of the then-building Panama Canal.

Soon, work began on the "Initial Development" of the Big Creek–San Joaquin River Hydroelectric Project, which was destined to become the largest progressive hydroelectric project in the nation to be financed entirely by private investment capital. From the beginning, it was a project of superlatives, incorporating the biggest and best that technology could produce: the most powerful Pelton wheels, the biggest hydro generators, the strongest pipes, the highest head power plants, and the longest and highest voltage transmission lines to carry the resulting electrical energy to Los Angeles.

As the construction effort gained momentum, the problem of access to the remote power sites that Eastwood had charted became an important concern. The thousands of tons of cement, pipe, steel, machinery and supplies for a growing workforce could be carried by ponderous freight wagons only at prohibitive

Just a few months old in 1912, the San Joaquin and Eastern Railroad is already busy with construction work on the Initial Development at Big Creek.
AUTHOR'S COLLECTION.

cost—over $20 a ton. To a railroad man, however, the decision was easy: build a railroad to Big Creek. Thus was born the San Joaquin and Eastern Railroad, (S.J.&E.) sometimes referred to as the "Slow, Jerky and Expensive," destined to become one of the most famous railways in the history of the West.

Stone and Webster built the 56-mile, standard gauge line from El Prado Station on the Southern Pacific 18 miles north of Fresno, to the site of Big Creek Power House No. 1, where a permanent town grew up. Construction of the railroad, including survey work and purchase of the right-of-way, was completed on July 10, 1912, in a record 157 days, remarkable when considered that this was done without benefit of modern earth-moving equipment. The route had over 1100 curves, and in one place, the tracks were laid on a trestle bolted to a sheer granite cliff.

A trip on the S.J.&E. was a memorable experience. On the steep grades above Auberry, it was possible to walk as fast as the laboring train itself could move. At the famous "Muleshoe Curve," which looped around nearly a full circle as the railway gained elevation, one conductor used to step off the uphill train, walk across the neck of the loop and board the same train on the other side. The "up" and "down" trains met at Stevenson Creek at noon, and the ticket price included a box lunch of sandwiches, pie, fruit and coffee put aboard both trains at that station. Because of the roughness of the ride, however, some patrons were known to refuse these hearty meals.

More than 400,000 tons of machinery and supplies were hauled to Big Creek during the lifetime of the railroad. The Saturday "down" train to Fresno was nicknamed the "Millionaires Limited" because it carried workers with fat paychecks bound for a good time in the fleshpots of Fresno. Sunday's "up" train, carrying broke, hung-over workers back to the camps, was known as the "Hobo Special". Between 1914 and 1918, years when the pace of construction at Big Creek temporarily slackened, the railroad began carrying tourists and vacationers to Huntington Lake Lodge and other nearby Sierra resorts.

The S.J.&E. was abandoned in 1933, having fulfilled Big Creek's need for dependable transportation in the era before good highways and powerful trucks. Today, a secondary automobile road has been built over much of the old rail route from Auberry to Big Creek, and the only evidence that it was once a railway is a mouldering watertank near Stevenson Creek, and the spectacular "High Bluff" trestle still firmly anchored to its granite cliff.

Big Creek's untamed upper reaches offered good sport to fishermen.
EDISON COLLECTION.

Something for the children: rides on a gentle burro.
EDISON COLLECTION.

Huntington Lake Lodge

Opened on July 4, 1915, the Huntington Lake Lodge was operated as a non-utility subsidiary of Pacific Light and Power Corporation, and later, of the Edison Company. Its first manager was H. M. Nickerson, from the famed Huntington Hotel in Pasadena, followed by Howard Brown, formerly of the Mount Lowe Tavern.

Because of its remote location, the lodge struggled until 1920, when completion of a good highway from Fresno up to Huntington Lake marked the beginning of the resort's prosperity. The rustic architecture of the building and its scenic location made it a favorite meeting place throughout the Roaring Twenties. Despite this popularity, the Lodge fell victim to the Depression, closing its doors to the public in 1931. In the late Thirties and early Forties, the vacant Lodge was briefly reopened to house construction crews and National Guard troops who protected Huntington Lake's dams during the War. Sadly, in 1949, just before it might have been renovated for postwar vacationers, it was demolished.

Main lobby of the Huntington Lake Lodge, 1919.
EDISON COLLECTION.

The Lodge at the height of its popularity, about 1923.
EDISON COLLECTION.

As had been envisioned by John Eastwood, the "Initial Development" at Big Creek involved the construction of three massive concrete dams each over 100 feet high to form a reservoir upon the upper reaches of Big Creek. From the lake, water would flow through a short tunnel, and drop more than 2100 feet in a steel penstock pipeline to Power House No. 1. A diversion dam below that plant would guide the water into a second tunnel and penstock with a nearly 1900 foot vertical drop to Power House No. 2. The only significant deviation from the engineer's original plan was in the penstocks that were to carry water under tremendous pressure down to the waterwheels. The great distance the water would fall would create pressures higher than could have been withstood by the steel pipe available in 1905, so Eastwood had proposed to drill a tunnel through the granite ridge topped by Kerckhoff Dome, and line it with steel and concrete. By 1912, however, the famous German steelmaker, Friedrich Krupp and Sons, was able to make pipe of sufficient tensile strength, enabling the laying of a much less expensive pipeline.

Even before the railroad was completed in the summer of 1912, surveyors were swarming over the area to lay out the facilities. As with any

A party of surveyors gauge the flow of Big Creek near its junction with Pitman Creek in 1910. These measurements, which corroborated John Eastwood's earlier work, determined the site of Big Creek Powerhouse No. 1.
EDISON COLLECTION.

Christmas Day, 1911, at a surveyor's tent at Big Creek.
AUTHOR'S COLLECTION.

construction job, men of many skills and vocations flocked to Big Creek to seek work. One engineer who drifted in was a young graduate of the University of Kansas named David H. Redinger, who was destined to become the project's resident engineer and later, superintendent of the Big Creek plants for nearly 40 years. With this huge army of men, rapid progress was made on the various dams, tunnels and structures, even continuing in the face of severe weather in the winter of 1912-13.

"The Other Half"

Just prior to her death in 1977 at the age of 92, Edith Redinger, widow of Big Creek's Resident Engineer David Redinger, finished writing her recollections of life at Big Creek. Her experiences in what was literally a man's world make fascinating reading, and were privately printed under the title "The Other Half," from which these excerpts have been taken, with permission.

"Born in St. Paul, Minnesota, I came from a life in the cities suddenly into an entirely new environment. In the spring of 1914 I was connected with a college in Fresno in the San Joaquin Valley. At the suggestion of the school's President, I went up into the Sierra Nevada mountains to look over the possibility of starting a summer school at the Big Creek Project. I returned thrilled with the idea of taking over an old, abandoned logger's camp, and by the latter part of June, we had completed the necessary preparations for the summer session.

"It was there that I met David Redinger, the man whom I was eventually to marry. I still think the mountain air had something to do with it, because marriage had been furthest from my thoughts. Three years later, when there was a work break and my future husband could get a few days off, we took the step. Not long before, I got a letter from Dave saying that if I expected to ride horseback, be prepared to wear a riding skirt rather than breeches, for the project superintendent had threatened to fire one of the boys whose mother wore breeches rather than a skirt when she rode over to the store at Big Creek.

"When returned to Big Creek as newlyweds, we had the best accommodations available—a tent with a woodburning stove and a corrugated iron roof to ward off the snow. Our first night in camp was not too restful. We had hardly retired when the stove began smoking because the chimney had been covered, and then began a shower of rocks on the iron roof thrown by friends and well-wishers. Since there was no other choice, we invited them in. They came with sandwiches, cakes and coffee, a wind-up Victrola and records, and spent the night with us.

"A month later, we were moved farther up into what was to me then an uncharted wilderness where the 'job' was in progress. There we had a house made of green lumber, which had been built for us in the fall before the snow came. A path had to be dug in the snow so we could get into the house and move in our belongings. We kept a big fire going to dry out the green lumber. We were occasionally startled by the cracking of the drying lumber. The house was of single-wall construction, just boards and bats, but we were lucky to have it. We had a wood stove in the room which served as kitchen and living room, and a real bathtub that was very popular with our friends and neighbors who did not have one. A galvanized tub was all right in a tent in lieu of something better, but it was a poor substitute for a real bathtub."

108 *David H. Redinger loved the mountains and refused any promotion which would have taken him away from Big Creek. As Resident Engineer and, later, Superintendent, he directed the construction and operation of the Big Creek hydro plants from 1915 to 1949. After his retirement, an important reservoir on the project was named for him.*
EDISON COLLECTION.

Then, suddenly, in the early summer of 1913, work slowed to a crawl. War jitters in Europe had depressed the international bond market, and Pacific Light and Power, which had been spending prodigious sums on the construction effort, found itself running out of cash. At the project, there was concern that a European war would delay delivery of the pipe from Germany, thus rendering useless all the facilities so far built. Huntington's financial partners grew nervous and uncertain.

Expressing his personal confidence in the future of Southern California, despite international events, Henry Huntington moved quickly to solve the financial crisis. He speeded up the separation of the various power interests he held with long-time associates Allan Balch and William Kerckhoff, exchanging his share in the San Joaquin Light and Power Corporation for complete control of Pacific Light and Power. Most importantly, he pledged his personal property as collateral to raise temporary loans to complete the Big Creek Project.

It had been hoped to put the first plant into operation by July 1, 1913, but equipment delays and the financial crisis pushed back that date. Nonetheless, in order to conserve the vital spring run-off, the dams that impounded Huntington Lake were rushed to completion in early April. Due to heavy winter snows, it had not been possible to cut down all of the trees within the new reservoir. As the water rose at the time of the first filling in the Spring of 1913, boats went out to cut off treetops. This explains why, for many years thereafter, tree stumps as much as 20 feet high would emerge from the lake at times of low water.

The concrete foundation for Power House No. 1 was poured in March 1913, followed a month later by that for Power House No.2. Work continued upon both into the summer, and No. 1 had been finished, when No. 2 met with disaster. Just as its roof had been poured, and before the concrete had set, a fire broke out in an adjacent workshop, spread to the wooden forms holding the concrete, and enveloped most of the structure. As a consequence, the roof fell upon the floors below, causing major damage and delaying the second plant from going into service until December.

Despite this mishap, work was restarted on the Big Creek Project following the financial crisis in the summer of 1913, and was pressed through to completion. On October 14, 1913, the first of Big Creek No. 1's two big Pelton waterwheel-driven generators began supplying power to local circuits around the project. Before deliveries could begin to Southern California, however, the transmission lines had to be completed. Consisting of two three-wire circuits supported on separate but parallel steel towers, in late 1913 this was the longest-distance and highest-voltage line in the world. From Power House No. 1 it extended 241 miles to Eagle Rock Substation near Los Angeles, where the electricity was fed into the distribution systems of Pacific Light and Power,

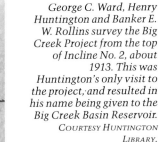

George C. Ward, Henry Huntington and Banker E. W. Rollins survey the Big Creek Project from the top of Incline No. 2, about 1913. This was Huntington's only visit to the project, and resulted in his name being given to the Big Creek Basin Reservoir. Courtesy Huntington Library.

Big Creek Powerhouse No. 1 under construction in 1913. Edison Collection.

It is fitting that the first delivery of Big Creek power to Los Angeles should involve an event of high drama. On the morning of Saturday, November 8, 1913—Saturday then being a regular work day—tens of thousands of Southern Californians were engaged in the ritual of the morning rush hour, which in those days meant a civilized journey by trolley car from suburb to work place. At the height of the traffic, when over 1,000 electric trains filled with commuters were hurrying over the lines of the Pacific Electric and Los Angeles Railways, a crisis arose. At the Redondo Steam Plant, which at that moment was supplying most of the energy to the trolley systems, a water pipe burst and flooded the boiler room. At 7:30 a.m., the flood snuffed out the fires under the boilers, steam pressure dropped, generators slowed, and all over Southern California, lights flickered and went out, and trolley cars came to a halt.

Edwin R. Davis, then General Manager of the PL&P system, received a phone message from Redondo that 20 minutes would be needed to restart the steam plant. When, after 45 minutes of agonizing delay, the power still had not come on, he decided to gamble on the as-yet untried powerline from Big Creek. The next day's *Los Angeles Times* described the result in lyrical prose a far cry from today's terse reporting style:

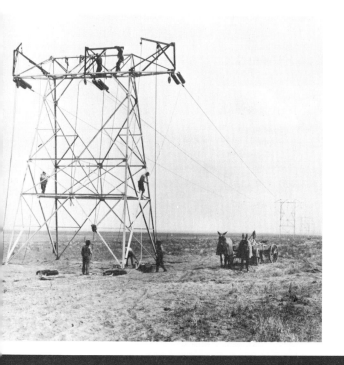

Stringing wires on the 243-mile long Big Creek to Los Angeles 150,000-volt transmission line, 1913.
Edison Collection.

Edison Stock Certificate.
Edison Collection.

Edison's Securities Department facilitated stock sales directly to the public at a time when millions of dollars had to be raised to finance the Big Creek Project.
Edison Collection.

110 Pacific Electric Railway and the Los Angeles Railway. Of widespread technical interest was the high "pressure" of 150,000 volts used by the new Big Creek lines. An entire new generation of insulators, transformers, circuit breakers and switchgear had to be designed for this great voltage. By the first week in November 1913, this record-setting powerline had been completed, but remained untested.

"Electrical energy from the far-off Sierras stretched a hand robed with lightning across the gulf of valleys and mountains to the doors of this city yesterday morning to kick the clogs from the wheels of a thousand stalled trolley cars. It was the debut of the Big Creek power into the Southland, the first employment of an undertaking on which over $12 million has been expended and which has required thousands of laborers for over two years.

"General Manager Davis of the Pacific Light and Power Corporation was the Moses at whose behest the first unit of the Big Creek power—20,000 horse—burst from the turbines in a canyon 241 miles north, to hurtle its way over a slender aluminum cable to this city. He took a chance on these cables, for the line was until then untested....

"At 8:38 or thereabouts, it came; first a tiny trickle of power, then a rippling wave...then the full swell from one unit of the mammoth revolving turbines at the upper plant at Big Creek. A tremor ran through the motors of the stalled trolleys...and the cars began to move...as the first juice from Big Creek began to work its way caressingly along the trolley connections and into the coils of the motors. Thus was broken a tie-up which threatened a long time to have been morning long..."

In the five weeks following this dramatic debut, the remaining generators were placed into service, providing a total of 60,000 kilowatts to Southern California. From that time until the 1950s Big Creek was to be the major source of electricity for the customers of Pacific Light and Power and its successor, Southern California Edison.

With a reliable supply of energy thus assured, Henry Huntington began to consider retirement from his many business activities in order to devote more time to his growing collection of rare books and fine art. On May 26, 1917, after months of planning and discussion, Huntington's Pacific Light and Power Corporation was purchased by, and merged into, the Southern California Edison Company.

The "Greater Edison," as one publication called the expanded enterprise, doubled in assets and properties to become the fifth largest central station power company in the United States. It now served over 100 cities, towns and rural communities with a population of over 1.25 million people. John B. Miller continued as president, but many former PL&P people took key posts in the larger Edison Company. Henry Huntington became a large stockholder and a director of Edison. As a result of the merger, Edison also acquired stock control of both the Ventura County Power Company and the Mount Whitney Power and Electric Company. The system of the former company was merged into Edison as its Ventura, Oxnard and Santa Paula Districts in 1917, while the latter became the San Joaquin Valley Division in 1920.

Following this great amalgamation, in order to ensure an even larger supply of low-cost power for the Southland's growing population, the Edison Company sought to expand the Big Creek Project. A dozen years of construction between 1917 and 1929 saw the completion of this vast project—America's first large-scale progressive hydroelectric development—

The Edison Building at Third and Broadway was headquarters for the Big Creek Project after the merger. The building also housed Sid Grauman's famous "Million Dollar Theater".
EDISON COLLECTION.

At the time of the merger between PL&P and Edison in 1917, work had just begun to raise the height of the dams impounding Huntington Lake. Here, work is proceeding on Dam No. 1.
EDISON COLLECTION.

The Shaver Lake Lumber Company's mill and pond. Edison bought this company in 1918 to gain a reservoir site to form today's larger Shaver Lake. Because of this purchase, the Company today owns a large tract of forest land around Shaver.
AUTHOR'S COLLECTION.

mill, operated a railroad, set up a weather and communications system, maintained a mountain resort and managed a score of construction camps.

Big Creek Powerhouses No. 1 and No. 2 were to be enlarged, and three new powerhouses were to be built. Dams would be poured to create or enlarge Huntington Lake, Florence Lake and Shaver Lake, thus providing greater water storage. A network of tunnels and steel and concrete pipelines were to be built to link the lakes with each other and with the hydro plants. This massive construction effort actually started a year before the merger with Edison, when Pacific Light and Power began raising the dams at Huntington Lake by 35 feet to double the capacity of that reservoir, which ensured an adequate supply of hydroelectric energy for Southern California during the years of World War One when fuel oil was rationed. It was in 1918, however, that Edison engineers mapped out the master plan for Big Creek Project construction that would be followed for the next decade.

The most important element of this plan was the drilling of a long water tunnel through Kaiser Ridge which, as originally had been

nearly to the size originally envisioned by John Eastwood. During this massive effort, Edison employed no outside contractors, but ran its own show. Guided by Edison's Vice-President of Construction George C. Ward and Executive Engineer H. A. Barre, Resident Engineer David H. Redinger directed a permanent staff of engineers, foremen and workers which exceeded 5,000 in number at its peak. They not only built powerhouses and transmission lines, but laid out roads, constructed dams, created artificial lakes, blasted tunnels, ran a lumber

proposed by John Eastwood, would divert water from the upper reaches of the South Fork of the San Joaquin River down into Huntington Lake. Eastwood had projected a 10 3/4-mile tunnel straight beneath the ridge. To dig this from its two ends would have taken more than six years, so instead, it was decided to drill a 13½-mile tunnel laid out on a "dogleg" with two angles in it. In this way, adits, or temporary access tunnels, could be driven, permitting work on the main tunnel to progress from six faces instead of two, which shortened the job

This photo of the camp at Florence Lake emphasizes the remoteness of these camps during the long winters.
VIC STAHL PHOTO.

was originally proposed to extend the San Joaquin and Eastern Railroad around the South Fork of the San Joaquin River to Florence Meadows, where a reservoir was to be built. By this time, however, the advance in automotive technology because of World War One led to a decision to build a road over Kaiser Pass and supply the tunnel camps by truck, moving everything during the summer months when the road could be cleared of snow. During winter, when snow closed the road, mail and medicines were moved to the tunnel camps by sled, using a team of seven dogs and a driver brought from Alaska.

by two years time. The Florence Lake Tunnel proved to be the biggest tunnel job of the 1920s, and when completed, the longest water tunnel in the world.

Before work on the tunnel could begin, a tremendous amount of preparation was necessary, because the construction camps established along the tunnel line were in an area isolated by snows for seven months of the year. To move the thousands of tons of supplies, food and equipment to these remote camps, it

Another way the isolation of the camps was mitigated during the long winter months was through the use of radio telephones and broadcast radio. A radio base station was built at Big Creek and by November 1920, broadcasts were being aired to camps all over the project. Programs were received "live" by telephone line from the East Coast or Los Angeles, and legend has it that "amateur night" programs even originated from Big Creek. The station's radio telephone services were intensively used, often exceeding a half-million messages per month during the busy years in the early Twenties.

The radio-telegraph office at Big Creek, taken in September of 1923, during which month the office handled more radio traffic than any other station on the West Coast.
EDISON COLLECTION.

The 2000 men who drilled the Ward Tunnel worked hard and ate voraciously. During the five-year life of the project, they consumed:
120 tons of butter
357 tons of sugar
200,000 pounds of coffee
4,175,000 eggs
106,000 gallons of milk
1,100,000 pounds of flour
885 tons of potatoes
1000 tons of fresh meat
450,000 pounds of smoked meat.
EDISON COLLECTION.

Transportation at Big Creek

Transportation was an essential element of the Big Creek construction effort. Many different modes were utilized, some of which were quite unusual.

SJ&E Railbus No. 501 passes Dam No. 4, just beginning its downhill trip to Auberry and El Prado, 1920.
EDISON COLLECTION.

The versatile Model T Ford was easily converted into a railroad "speeder" for the benefit of official inspection tours and unofficial hunting trips.
EDISON COLLECTION.

Heavy trucks like this eventually began to supplant the picturesque but expensive railroads for transport to remote construction sites.
EDISON COLLECTION.

114

Alaskan "sourdough" Jerry Dwyer provided a unique transportation service to remote Big Creek construction camps during winter months. With a sled and a spirited team of dogs named Babe, Patsy, Dooly, Riley, Barney, Whiskey and Trim, he carried mail and news to snowbound camps.
EDISON COLLECTION.

These Mack Bulldogs are at the foot of the Kaiser Pass Road at Huntington Lake, laden with pipe for the Mono-Bear Siphon near Florence Lake. Heavy snows kept this road closed much of the year, limiting truck travel to the brief summer months.
EDISON COLLECTION.

Jerry Dwyer's dog team on Kaiser Pass Road, March 1924.
EDISON COLLECTION.

Electric construction train inside Florence Lake (Ward) Tunnel, 1925.
EDISON COLLECTION.

The Florence Lake Tunnel project generated international interest as Edison men raced the calendar to complete it. Tunnel crews at the six headings vied with one another to excavate the most rock on a weekly basis, and an unofficial race was held with the workers drilling the Simplon Tunnel through the Swiss Alps, a railway tunnel similar in size and length to the Florence Lake bore. Cabled messages were exchanged daily between Big Creek and Simplon, comparing the rate of progress on these two tunnels.

Florence Lake Tunnel was built to generous size to allow for a double track construction railroad, but big shovels had to be cut down to fit the tunnel.
EDISON COLLECTION.

To speed the work, new explosives were developed that did not create a large volume of corrosive gas when detonated, and a new type of rock drill was introduced. With these innovations, and with the friendly rivalry as a spur, several records for hard-rock drilling were established, the most impressive of which was 692 feet in one month. It came as no surprise therefore, that Florence Lake Tunnel was "holed through" nearly two years ahead of schedule, on February 18, 1925.

The holing through of the Florence Lake Tunnel was a major milestone on the Big Creek Project. Here, E. R. Davis (wearing glasses, squatting in center) supervises the placing of the last few charges of dynamite to break through.
EDISON COLLECTION.

After the tunnel was completed, a dam was constructed at its upper end to impound a reservoir at Florence Meadows. The dam was of the multiple-arch type invented by John Eastwood for use at remote locations just such as Florence. The design required less cement than other types, which substantially cut transportation requirements. Aggregates for the concrete were made by processing the granite spoil from the tunnel, while the dam's reinforcing steel came from the railroad tracks that had been used inside the tunnel during its construction. With these advantages, work on the dam was completed in two brief working seasons. Water was impounded behind the new dam and delivered to Huntington Lake through the long tunnel late in 1926.

In 1936, the Florence Lake Tunnel was renamed Ward Tunnel to honor George C. Ward. As Edison's Vice-President of Construction in the Twenties, Ward personally oversaw the massive Big Creek construction effort. Ward also had a brief tenure as President of the Company before his untimely death in 1933.

To make use of all the water impounded by Florence Dam, and by Shaver Dam when it was finished in 1927, three new power houses were

1928, the last during the great construction effort of the Twenties. With its 2419-foot head, it supplanted Powerhouse No. 1 as the highest-head hydro plant in the world. Portions of the penstock came variously from steelmakers in the United States, Germany and Poland.

Powerhouse No. 8 rises from the steep cliffs at the junction of Big Creek and the San Joaquin River.
EDISON COLLECTION.

built. The first, Power House No. 8, was not in Eastwood's original plan, thus its out of sequence number. Plant Eight's first unit went into operation in August 1921, and it was the first hydroelectric plant to be built for 220,000-volt transmission.

Big Creek No. 3, the so-called "Electric Giant of the West," originally had three units totalling 75,000 kilowatts which were completed in 1923. Subsequently two more units were added. Plant No. 2A was finished in

117

Construction of Florence Lake Dam in the summer of 1926. This was the largest multiple-arch dam ever built to John Eastwood's plans.
VIC STAHL PHOTO.

To defer the substantial cost of building a new power line down to Los Angeles, the courageous decision was made to instead raise the voltage, and hence the carrying capacity, of the existing lines. Electrical engineer Jim Lighthipe is credited with selecting the new pressure of 220,000 volts and with designing the switch gear to be used. For two years, transformers, oil switches and insulators were tested by Dr. Harris Ryan at Stanford University's High Voltage Laboratory, and later at the "Million Volt Lab" endowed by the Edison Company at Pasadena's Cal Tech.

Handsomely proportioned Big Creek No. 3 justified its nickname as the "Electrical Giant of the West", bestowed upon its opening in 1923.

118

Camp 35 on Stevenson Creek was on the line of the water tunnel being dug to Powerhouse No. 3. Perhaps the most remote of any camp below Huntington Lake, the tent-cabins were built on stilts and lashed by cables pegged into the cliff.

As these new facilities were being built, plans were being made to carry the resulting electricity to Southern California. As noted above, when the Initial Development at Big Creek was finished in 1913, the 150,000-volt power line to Eagle Rock Substation was the longest-distance, highest-voltage line in the world. By 1922, with substantial new generation coming on line and more planned, the capacity of these original transmission lines was inadequate.

The change-over to "220 KV" began in the spring of 1922. New "switch gardens" containing new transformers, bigger switches and circuit breakers had to be installed at all the Big Creek plants and at Eagle Rock. The most difficult single aspect of the job was converting the transmission towers themselves. New, longer insulators had to be installed, and most of the towers physically raised from 10 to 30 feet so the power lines would adequately clear the ground, all while the lines remained "hot"—energized at 150,000 volts—for the vital flow of energy to

Reconstructing the Big Creek lines to handle 220,000-volts was not easy. First, longer insulators had to hung on the towers. Then the towers had to be raised from ten to thirty feet so the power lines would adequately clear the ground. Though the lines were energized during the tower raising phase, the job was done without accident or injury. Here, the elevators are in place to begin a ten-foot lift.
EDISON COLLECTION.

As part of the conversion of the Big Creek lines to 220,000-volts, Eagle Rock Substation had to get new transformers. As a legacy from the days of Henry Huntington, the only access to the station was via a little-used narrow-gauge branchline of Los Angeles Railway. Here, an L.A. Railway freight motor prepares to leave Verdugo Junction with a flatcar carrying the new transformer.
EDISON COLLECTION.

Los Angeles could not be interrupted. On Sunday morning May 6, 1923, the line was cut over to 220,000-volt operation, establishing another technological first for Edison. For this achievement, the Southern California Edison Company in 1923 became the first winner of the Charles A. Coffin Medal, today known as the Thomas A. Edison Award.

When the great construction effort of the 1920s finally was completed, 360,000 kilowatts of electrical energy could be produced in Big Creek's generating units, which, in 1929, represented slightly more than half of the Edison Company's total capacity. After cascading through the chain of power plants, the water from Big Creek goes into the agricultural irrigation systems of the San Joaquin Valley. This efficient reuse of the same water earned a nickname for the Big Creek Project which it still bears today: "The Hardest Working Water in the World."

119

With an abundance of low-cost energy from Big Creek, Edison solicited large manufacturing accounts with exhibits such as this for the Western Metals Congress, held at the Shrine Auditorium in January of 1929.
EDISON COLLECTION.

Power and Ice

As the Twentieth Century dawned, the arid Imperial Valley of Southeastern California was in the process of developing into a major agricultural district, thanks to the efforts of entrepreneurs and hardy pioneer farmers. There were many problems encountered along the way, not least of which was a "Catch-22" tangle of Federal regulations. Under the terms of the Desert Land Act of 1877 and the earlier Homestead Act of 1859, the amount of public land any individual could file upon was limited to 320 acres. Unfortunately, this land could not pass into the settler's ownership and legal title, that is, it could not be "patented," until certain improvements were made. One of the requirements was the provision of water for farming, usually by drilling wells. The problem with developing the Imperial Valley was that no farmer could gain title to his land until he obtained water, yet because no wells could be drilled successfully in the arid valley, water could be provided only through expensive irrigation projects, which, in turn, only could be built by raising money by mortgaging farms.

Southern Sierras Powers' El Centro Substation was the terminus of a transmission line from the Bishop Creek hydro plants. It started life as Holton Power Company's gas-electric power plant.
EDISON COLLECTION.

Paradoxically, no mortgage money could be raised to build a water system until the farmer had received title to his land, which he could not get until water was brought in. Complicating this was the fact that both the 1859 and 1877 Acts specifically forbade the purchase of large blocks of public land by large companies or associations that would have the financial resources to bring in water and make other improvements.

To overcome these problems, in the spring of 1900, George Chaffey, S. W. Ferguson, J. H. Beatty, Anthony Heber and C. R. Rockwood formed the California Development Company and offered an irrigation proposal that circumvented the technicalities of the law. As homesteaders heard of the agricultural potential of the Imperial Valley, they arrived by the trainload. Chaffey's company assisted the settlers in filing for government land and sold them water rights in the form of stock in local Mutual Water Companies, whereby title to the land could be patented. With the money thus raised, the various mutual water companies in turn purchased water entitlements from the California Development Company, which filed

Stately rows of date palms near Coachella were irrigated by water pumped electrically.
EDISON COLLECTION.

As early as 1913, the Imperial Irrigation District took advantage of the Company's low power rates to operate electric dredges to maintain its vital water canals.
EDISON COLLECTION.

before discharging into the Salton Sink north of the Imperial Valley. To save money, the Alamo River was cleared of brush and channelized to carry the irrigation water much of the distance into the Valley. Thanks to this short cut, the

to appropriate 20,000 acre-feet of Colorado River water and proceeded to build a canal into the Valley.

This entire proposal depended upon water being delivered to those farmers in the Imperial Valley who had paid for it. Work on the canal began in August 1900 at Pilot Knob, less than a mile above the border with Mexico. An eight-mile canal was cut from the Colorado to the Alamo River, a normally dry runoff slough of the Colorado River that looped through Mexico

water system of the California Development Company was completed in under a year; the first water being delivered to Imperial Valley farmers in June of 1901.

Soon after, George Chaffey was squeezed out by his partners, who then proceeded to sell more water than the canal could deliver. To make matters worse, the irrigation supply was jeopardized by the extreme siltiness of the Colorado's water. Even though dredgers and draglines were brought in to keep the canal

At the height of the flooding, as much as 75,000 cubic feet of water per second swept into the Imperial Valley. Late in 1906 a massive effort was mounted to close the breach. While a trestle was built across the break, mattresses of straw and wire netting were placed to slow the rapid erosion.

Then thousands of trainloads of rock were dumped until the Colorado returned to its old course.
FOUR PHOTOS THIS PAGE
COURTESY SOUTHERN PACIFIC
TRANSPORTATION COMPANY.

Saving the Valley

The closure of the huge breach in the banks of the Colorado River and the turning of it back into its old bed is one of the great engineering achievements of all time. The floods of February 1905 diverted much of the river's flow into the Salton Sink and initial efforts to redirect it failed during the ensuing months.

Late in the summer of 1905 the Southern Pacific Company took over the task, in part because the formation of the Salton Sea had inundated long stretches of its main line between Los Angeles and New Orleans. The first dam built by the railroad's engineers failed in a flood in November 1905. Another flood in April 1906 turned the entire river into the breach, with water pouring through at the rate of over 6 billion cubic feet per day!

Then S.P. civil engineer Harry T. Cory was brought in. He proposed a dramatic and desperate measure: to build two parallel railroad trestles across the break and dump carloads of rock without let-up until the gap was closed. In July 1906, as the Colorado's waters receded from the annual spring flood, work began. A railroad branch from Yuma reached the site of the break in August, and, with a pile driver mounted on a flat car, a trestle was built out into the roaring current. On September 14, 1911, trains of "battleships," huge side-dump hopper cars, began running onto the trestle and dumping their loads into the water. Nearly 1700 carloads of rock, most

quarried at Pilot Knob, were dropped to build up a solid dam. On November 4, 1906, the flow into the Imperial Valley stopped, and wild celebrations were held all over the Valley.

But the Colorado was not yet tamed. On December 7, another flood roared down the river and broke through again, just south of the new levee. Within hours the entire river had turned into the Valley, leaving a steamboat stranded downstream in the dried up old bed. A few days later the entire dam building process began again. Three times the railroad trestles were torn out by flood waters, but the fourth time they held, and again thousands of carloads of rock were poured into the breach. Regular train movements over the Southern Pacific's Los Angeles and Yuma Divisions virtually halted as hundreds of special trains brought rocks from many quarries to the site of the new break.

Day and night the dumping continued: big boulders followed by sand and gravel to fill in the cracks. At first even big stones washed away in the current, but gradually the dam was built up once again. At last, on February 11, 1907, the flood waters were stopped and the Imperial Valley was saved from further flooding. Today the dams built in 1906 and 1907 are the core of a larger system of levees on the west bank of the Colorado River in Mexico and California that still protect the Imperial Valley.

cleared, it began to silt up just below Pilot Knob, threatening to curtail water deliveries. An ungated intake was cut from river to the canal below the most heavily silted section of the original ditch. This expedient ultimately resulted in tragedy. Unseasonable floods in February of 1905 turned virtually the entire flow of the Colorado River into the irrigation system. Deep canyons were carved through the Valley and the Salton Sink was flooded to form a huge inland sea.

The closure of this vast breach to return the Colorado back into its old bed is one of the most dramatic stories in California history. The Southern Pacific Company voluntarily poured its resources and engineering skill into this project when the Federal Government itself would not do so. Even before the final closure on February 11, 1907, the Imperial Valley was recovering from the disaster. An improved irrigation system was constructed and placed into operation by the Imperial Irrigation District, formed by Valley farmers to succeed to the properties of the bankrupt California Development Company. By 1910, the Imperial Valley was well on its way to becoming the major source for winter vegetables and melons in the United States.

The Kamura Brothers near Holtville shipped tons of cantalopes to market via the Holton Inter-urban Railway, iced by Imperial Ice, of course.
COURTESY FRED OLDENDORF.

123

One early valley resident who saw the need for many other types of enterprises to support the region's spectacular agricultural growth was William F. Holt. In addition to founding the town of Holtville, Holt started banking, mercantile and cotton ginning activities. Even while flood waters were still pouring through the Valley in 1905, Holt had enough faith in the future to establish a series of utility enterprises. The Holton Power Company, the Imperial Valley Gas Company and the Holton Inter-urban Railway were all formed by him to

W. F. Holt standing next to the Holtville Substation, 1910.
EDISON COLLECTION.

Two section hands on the Holton Inter-urban pose with their gasoline speeder car.
COURTESY FRED OLDENDORF.

provide public utility services to the new towns of Holtville, El Centro, Imperial, Brawley and Calexico.

Holt realized that the growth of Imperial Valley's fledgling towns and businesses would be hampered without utilities service, most importantly electric power. Holt negotiated an agreement with the California Development Company to divert sufficient water out of a lateral canal near Holtville to generate electricity at a low head hydro plant. A back-up steam power plant was built at El Centro. Curiously, some of the generating equipment for these facilities was purchased second hand from the Edison Electric Company of Los Angeles.

Over the next five years, despite the physical damage and business recession caused by the Great Flood, the Holton Power Company extended its service to several communities in the Imperial Valley. Insofar as the generating capacity of the company was very limited, little attempt was made to solicit residential or rural electric business. Rather, the Holton Power Company concentrated primarily on providing

The main road between El Centro and Holtville in the Imperial Valley, now Highway S-80.
EDISON COLLECTION.

124

Looking east on Main Street, El Centro in 1910, showing the Holt Block, headquarters of W. F. Holt's extensive commercial enterprises.
EDISON COLLECTION.

service to the agricultural products processing industry and other businesses in the Valley. Indeed, the Power Company itself soon engaged in a subsidiary business of operating ice manufacturing plants, which made ice to chill the railroad cars of produce shipped from the valley.

By 1911, the demand for electricity in the Imperial Valley had outstripped the Holton Power Company's ability to provide service, primarily because W. F. Holt had also reached the limit of his ability to personally finance needed improvements in his many growing enterprises. In November 1911, Holt invited noted engineer James Dix Schuyler on a tour of his Imperial Valley properties in the hope of attracting the interest of outside investors. Schuyler's report noted that the power business was growing and represented a stable market for the future, but that the Holton Power Company's physical plant, especially the generating stations, was in need of complete renewal. Further, Schuyler noted, the gas business was a total failure due to the high cost of the manufactured gas it sold.

Schuyler also toured the Holton Inter-urban Railway, which extended from Holtville to a connection with the Southern Pacific at El Centro, and reached further westward to Seeley, where a connection was made with John Spreckels' San Diego and Arizona Railroad. Despite its name, the railroad was not an "interurban" in the conventional sense of an

Holton Power Company's two hydro plants near Holtville. The brick Plant One, behind, was built in 1905, concrete Plant Three, foreground, was built after the Great Flood of 1905-07 lowered the grade of the New River by 40 feet.
Edison Collection.

One benefit of the Great Flood was the substantial deepening of the channel of the New River near Holtville, which allowed the Power Company to construct a second hydro plant adjacent to its existing one. The new plant, with its much higher head, virtually doubled the Company's generating capacity. It should be noted, however, that the extreme siltiness of the irrigation water used at the hydro plants caused frequent damage to the water turbines.

Two workmen load blocks of ice into a domestic delivery wagon in El Centro.
Courtesy Fred Oldendorf.

125

electrified inter-city trolley line, but operated a steam-powered passenger and freight service. Schuyler noted that the growth of produce sheds, packing plants and car-icing facilities along the railroad promised for it a profitable future.

The desire of W. F. Holt to find outside financing for his Imperial Valley utility properties coincided with the expansion of the Southern Sierras Power Company into the Southern California marketplace, as has been described in an earlier chapter. Eager to find a substantial market not overshadowed by competition from large existing utilities, the Southern Sierras management viewed with interest the potential inherent in the Imperial Valley. In 1913, they entered into a 43-year contract to provide electric energy to both the Holton Power Company and the Coachella Valley Ice and Electric Company. This latter company, another of W. F. Holt's many enterprises, had a small power and ice manufacturing business in Indio, Coachella and Niland.

Holton Inter-urban No. 7 switching in Holtville in 1918. Despite its name, the railway never operated electric trolley cars.
Courtesy Fred Oldendorf.

Holtville Depot of the Holton Inter-urban Railway, about 1918. This building still stood in 1980.
Author's Collection.

To fulfill the terms of the power contract, Southern Sierras Power constructed a 55,000-volt power line from San Bernardino to Banning. From that connection point, the Coachella Company extended its 55,000-volt transmission ''backbone'' line south through Indio and Niland to El Centro to connect with the Holton Power Company's existing system. Energy deliveries from the Southern Sierras Power Company to the Coachella and Holton companies began early in 1914.

With the establishment of power service to the Coachella and Imperial Valleys, the Southern Sierras Power Company began a very close operational and financial relationship with the Coachella Valley Ice and Electric Company and the Holton Power Company. Although still nominally independent, the two companies became referred to as "Allied Companies." After two years of this close working together, the Southern Sierras management purchased outright both the Coachella and the Holton Companies, and W. F. Holt retired from the utility business.

As a precondition of selling his Holton Power Company, Holt wished also to sell his gas and railroad properties. Southern Sierras would have nothing to do with the gas business, and the Imperial Gas Company subsequently floundered through independence until it was purchased years later by the Southern California Gas Company. The railroad was another matter, and as part of its power system purchase, Southern Sierras also became proud owner of the Holton Inter-urban Railway, and operated it until 1925, when it was sold to the Southern Pacific Company, which has owned it ever since.

The Company's Mexicali office about 1955. Service to portions of Baja California continued until 1965.
EDISON COLLECTION.

Raising a pole by "horse-whim" during building of the 55,000-volt line to Banning in 1913. This was the first leg of Southern Sierras' extension into the Imperial Valley.
EDISON COLLECTION.

127

A series of corporate streamlinings between 1916 and 1923 reduced this plethora of "Allied Companies" until at last the Southern Sierras Power Company remained as the sole operator of a power system extending from Bishop through San Bernardino to the Mexican border. Power operations in Baja California were begun in 1916 under the name of Industrial Electrica Mexicana.

Imperial Ice's huge Brawley No. 3 Ice Plant was center of railroad car icing operations of Pacific Fruit Express.
EDISON COLLECTION.

The freezing cans for the 50-pound domestic ice blocks.
EDISON COLLECTION.

As part of this restructuring, in 1916, all of the ice manufacturing and distribution operations inherited from the various predecessor companies were consolidated in a new subsidiary, the Imperial Ice and Development Company. Although the ice business was at first a sideline, it quickly grew in importance. At a time when mechanical refrigeration was in its infancy, and home refrigerators unknown, local ice plants were an essential part of a

The most popular work in the Imperial Valley may have been in the ice storage room, where blocks of ice were stockpiled between layers of sawdust to await harvest season demand.
COURTESY FRED OLDENDORF.

The Ice Plant in Imperial made ice for domestic use.
EDISON COLLECTION.

As late as 1950, most homes in the Imperial and Coachella Valleys relied upon frequent ice deliveries.
EDISON COLLECTION.

community's economy, maintaining a continuous supply of 25-pound blocks of ice that were placed in the old "ice-boxes" that were the only method of preserving the freshness of perishable foods. To an agricultural region such as the Imperial Valley, the ice plants were of even greater importance to provide the ice needed to chill the refrigerator car-loads of fresh produce shipped by rail to markets near and far.

When established in 1916, the Imperial Ice and Development Company had but two small manufacturing plants, those at El Centro and Coachella. Within two decades, these had grown to a dozen plants manufacturing nearly a third of a million tons of ice each year used in homes, railroad refrigerator cars, creameries and cold storage plants throughout the Coachella and Imperial Valleys. Just as important, the big electric motors that ran the ammonia compressors at the ice plants comprised the largest single load on the Southern Sierras Power system, thereby making possible lower electric rates in the Imperial Valley than otherwise would have prevailed.

In 1917, at the request of the local Indian agent, Southern Sierras crews built a power line from El Centro to Hanlon Heading on the Colorado River to provide service to the Yuma Indian Reservation. Interestingly, the wooden poles, insulators and copper wire used to build this extension had been salvaged when an unused transmission line from Palmetto Substation near Goldfield to the abandoned town of Rhyolite was dismantled. Although the

insulators removed from the Rhyolite line were rated for 55,000-volt operation, on the new line to Hanlon Heading they were able to carry electricity at 88,000 volts because of the much drier air and virtual absence of rainfall in the

The new Ice Depot at Imperial, where customers could drive up to buy blocks of ice.
COURTESY FRED OLDENDORF.

130 *The Company's facilities at El Centro in 1918 included railroad car icing platforms (left), and ice plant (center), and a gas-engine powered generating plant and substation (extreme right).*
EDISON COLLECTION.

Prior to small mechanical refrigeration units, real ice was used to make drinks "ice cold". EDISON COLLECTION.

region. The most difficult problem encountered during the construction of the new line was the provision of stable footings for the wooden poles as they crossed the sand dunes on the east side of the Imperial Valley. Eventually, wooden "outriggers" were developed that enabled each pole to "float" over the shifting sands.

After World War One, this transmission line was carried across the river, and the company gradually extended its lines throughout the Yuma agricultural district. An emergency energy interconnection was provided to the

A Southern Sierras line crew in the 1920's. EDISON COLLECTION.

One of the big electric motors which ran the ammonia compressors at the El Centro Ice Plant. COURTESY FRED OLDENDORF.

Yuma Light, Gas and Water Company, an independent utility serving the City of Yuma. In 1926, Southern Sierras rounded out its expansion into the lower Colorado River region, first by successfully bidding for the energy output of the Siphon Drop Hydro Plant operated by the (then) U. S. Reclamation Service, and then by purchasing the Yuma Utilities Company, which operated a distribution system in the agricultural area around Yuma and south to Gadsen, near the Arizona-Mexico border.

The two diesel engine generators at Blythe. At left is the larger unit added in 1919, at right the original single cylinder 75 H.P. unit. This photo was taken in 1930, upon the plant's retirement.
EDISON COLLECTION.

Blythe Diesel Plant, center, and the operator's house, at right.
EDISON COLLECTION.

A Diesel Generator for Blythe

In 1916, the Colorado River community of Blythe, the commercial centre of the thriving Palo Verde Valley agricultural district, boasted a population of 600. There was, however, no electric service except for a gasoline-powered generator to run the town's movie theatre and another at a nearby cotton gin. Late in that year, however, Southern Sierras Power Company installed a small 75-horsepower diesel engine connected to a 50-kilowatt generator in a corrugated iron building beside the bank of the river.

Despite this welcome improvement, the pace of life in Blythe was slow: so much so that the plant operator was frequently able to shut the engine down and go fishing without raising a hue and cry from the townspeople. Daytime electric service was still viewed by most as a luxury, and the diesel plant engineer's love of fishing became a local legend.

In 1919, the original plant caught fire and burned, but was promptly replaced with a larger diesel engine. Within a decade, despite floods and crop failures, the economy of the Palo Verde Valley had prospered and electric service expanded to keep pace with the needs of a population that now exceeded 6500. Three diesel units offered service from 6 a.m. to midnight, but the operator still was able to get in some fishing.

In 1930, the diesel plant was retired when Southern Sierras built a 70-mile long transmission line to connect Blythe with its main system at Calipatria. Thirteen years later, though, the Palo Verde district was again isolated from the rest of the Power Company's system by the sale of its Imperial Valley properties to the Irrigation District.

Today the region is one of California's most important agricultural areas, but remains isolated from the main Edison system to the west. Energy for Blythe now comes primarily from nearby Parker Dam, where the fishing is still reported to be very good.

By the late Twenties, Southern Sierras Power and its subsidiaries were operating an integrated electric utility system that was providing the Palo Verde, Coachella and Imperial Valleys, Yuma and Mexicali with highly reliable service at a cost not just below that of many urban areas, but among the lowest anywhere in the nation. It is all the more surprising, therefore, that much of this important market, which Southern Sierras had done so much to develop, would be torn away from the Power Company within the space of a few years.

The loss of the electric utility business of the Imperial and Coachella Valleys is a story of bitter conflict between the opposing philosophies of investor ownership and government ownership of utilities. The spark that triggered this dissention was the long-deferred decision to build the All-American Canal. The canal, with its power drops where irrigation water would be diverted through low-head stream flow hydro plants to produce electricity, was a crucial part of the compromise formalized by the Boulder Canyon Act of 1928.

By 1923 the desert community of Palm Springs was attracting the notice of the wealthy. The famed Desert Inn catered to an exclusive clientele.
EDISON COLLECTION.

from federally built power plants. The announced intention of this program was to encourage rural electrification, traditionally a market many investor-owned power companies were reluctant to serve because of low rates of return. It is unfortunate that in some cases these rural electrification projects turned into vendettas against existing power systems.

Southern Sierras Power had always believed that it would either operate, or receive energy from, any power plant built along the new canal whenever it was built. When construction of the All American Canal began in the mid-1930s, the Depression-era Administration of Franklin Roosevelt had begun to encourage alternatives to traditional power enterprises. One tenet of Roosevelt's New Deal program was to support the development of rural electric co-operatives, financed by low-cost federal loans and often receiving bulk energy

133

The switchyard of the big terminal station in El Centro after its 1926 reconstruction.
EDISON COLLECTION.

As noted earlier, the Imperial Irrigation District had been formed in 1906 to sustain water service to the Imperial Valley's farmers. For two decades and more, the investor-owned electric utility and the farmer-owned water utility worked side by side to insure the prosperity of the region. In 1935, however, the management of the District determined to enter the field of electric utility service, hoping that federal funds could be solicited for this purpose. Interestingly, at that time, due to the business depression, the District had been in default of interest and principal payment on its existing outstanding bonds for three years and so apparently had no money or credit with which to establish a power system without federal help.

At this late date it is difficult to understand why the District believed such an expensive project to be necessary. The Southern Sierras Power Company had been providing a highly reliable, low-cost service for two decades, and the only apparent criticism of the Company's service was over a reluctance during the Depression to extend electric service to remote farms, when in many cases those farmers could ill-afford the cost of providing such service.

The "Brawley" was one of Imperial Irrigation District's several electric dredgers, shown here in about 1920 removing silt from the main canal in Baja California.
EDISON COLLECTION.

Southern Sierras' dispatcher's office at San Bernardino, about 1928.
EDISON COLLECTION.

Whatever the motive, early in 1936 the Irrigation District secured a federal Rural Electrification Administration loan bearing a one percent interest rate, and following unsuccessful court challenges by the Power Company, constructed a diesel engine power plant at Brawley to provide service until hydro drops on the All American Canal could be completed. Service over the District system to its few initial customers in Brawley began on May 18, 1936.

Southern Sierras' Annual Report for 1936 described the opening salvos in what would be a bitter seven-year battle with the new District system:

"For over 60 days the District operated without published rates, except that customers were advised that the District rates when established would be much lower than those charged by the Corporation. When such rates were finally announced they were approximately 1-% under the rates of the Corporation in effect at the time, the reduction approximately equaling the per cent of the Company's rates representing taxes paid by the Company, from which the District will be free.

"At the outset a large number of consumers were influenced to leave the Company's service, but by October the tide had turned to a point where new connections with the Company's service exceeded disconnections. Since October the situation from the Company's standpoint has slowly but progressively bettered, with an increased number of former consumers leaving the District's service to return to the Company."

Southern Sierras' handsome Brawley office, as it looked in 1928.
EDISON COLLECTION.

Southern Sierras' San Bernardino Substation was the operating nerve center of the system. Electricity from the Bishop Creek plants was routed through here on its way to the Imperial Valley.
EDISON COLLECTION.

The following year the conflict intensified. Despite repeated offers from the company to submit the dispute to mediation—calls that were echoed by most responsible people in the community—the District persisted in its aggression. Using additional federal grants and loans, work was begun on the Canal hydro-drops and enlarging the Brawley Diesel Plant. Another Rural Electrification Administration loan was secured to construct 600 miles of rural lines in the Imperial Valley, much of which would be merely duplication of existing

The photographer labeled this one "a bunch of Meloland beauties".
COURTESY FRED OLDENDORF.

Company lines. Thus, the District extended its assault on the company's system from Brawley to the Valley at large.

By November 1938, the District had finished its frantic line extension program and began active solicitation for customers throughout the Valley. Old-timers tell stories of District crews going out in the dead of night to switch customer meters, smashing Company meters in the process. There were also rumors of violence carried out against the families of company employees. Even given the bitter emotions involved in this conflict it is difficult to give credence to these legends. Nonetheless, the District spent over $5.3 million, a huge sum for that era, in an aggrandizement that did not have the clear support of a clear majority of Imperial Valley residents.

This lack of overwhelming support is demonstrated by the fact that by 1939 the competition between the two systems had reached a point of stalemate. Having lost in three years substantially less business to the District than it at first feared, the Company intensified attempts at reconciliation, hoping to replace argument with agreement and cooperation, without surrendering the independence or competitive position of either system. The 1939 Annual Report noted:

> "Our month by month revenue figures from Imperial Valley for the six months ending January, 1940 showed that revenue on our lines at no time fell below 70% of that on the lines previous to competition. We have Valley-wide in March 1940, 65% as many meters connected as we had in November, 1938. These are facts all pointing toward the conclusion that a point of stabilization is being reached in the Imperial Valley."

In 1950, most produce was sent to market by rail and required elaborate icing to stay fresh.
EDISON COLLECTION.

This stagnation continued through 1940 and 1941, until in April 1942, competition was frozen at the insistence of the War Production Board. Neither utility was allowed to solicit business from existing customers of the other utility, in order to reduce waste of manpower and material. Active competition was never resumed, for late in 1943 the Company, which in 1941 had changed its name to the California Electric Power Company, sold its Valley system to the District.

Railroad Comission. With this agreement, the Company retired in 1943 from the Imperial and Coachella Valleys in an honorable fashion, having shown that an established utility system could survive the attempts of federally financed public power systems to drive them out of business.

Blythe and the Palo Verde Valley District, although isolated by the sale from the rest of the Company's system, continued to be served by the Power Company through power interchanges with the Irrigation District and with energy received from Parker Dam. The Yuma properties were sold to the Arizona Edison Company effective April 1, 1948, and that company was itself sold to Arizona Public Service a year later.

After 1943, California Electric Power's system in Northwestern Baja California was isolated from the balance of its territory and was served by an exchange of power with the District through connections in Calexico and at Andrade on the Colorado River. This Mexican system in 1960 was sold to the Mexican Government's Comision Federal de Electricidad.

In the face of the Company management's strong philosophical stance in opposition to government ownership of electric utilities, the sale can only be explained by crushingly strong pressure from Washington, using as an excuse the war emergency. Thus, the Power Company lost what once had been its most important market area. As part of the sale agreement, however, the Company did secure an important promise from the District never to invade the Company's territory outside the area sold, which was reinforced by an order of the State

California Electric Power retained the ice business after sale of its Imperial Valley electric system. Following the development of precooling and field packing of produce in the early 1950s, however, this business quickly declined. By 1956, even this last remnant of the Power Company's once extensive Imperial Valley operations had disappeared.

Big Creek Hydroelectric Plants

Ward Tunnel

San Joaquin and Eastern RR

Bishop

Owens Valley

San Joaquin Valley

Bishop Creek
Hydroelectric Plants

Fresno

Visalia

Big Creek Transmission Line

Borel Hydroelectric Plant

500 KV Intertie

Kern River No. 1
Hydroelectric Plant

Tehachapi
Wind Farm

Service Area Boundary Kern River Transmission Line
Santa Susana Experimental Station

Santa Clara River

Mt. Lowe Railway

Santa Barbara

Ventura

Pacific Electric Railway

Pasadena

Miles of History

El Segundo Generating Station
Redondo Beach Generating Station

Los Angeles

The service territory of the Southern California Edison Company today includes an area of some 50,000 square miles in all or part of 14 Central and Southern California Counties. The Company's former service area in Nevada, which was sold to Sierra Pacific Power Company in 1969, is shown on this map for reference purposes. Similarly, the former franchised Imperial Valley service territory of Edison predecessor, the Southern Sierras Power Company, is indicated by an outline even though it was sold to the Imperial Irrigation District in 1943. The Cities of Los Angeles, Pasadena, Glendale and Burbank operate their own power systems, and certain other cities and agencies purchase energy from Edison for resale to their own customers. Please note that many modern facilities have been omitted; for reasons of space, only events and facilities mentioned in the text are shown on this map.

Santa Catalina Island

PACIFIC OCEAN

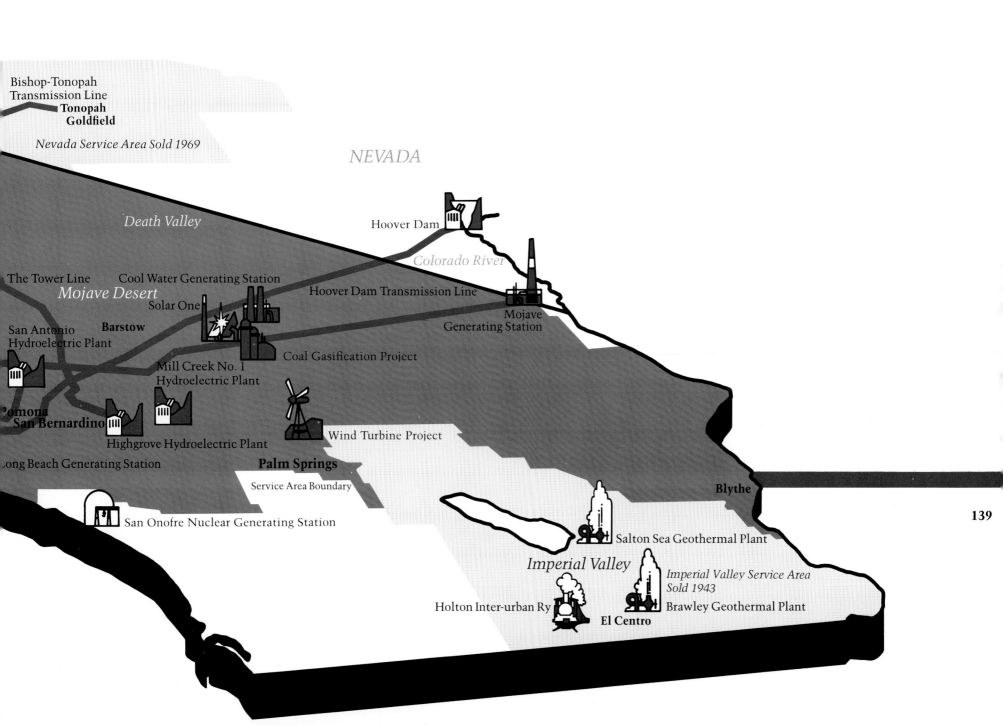

Bishop-Tonopah
Transmission Line
Tonopah
Goldfield

Nevada Service Area Sold 1969

NEVADA

Death Valley

Hoover Dam

Colorado River

The Tower Line   Cool Water Generating Station

Mojave Desert   Solar One

San Antonio   **Barstow**   Hoover Dam Transmission Line
Hydroelectric Plant

Mojave
Generating Station

Coal Gasification Project

Mill Creek No. 1
Hydroelectric Plant

Pomona
San Bernardino

Highgrove Hydroelectric Plant   Wind Turbine Project

Long Beach Generating Station

Palm Springs

Service Area Boundary   **Blythe**

139

San Onofre Nuclear Generating Station

Salton Sea Geothermal Plant

Imperial Valley   *Imperial Valley Service Area*
Sold 1943

Holton Inter-urban Ry   Brawley Geothermal Plant

El Centro

The busy intersection of Fair Oaks and Colorado in Pasadena, 1902. Red Cars trundle down the streets and Edison is the City's electric utility.
AUTHOR'S COLLECTION.

A Pawn of Politics

The issue of investor ownership versus government ownership of electric utility systems has been an emotional one, widely debated during many years of the Twentieth Century. Southern California became one of the principal forums for this debate, not just because of the bitter controversy in the Imperial Valley, but because the City of Los Angeles itself developed what became the nation's largest municipally owned electric utility. Despite the conflict by which some such systems were born, however, many

municipally owned utilities were quietly created out of a real need to provide electric service to communities when no company was willing or able to do so.

The growing agricultural community of Riverside received some of the output from the pioneer Highgrove Hydroelectric Plant when it began operation in 1887. The small amount of energy available was used exclusively for arc-type street lighting systems. The demand for electricity quickly outstripped the supply, however, and before long the Riverside City Council was demanding a more reliable and adequate source. Entrepreneur Charles Lloyd, who had built the Highgrove plant, had little money for a larger undertaking, and indeed did not even have a corporate structure with which to attempt such a project. In the absence of a group of investors willing to risk their capital, many influential citizens in Riverside urged that a municipal project would benefit the community. Curiously, this concept received the endorsement of none other than Cyrus Baldwin, President of the San Antonio Light and Power Company, who suggested that power could be generated with the ample water supplies of surrounding streams. An election was held on June 5, 1895, and Riverside's citizens voted to bond the city for $40,000 to create an electric light plant. Thereby, Riverside became the first city in California to develop a municipal electric system.

Because the bond issue proved too small to construct an adequate power plant, the money was instead used to build a distribution network. Hydroelectric power was purchased from the Mill Creek No. 1 plant of the Redlands Electric Light and Power Company,

The intersection of Ninth, Spring and Main Streets, about 1910. Los Angeles is beginning to sprawl, with a population of nearly 200,000 people. AUTHOR'S COLLECTION.

some 20 miles away, delivered over a 10,000-volt transmission line built by the Company. Service on the Riverside municipal system began on December 8, 1896. Three years later a steam station was constructed at a cost of $34,000. Contrary to the hopes expressed that Riverside would no longer have to purchase its energy, the tiny plant helped the situation very little, as demand for power reached new heights in the growing town.

The same intersection in 1925. Los Angeles has grown up, and her population will soon surpass a million people. AUTHOR'S COLLECTION.

Dissatisfaction with the very poor service rendered by small local private power plants persuaded three other Southern California communities to begin municipal electric systems. Glendale pioneer Leslie C. Brand organized the Glendale Light and Power Company in about 1904. Shortly after the City of Glendale was incorporated in 1906, Brand found it difficult to continue the activities of his small power system. Having little interest in the power business, he offered his utility for sale to the City. His offer was accepted only after a long delay. On November 1, 1909, the Glendale Light Department began operation to 190 customers. Energy was purchased from Pacific Light and Power.

Although the steam plant was retained by the municipal utility for many years for standby service, virtually all of the energy used by its consumers was purchased from neighboring electric companies. In 1902, Edison succeeded the Redlands Company as Riverside's supplier, and when Southern Sierras built lines through the area in 1912, that company, too, wholesaled electricity to the City. Riverside today remains a resale customer of Southern California Edison.

In 1896, the City of Anaheim in Orange County began a municipal power plant, again because no other energy supply was available. Anaheim's steam plant operated until about 1918, when, hopelessly inadequate to meet the community's needs, it was shut down in favor of purchasing power at wholesale rates from Edison. The City still purchases most of its energy from Edison today.

The small cities of Azusa and Colton each started municipal systems in 1900, primarily at first for street lighting. Azusa originally purchased its power from the San Gabriel Electric Company, while Colton has always been a resale customer of the Edison Company.

Late in 1911, the residents of the town of Burbank were pleased to learn that the Burbank Light and Power Company had been formed to bring electricity to them. Before service could begin, however, the company sank into financial difficulties. Pacific Light and Power offered to buy the incomplete system, but the City trustees instead decided to organize a city utility patterned after that in Glendale. With the unfinished company system as its nucleus, the Burbank Light Department began electric service on August 5, 1913. It, too, purchased electricity from P. L. & P.

In 1914, a small electric system was begun in Banning. While information is sketchy, it appears that this company purchased its power from the Southern Sierras Power Company, tapping off their 55,000-volt Imperial Valley line that had been built through Banning in that year. On October 14, 1922, the City of Banning bought out the private company, but continued to purchase its energy from Southern Sierras, and later from successors California Electric Power and Southern California Edison.

The creation of these municipal utilities was amicable insofar as they fulfilled important needs in the community. When the City of Pasadena established its municipal lighting plant, however, a bitter controversy erupted. Pasadena had been the first city outside Los Angeles to be served by Edison, when the local Pasadena Electric Light and Power Company was purchased in 1899. Edison spent substantial sums to reconstruct and modernize the dilapidated system of its predecessor. In addition, rates were reduced. Edison President John B. Miller lived in Pasadena and was proud of the way in which these material improvements could be made even while

lowering the cost of service. Pasadena appeared to him to be ample proof of his philosophy of the benefits of amalgamation.

This notwithstanding, late in 1905 the City Board of Directors expressed dissatisfaction with the slow pace at which Edison had been extending street lighting to all districts of the city. When the company responded that it was absorbing a loss in its street lighting service in areas below a certain population density, the City replied that Edison rates were too high.

Interior of Edison's Pasadena Steam Plant at Broadway and California, about 1902. Cheap hydroelectric power had already relegated this plant to standby status, and it would be scrapped in 1906.
EDISON COLLECTION.

Colorado Street in **143** *Pasadena in 1903.*
AUTHOR'S COLLECTION.

Pasadena's first Municipal Steam Plant on Glenarm Street, as it appeared in 1914.
COURTESY PASADENA D.W.P.

Workmen unload a new turbine for the Pasadena plant during its expansion in 1914.
COURTESY PASADENA D.W.P.

This ruinous competition continued for over a decade. Pasadena hoped to buy inexpensive hydroelectric power from Los Angeles' aqueduct plants, but was disappointed when instead Edison secured their output. When Edison further lowered its rates, the city sought state legislation to compel them to be raised again. To cap this, the City of Pasadena began extending its power lines outside the city limits to serve customers in adjacent incorporated communities. Such unethical invasions of franchised service areas were forbidden to investor-owned utilities by the State Railroad Commission, today's Public Utilities Commission, but as a "people's utility," Pasadena was exempted from following the same rules.

The outbreak of World War One finally persuaded the two utilities to mediate a compromise in order to eliminate wasteful competition. In 1917, Pasadena offered to sell to Edison its distribution lines outside of the city limits, and to buy surplus energy from the Company, if in return, Edison would sell to the city its Pasadena distribution system at a price to be set by the Railroad Commission. The agreed upon sale was completed in 1920.

144 Quickly attitudes hardened. Before long, a municipal street lighting plant was being proposed, and in May 1906 bonds for such a system were approved by the voters.

Almost before it knew what had happened, the Edison Company was faced with the loss of an important marketplace. Once the city plant was operating, bitter competition ensued. The city called Edison rates too high, but when completion of the huge Kern River Hydroelectric Plant in 1907 enabled the

company to pass along to customers a substantial rate reduction, Pasadena officials charged Edison with unfair rate cutting. Admittedly, the Pasadena municipal system met and beat each Edison rate decrease, but at first was forced to operate at a loss to do so. Such practices would have bankrupted a corporation, but the City of Pasadena simply persuaded its citizens to pass more bond issues, and even levied a temporary increase in the local property tax to sustain its power system.

The dispute with Pasadena was prolonged and bitter, during which, to many, the concept of public service became a pawn of political expediency. Before it was resolved, however, Edison had become involved in an even greater crisis, one that threatened for a time to destroy the company altogether. This new crisis was the impending loss of Edison's most important single marketplace, the City of Los Angeles, which the company and its predecessors had served since 1896.

Los Angeles' first Board of Water Commissioners, 1902. Railroad builder Moses Sherman, center, was Chief Commissioner.
COURTESY LOS ANGELES D.W.P.

A view of northwestern Los Angeles from the Court House, about 1900. This was part of the district served by the Edison Electric Company.
AUTHOR'S COLLECTION.

The reason for this loss is closely tied to the City of Los Angeles' desire to develop an adequate water supply for its rapidly growing population, which had soared to 100,000 residents by 1900. On February 3, 1902, faced with impending water shortages, the people voted for a $2 million bond issue to buy out the private water company. Three days later, the City Council passed an ordinance creating a Board of Water Commissioners, the beginning of today's Department of Water and Power. William Mulholland, who had begun his career as a "Zanjero" (ditch tender) for the old water company, became Chief Engineer of the city system. When it was suggested that the Owens River might be tapped as a source of water for the city, Mulholland spent 40 days on horseback surveying the river, checking stream flow and reconnoitering a route for an aqueduct. He proposed a 250-mile long, entirely gravity-flow aqueduct to cost $24.5 million.

A steam shovel clears away big boulders on the open section of aqueduct near the Alabama Hills.
COURTESY LOS ANGELES D.W.P.

Early in 1913 concreting of the Owens Valley section of the aqueduct was nearly completed.
COURTESY LOS ANGELES D.W.P.

In 1905 Los Angeles voters approved another bond issue, this one for $1.5 million to purchase of water rights in the Owens Valley, and to pay for a formal engineering survey. The city hired three eminent consulting engineers to check Mulholland's preliminary figures. Their report confirmed his earlier estimates and agreed that despite the aqueduct's record length, there were no insuperable problems involved in its construction. Buried in this report was a proposal to develop electric power along the aqueduct, the sale of which, the engineers stated, might pay for the entire project.

This last proposal, buried in the technical data of the report, was soon to inflame passions. The ensuing controversy over the development of municipal power was to engulf the city and its three investor-owned utilities in political storms and legal quicksand for over a decade. Eventually, it led to the complete withdrawal of the Southern California Edison Company from the city limits of Los Angeles.

Mules haul a large pipe section into place during construction of the Jawbone Siphon.
COURTESY LOS ANGELES D.W.P.

Thousands turned out to see the first delivery of water through the Owens River Aqueduct in 1913.
COURTESY LOS ANGELES D.W.P.

city's history. Although no expenditures were specifically earmarked for power development, the final route of the aqueduct was located with an eye to siting future hydroelectric plants.

Actual construction of the Owens River Aqueduct began in 1908. Almost immediately a small hydro plant was built on Division Creek, just north of Independence, to provide power to the project. While work progressed, Los Angeles newspapers ignored the growing bitterness among Owens Valley residents resulting from the heavy-handed appropriation of their water, and instead focused upon the development of a municipal power system.

In 1910, a fourth bond issue, this of $3.5 million, was passed by the voters. These funds specifically were to be used to build San Francisquito power house No. 1 along the aqueduct, and a 110,000-volt transmission line to Los Angeles. How the power would be distributed was not specified. During the campaign, some incredible claims were made by municipal power advocates. The City's Public Service Commission stated: "We may never require another bond issue for this one may lay a foundation that will itself pay for the

Los Angeles' voters were asked to approve yet another bond issue in 1907, for $23 million to build the Owens River Aqueduct. Edison, Pacific Light and Power, and Los Angeles Gas and Electric were not opposed to the water project, but they feared that a municipal power system would destroy them by removing their principal marketplace. During the campaign the *Los Angeles Times*, in strident editorials, painted the power companies as villains, and when the ballots were counted, the aqueduct bonds had passed by the largest majority in the

rest of our future improvements. This great project will be completed without the expenditure of another cent." Mayor George Alexander went completely overboard. He declared that the city power plant would be a money-earner, and predicted that the bonds would not just finance the power plant but would wipe out the entire city indebtedness. The bonds passed by a nine-to-one margin. The question of how to dispose of the energy was ignored while work on the aqueduct continued and ground was broken for the power plant.

In 1910, the state-wide Progressive movement swept reform-minded Hiram Johnson into the Governor's office. He was responsible for introducing many needed reforms into the state government, including state regulation of public utilities, a move welcomed by the power companies who were weary of bitter harassment they received from most municipal public service commissions. Unfortunately, in Los Angeles, a number of Socialists rode into city offices upon the coattails of the progressive landslide, bringing with them an anti-business rhetoric that inflamed the municipal power issue.

In the fall of 1912, the Los Angeles City Council began negotiations with representatives of the Edison Company, Pacific Light and Power, and L. A. Gas and Electric to purchase their distribution systems within the city limits. The electric companies made a counter offer: they would purchase power that the city developed along the aqueduct and retail it to customers within the city. This created an impasse from which neither side would budge. So, a $6.5 million bond issue to build a city-owned distribution system was put on the April 15, 1913 ballot.

supported building the aqueduct were set against the city getting into the power business. In the election, the distribution system bonds failed to receive the needed two-thirds majority.

This setback persuaded the city to go back to the bargaining table. In October, the companies offered to lease their distribution systems to the city and to ultimately work out a sale. This proposal failed, however, when the companies could not secure releases from their bondholders, and provisions of the city charter did not allow a lease under any other conditions.

Meanwhile, construction of the San Francisquito power plant came to a halt due to lack of funds. Still another bond issue was proposed: $1.25 million dollars to finish the plant, and $5.25 million to purchase Southern California Edison's distribution system. Edison's system was singled out because it was the largest in the city, serving some 45 percent of Los Angeles' power consumers. On May 8, 1914, after a very brief campaign that generated little public interest, the bonds narrowly passed. Many analysts believed that the passage

Los Angeles' old Buena Vista Pumping Plant, made redundant after arrival of Owens River water.
COURTESY LOS ANGELES D.W.P.

Having lost the power bond fights up to this point, the electric companies decided to speak directly to the voters through a series of straightforward advertisements placed in prominent newspapers before the election. These advertisements reviewed the attempts to mediate the issue and put forward a list of four compromises any of which the companies would accept. In this campaign, such calm and reasonable explanations gained much public understanding for the electric companies' point of view. Many community leaders who had

was due to the fact that women were voting for the first time. They also felt that most women may not have been well informed on the issue because of the short election campaign.

As a first step towards purchasing the Edison system or acquiring it by condemnation, the City of Los Angeles petitioned the State Railroad Commission to fix a just price. Lawyers and utility managers all over the nation watched these proceedings, for it was the first case of its kind. Most importantly, it

would establish a precedent for fixing severance damages: in this case, the damage suffered by the rest of the Edison system by the excision of the Los Angeles area.

After two years of deliberation, a decision was rendered that pleased neither party. The plant valuation and damages were fixed at $6.4 million, much less than what Edison had asked for, but nearly double what Los Angeles had thought reasonable.

The City Council rejected the offer and promptly set about building a duplicate distribution network in Hollywood and Garvanza, areas served by P. L. & P., and in that part of East Los Angeles then served by L. A. Gas and Electric. The first pole in the city's system was set at the corner of Pasadena Avenue and Marmion Way in Highland Park (Garvanza) on March 30, 1916. Beginning in November, power service was offered to customers solicited by the promise of substantially lower rates. The electricity was purchased from the City of Pasadena's municipal power plant.

During this difficult time, Edison President John Miller privately confided his fears to an associate. The Edison management believed that because the business within the city accounted for nearly 75 percent of the company's total income, loss of that business would bankrupt and destroy the company. This may have been one reason behind the relatively quick negotiations leading to the merger with Pacific Light and Power.

Immediately upon completion of that merger in the spring of 1917, the company's combined distribution system within Los Angeles was offered for sale to the city for a price of $12 million. This offer was accepted. Insofar as the city would not have the generating capacity to serve its new system for several years, it was also agreed that for five years Edison would continue to operate the system under lease, sharing its revenue with the city. Another part of the lease agreement came into effect after the city's San Francisquito No. 1 hydro station came on line in mid-1917, whereby Edison received the plant's output and sold it within Los Angeles as an agent for the city.

Los Angeles' Board of Water and Power Commissioners, about 1917. William Mulholland is second from left, E. F. Scattergood is far right.
COURTESY LOS ANGELES D.W.P.

San Francisquito No. 1 hydro plant under construction, 1913. Shortages of funds delayed its completion until 1917.
EDISON COLLECTION.

A large party visits San Francisquito No. 1 hydro plant in 1924.
Courtesy Los Angeles D.W.P.

This relatively amicable settlement gave Edison the breathing space it needed to build up its load outside the City of Los Angeles. Within five years, the growth of population in surrounding Southern California communities was so spectacular as to eclipse the importance of the Los Angeles City marketplace, which dropped to only 25 percent of total system sales.

Moving the generator rotor to San Francisquito No. 1, about 1916.
Courtesy Los Angeles D.W.P.

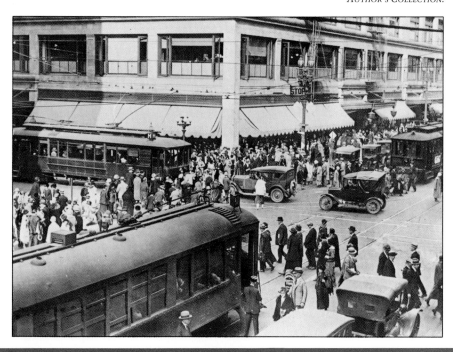

On January 31, 1937, the City of Los Angeles purchased the entire electric system of the Los Angeles Gas and Electric Corporation, ending nearly a decade of litigation. Two and-a-half years later, in August 1939, Edison and the city concluded an exchange of facilities, whereby

On May 16, 1922, the Edison Company completed transfer of its Los Angeles distribution system to the city's Bureau of Power and Light. As part of this final agreement, Edison contracted to supply substantial blocks of energy to the chronically power-short municipal utility for a period of up to 30 years. Curiously, as a legacy from the days of Henry Huntington, all of the trolley lines within the city continued to receive their power from Edison, an arrangement that continued until the last streetcar ran in 1963.

Edison received those distribution facilities formerly belonging to L. A. Gas and Electric that lay outside the Los Angeles city limits, while turning over to the city its distribution system in areas that had been annexed by Los Angeles since the original electric system sale in 1922. By these agreements the City of Los Angeles acquired the last large groups of customers within its borders still being served by investor-owned utilities.

The City of Vernon got into the power business when John Leonis, the flamboyant and popular mayor of that small community, determined to convert Vernon from a sleepy suburb into a major manufacturing district. Sometime early in 1932, Leonis approached Edison's President Russell H. Ballard about the possibility of a special power rate for manufacturing concerns who relocated to Vernon. Due in part to the deepening depression, but also because of an understandable dislike of such "special favor rates," Ballard refused Leonis' request, perhaps not as diplomatically as might have been done. Angered, Leonis departed with a threat to start his own power system.

True to the Mayor's word, the City of Vernon quickly sold bonds and let contracts in 1932 to construct a power plant and distribution system. In a significant departure for the time, the power station was to house five 7500-kilowatt generators driven by huge diesel engines. Never before had such a large power system relied exclusively upon diesel generation with the expectation that the energy produced would be cheaper than that from commercial utility systems. The distribution

system was operated at the unusual line pressure of 6600 volts. This was considered to be the highest line voltage that could be worked "hot", by men wearing insulated gloves. Those lines supplied energy directly from the power plant to customers, thus saving the expense of a separate transmission network.

Despite these non-standard aspects, Vernon's system was successful—indeed, too much so. It started service on June 19, 1933, and as the manufacturing concerns that had located in Vernon began to shrug off the torpor of the depression, demand soared. Soon the five

Los Angeles Gas and Electric's Seal Beach Generating Station, under construction in 1924. This was among the properties sold to the City of Los Angeles in 1937.
COURTESY W.B. MILLER.

The Vernon Diesel Plant

Although small diesel engines had been used since World War One to generate electricity in private plants and very small commercial systems, the decision by the City of Vernon in 1932 to rely exclusively upon that technology for their new municipal power system was considered daring. Carl Heinze, the engineer who made that decision, believed that two factors would enable diesel generated electricity to be cost competitive: first, that diesel fuel then cost only 6 cents per gallon, and secondly, that the big slow-speed machines he had in mind would prove very economical of fuel.

The diesel engines chosen as prime movers for the Vernon plant were giant, double-acting, two-cycle, eight cylinder, solid-injection types operating at 167 revolutions per minute. Built by the Hamilton Machine Works in Ohio, under a manufacturing license from Masheinenfabrik Augsburg-Nuremburg of Germany, the engines were identical to those used in Germany's famous "pocket battleships" built in the inter-war era. In fact, some of the precision-machined parts, including the massive 45-ton crankshaft forgings, were made in Germany.

The engines began running in June 1933 and operated almost continuously for four years. After Edison leased the Vernon system in 1937, the diesels were still running from time to time even though maintenance outages were scheduled by necessity and thanks to back-up power available from other Edison power plants.

Made obsolescent by more modern post-war generating plants, the Vernon diesels were used less and less. Age, rising fuel prices and smog regulations all caught up with the plant until it was used only for emergencies. During a series of very hot summer days in August of 1972, the plant was run to help meet a record peak demand on the Edison system, but not long afterwards, the plant was retired with sentimental ceremony.

All was not over, however. The City of Vernon decided to give the plant another chance. After extensive overhauling by Vernon, Unit 5 came back to life in 1982. It was the first of the five units slated for overhaul by the City. The extent of available usage of these historic engines is a question only time will answer.

The art-deco facade of Vernon's Diesel Plant in 1938. Plant was then being operated by Edison.
Edison Collection.

Edison crew rewiring one of the Vernon generators for 60-cycle operation, 1947.
Edison Collection.

One of Vernon's massive engines under construction in 1933.
EDISON COLLECTION.

This switchboard controlled the entire Vernon City power system, and matched the decor of the building's exterior.
EDISON COLLECTION.

engines had to be run constantly to meet the demand, leaving no margin for emergencies or scheduled repairs. After four years of increasingly strenuous operation, the City of Vernon leased its system back to the Edison Company, which to this day continues to operate the distribution system as an agent for the city.

Despite these losses of customers to municipal power systems, the vast majority of Southern Californians continued to approve of both the quality and the cost of Edison service. For some 40 years following the start of state regulation of rates in 1912, except for one brief, temporary rate hike in 1920 caused by the high inflation which followed World War One, the Edison Company continually and voluntarily reduced its rates to all classes of customers, including the municipal resale cities, as its huge investment in hydroelectric facilities, coupled

with economies of scale, significantly lowered the cost of service. During this period, Edison's rates in all the cities it served were only fractionally higher than those of the City of Los Angeles for comparable classes of service, the marginal difference reflecting the expense of a much larger transmission network to serve remote customers, greater capital costs and a high rate of corporate taxes, expenses the city did not incur.

The Difficult Decades

Although the Southern California Edison Company relied on steam plants for some of its electricity, until the mid-Twenties it was predominantly a water power company deriving most of its energy from hydroelectric plants in the Sierra Nevada, San Gabriel, and San Bernardino Mountains. In California, coal was scarce and very expensive, and although oil was plentiful, steam power plants still cost more to operate than did hydro plants. Unfortunately, the winters of 1921-22 and 1922-23 had lower-than-normal rainfall, and

the winter of 1923-24 was the driest on record throughout the State, with the snow pack in the Sierras only one-eighth of normal. At the end of the runoff in the spring of 1924, Edison operating officials knew that not enough water was available in storage to meet the summer's load demand.

This was only the beginning of a desperate summer all over the West Coast, for the drought was not confined to Southern California alone. Every electric system in the state was faced with shortages, so, under the guidance of the State Railroad Commission, all worked together to solve the problem.

The first step for Edison was to make full use of existing steam generating capacity. Plants at Long Beach and Redondo, which normally carried only peak loads, were put on 24-hour duty. Long Beach's capacity was increased by quickly adding three small generators at one end of the building. Two older plants at Visalia and Santa Barbara, neither of which had been used since 1918, were rehabilitated and returned to operation.

Kern River No. 3 hydro plant showing low water conditions in the spring of 1924.
EDISON COLLECTION.

Edison's photographer G. Haven Bishop took this haunting 1932 portrait of the 300 foot high towers which carried Long Beach Steam Plants power lines across Cerritos Channel.
EDISON COLLECTION.

Second, arrangements were made to establish interconnections with other California utilities for emergency exchanges of power. During the drought, regular power interchanges were made with the Los Angeles Gas and Electric Corporation, Southern Sierras Power Company, San Joaquin Light and Power Corporation, Great Western Power Company, the City of Pasadena and San Diego Consolidated Gas and Electric Company. Edison even arranged to purchase the output of the obsolete and long-idle municipal steam

plant of the City of Alameda and surplus capacity from a sawdust-fueled power plant belonging to the Sugar Pine Lumber Company near Fresno. This energy was imported through San Joaquin Light and Power's transmission system.

Third, Edison engineers sought to lease small private steam plants owned by industries throughout Southern California. Mostly obsolete facilities that long ago had been relegated to stand-by status by less expensive

157

During the 1924 drought, many Southern California industries generated electricity to help Edison with the power shortage. The Monolith Cement Plant near Tehachapi was one such good samaritan.
EDISON COLLECTION.

Construction of the Long Beach Steam Plant No. 2 was speeded up in the hope the Plant's capacity would be available to alleviate the power shortage.
EDISON COLLECTION.

Los Angeles Railway went to great lengths to explain to its patrons the service changes imposed by the drought-caused power shortage. No one could then know that trolley service would never return to pre-drought levels.
AUTHOR'S COLLECTION.

The problem was two-fold: not only was the amount of available power reduced, but more energy was required for pumping inasmuch as water levels had been lowered by several years of subnormal rainfall. This power had to be allotted to save farmer's crops. Chambers of Commerce, merchants' associations and newspapers enlisted in the campaign to reduce power consumption by 25 percent. Restaurants, theaters and stores cooperated by using fewer lights. The rock and gravel companies of Orange County shut down operations during June. The Santa Fe Railway closed its San Bernardino repair shops for two weeks. Members of the Long Beach Chamber of Commerce agreed to discontinue all sign and decorative lighting.

Frequent complaints were launched against the big "HOLLYWOODLAND" sign, said to be the world's largest electric sign, which remained brightly lit in the Hollywood Hills, until it was explained in the papers that the sign got its energy from a private gasoline generator. Similar complaints about the lights on Long Beach's pleasure pier were quieted when it was revealed that they were gas lights.

Edison service, these plants had to be cleaned up or extensively rebuilt before they could be placed into around-the-clock service. Of the 15 power plants so conscripted, one was the City of Riverside's antique municipal generator, six belonged to local sugar processing companies, two were owned by cement manufacturers, two by oil companies, one by a tool forging company, one by an electric dredging concern in Long Beach Harbor; the two largest stations were owned by the Pacific Electric Railway, and ironically had not been used since Big Creek power arrived in Los Angeles a decade earlier.

Having searched for every available source of electric power, the Edison Company still found itself 15 percent short as summer began. The only option left was the distasteful one of curtailing service to customers. Inasmuch as the shortages were statewide, the Railroad Commission appointed a Power Supervisor, H.G. Butler, to administer a voluntary and mandatory rationing program. Butler had performed the same duty during World War One, when oil conservation measures had threatened to curtail electric service, but now the need was much more urgent.

Tragically, Southern California's great trolley systems were hard hit. Power consumption was reduced by skipping stops, curtailing routes and frequency of service, and by replacing many lightly patronized lines with motor buses. Though no one could then know it, this was the first step into oblivion for the region's magnificent public transit network.

To keep employees and the public informed about the crisis, the Edison Company issued a weekly "Power Conservation Bulletin" that was excerpted in newspaper advertisements. While telling of the efforts that were being made to return the electric supply to normal conditions, the bulletins also passed along the latest State-ordered conservation rules, some of which make interesting reading today:

All light and power loads to be reduced by 25 percent;

Only one watt per square foot allowed for display window lighting;

No billboard lighting;

No pumping of water to fill duck ponds or to water golf courses;

No new business accepted by electric companies except domestic lighting loads not to exceed 2 kilowatts;

Theatre marquee lighting allowed only between the hours of 7:30 and 9:30 p.m.;

Street lighting to be reduced 50 percent in congested business districts;

Daylight savings time to be inaugurated.

For 144 power-short days, Southern Californians wrestled with the shortages and with the hot, dry summer. Many watched with

Designated Plant No. 2, the expansion at Long Beach had been decided upon in the fall of 1923, before the serious water shortages had developed. When the drought threatened, however, plant construction was speeded up in an effort to alleviate the situation. This 70,000-kilowatt facility was to be the first modern high-pressure steam plant on the West Coast, yet despite its complexity, work was pushed way ahead of schedule.

Construction of the plant began on January 15, 1924, when the first of 7000 long wooden piles were pounded into the unstable, sandy soil of Terminal Island to prepare a foundation for the structure. For months, as trainloads of materials poured in from factories all over the nation, the steel and concrete giant took shape upon the mudflats. In August, American railroads set a never-bettered record when a train of 22 cars filled with electrical machinery from General Electric rolled across the continent from Schenectady to Terminal Island in just five days. In a saga of construction without equal in the history of the electric power industry, Edison's Long Beach No. 2 plant began producing power on November 15, 1926, just 303 days after work started.

interest two developments that would hopefully prevent a future recurrence of 1924's problems. One was the continuing rapid progress made in drilling the Florence Lake Tunnel, designed to keep Huntington Lake full and the Big Creek plants running at capacity even in the driest years. The other event was the dramatic progress on a substantial new addition to the Long Beach Steam Plant.

159

Work on the Long Beach Steam Plant No. 3 continued despite the deepening depression as the Company sought to keep its workforce employed.
EDISON COLLECTION.

The Long Beach Steam Plant complex on Terminal Island, viewed from the mouth of Cerritos Channel.
EDISON COLLECTION.

Ironically, only four days earlier, State Power Supervisor Butler had declared the water and power shortage at an end, thanks to a torrential rainstorm that had inundated much of California. Southern California Edison learned a valuable lesson from this confrontation with whimsical nature. Hydro was still the preferred generation resource, of course, and would continue to be so for many years, so the water storage capacity at Big Creek, the Company's

Damage to the Van Ness Hotel on State Street.

principal source of hydroelectric power, was to be further enlarged. It was also decided that, to improve system reliablity, steam generation should be increased to meet much more of the system demand in emergencies. A third turbo-generator was to be added alongside the two just built at Long Beach Plant No. 2, and plans were developed for a third complete plant to be built. By the time this construction program halted in 1930, the total of eleven generators at Long Beach Plants One, Two and Three produced 419,000 kilowatts, making them the major power resource on the Edison system.

The drought was only the first natural disaster of the Twenties. At 6:44 a.m. on June 29, 1925, an earthquake rumbled through Santa Barbara, heavily damaging the city's business district and destroying Edison's local generating station. Although the steam plant was for standby service and had not been used since the end of the drought, the same building housed a substation that received power over a 66,000-volt high line from Ventura. The earthquake caused lighting arrestors to collapse upon the station bus bars, interrupting all power service west of Carpinteria.

The Santa Barbara Steam Plant was a total write-off as a result of the 1925 temblor.

Although no Edison facilities were significantly damaged in the 1933 Long Beach Quake, Pacific Electric's North Long Beach Substation was virtually destroyed.
AUTHOR'S COLLECTION.

Edison employees loaned their electric cooking appliances as the Company spearheaded relief efforts following the 1933 quake. Here Red Cross volunteers staff an Edison-supplied food station.
EDISON COLLECTION.

Station operator William N. Engle, on duty that morning, was just outside of the building when the quake struck. In spite of falling bricks and debris, and the danger of explosion from the oil switches, he ran back into the station to disconnect all switches. He was hit on the head by falling brick but completed his task and escaped from the building. Engle's bravery was credited for saving Santa Barbara from the danger of a conflagration caused by sparks from downed power lines igniting gas escaping from broken mains.

Shaken, but determined to restore service quickly, Santa Barbara District crews immediately assembled to begin repairs. One group went to work at the substation, and within a few hours, despite danger from aftershocks and weakened walls, had cleared away damage and reconnected to the transmission system. Damage to street lights was extensive, but another crew put up a temporary pole line along State Street, and street lights went on all over town that evening. Still another crew quickly restored service to the city's only hospital and to the telephone company.

With the assistance of crews sent up from Ventura, work began to return the trolleys to operation and to restore general light and power service. On Saturday the Fourth of July, only five days after the temblor, the Santa Barbara and Suburban Railway's trolleys were threading their way between piles of rubble from the ruined buildings on State Street. That same day saw electric service restored to most customers whose homes and buildings still stood, this work having been slowed only by the need to wait for city building inspectors to check each structure prior to reconnection.

Catastrophe at Kemp Camp

(Excerpted from an article by Leo Smith in the *Santa Paula Chronicle*, March 13, 1928)

Twisted company cars mark site of Kemp Camp.
EDISON COLLECTION.

Survivors from Kemp Camp at seven o'clock the next morning.
EDISON COLLECTION.

"Grim death dealt a cruel blow at the construction camp of the Southern California Edison Company about four miles east of Piru, when a wall of water from the ruptured St. Francis dam without warning hit the narrow gorge which narrows the Santa Clara River at 1:30 o'clock this morning, and is believed to have trapped 96 of the 140 men as they slept in their tents. Ed Locke, heroic night watchman who was on duty, gave his life in a vain attempt to warn the men, but to no avail. Where the camp stood last night there is nothing but a sea of mud, littered with 50 autos either buried or partially submerged, and freight cars that had been bowled over, remnants of buildings, tents, great rolls of copper wire and a mountain of debris.

"When the wall of water descended on the slumbering camp the roar deafened the warning cries of the watchman. Men who were awakened endeavored to get out, but in the darkness could not find their way through the canvas of their tents, being unable to claw holes through it. There they were, forced to take their chance with fate...If they were fortunate, they weathered the experience....

"Perhaps the most thrilling story was told by Russell Roth, whose bunk in the camp was nearest to the riverbed. Roth said he heard a roar and thought it was an explosion or a terrible storm. He put his hand out and found it was not raining. As he turned around he found his bed starting to move in the water milling into his tent. Before he could think, as he stated, 'I was on top of a raft composed of part of the tent, and was being tossed about. Finally I got aboard a big metal object which proved to be a water tank, and this saved my life. I rode this until finally it was pushed up onto the shore.'"

A program of emergency procedures developed by Edison as a result of the Santa Barbara quake was put to the test just eight years later. On March 10, 1933, most of Southern California was shaken by the Long Beach Earthquake, which left 120 people dead in its aftermath. Edison's Long Beach Steam Plant was near the epicenter, but damage was moderate, confined mostly to one 220,000-volt substation bus structure. Fortunately, hydro plants were carrying most of the load at that moment; only Long Beach Unit No. 9 was on line, supplying power to the City of Los Angeles.

There was a 30-second outage in Los Angeles until system stability was restored. After that, service was normal in all areas except Long Beach and Compton, where all circuits were restored within an hour-and-a-half. Because Company telephone lines were damaged, at first the only way Edison's power system dispatchers could determine that the Long Beach Steam Plant was uninjured was by its ability to pick up load as required by the emergency.

As conditions became known in the stricken areas, relief efforts were mounted. Because Long Beach's municipal gas system had to be shut off due to the fire hazard, one of the first

The St. Francis Dam as it appeared in 1926.
COURTESY LOS ANGELES D.W.P.

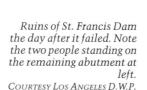

Ruins of St. Francis Dam the day after it failed. Note the two people standing on the remaining abutment at left.
COURTESY LOS ANGELES D.W.P.

needs of the shaken city was for cooking equipment. From warehouses all over the Pacific Coast, as well as from its own General Store in Alhambra, Edison located and brought to Long Beach electric ranges, hotplates, air heaters and heating pads. Electric ranges already in service in the homes of Edison employees living in the area were made available for community use. Tents and a portable kitchen, used by Edison in its construction camps, were sent to Long Beach and Compton for the use of the Red Cross and other relief agencies. For their tireless efforts to

restore service and provide relief assistance, Edison people received many expressions of thanks in the ensuing days.

Earthquakes must be endured at the caprice of nature, but one great tragedy in this difficult time could easily have been prevented. Forty-five miles northwest of Los Angeles lay the St. Francis Dam, built in 1926 by the Bureau of Power and Light to store Owens River Aqueduct water and to generate electricity. At two minutes before midnight on March 12,

1928, the dam collapsed with a thunderous roar and a mighty rush of water. A 110-foot high wall of water poured death and destruction for 50 miles down San Francisquito Canyon and the Santa Clara River Valley. Of the 700 people who lost their lives that night, 84 were Edison employees who had been working on a transmission construction project. At Kemp Camp, where the workers were housed, night watchman Ed Locke tried to rouse as many of the sleeping men as possible before he was swept away and drowned.

Aftermath of the St. Francis Flood: a home washed partly across Harvard Blvd. in Santa Paula.
LUTHER S. LOTHRIDGE COLLECTION.

The first positive indication of the magnitude of the disaster was received by the dispatchers at 12:20 a.m., when Edison line patrolman Ray Starbard called over the Company telephone from Saugus Substation. This lucky man had gone out to investigate the cause of the original 66,000-volt line interruption, only to be caught in the edge of the onrushing water, but had escaped. Returning to Saugus, he phoned in a report that the St. Francis Dam had indeed failed. Starbard coolly noted to the dispatcher that even as he talked, water was waist high around the substation. Ordered to abandon his post, the patrolman had to swim to safety on higher ground.

Immediately upon receipt of this warning, Senior Dispatcher J. D. Poe recognized the seriousness of the situation and began phoning warnings to Edison substations in communities in the path of the oncoming flood. These phone calls, quickly passed on to local authorities, were the first, and in some cases the only indications received by many communities downstream of the disaster racing towards them. Poe's prompt action was later credited with having saved many lives.

Only seconds after the dam failed, Edison power system dispatchers in Los Angeles had their first indication of trouble, when the Saugus-Lancaster 66,000-volt line, which crossed the canyon at the foot of the dam, failed, causing an oil circuit breaker at Saugus

State Highway bridge washed out near Santa Paula, March 13, 1928.
EDISON COLLECTION.

Substation to explode. Four minutes later, the entire load of the City of Los Angeles was instantly dumped onto the Edison system by emergency relays as the City's main transmission lines and the Francisquito No. 2 hydro plant were destroyed by the onrushing wall of water. Unaware of what was causing these disturbances, the shaken dispatchers began telephoning into the district unaware that millions of gallons of water rushing towards the sea were quickly washing away communications into the area.

Boy Scouts and the ladies of Santa Paula make soup and coffee for the victims of the flood and rescue workers.
COURTESY CARL IRWIN.

Remains of one of the Big Creek lines near Saugus Substation. Much of the Edison system in the Los Angeles area was briefly blacked out when the St. Francis flood hit these towers.
EDISON COLLECTION.

Luther Lothridge, Edison's Santa Paula District Manager, and Operating Department officials were also notified. As early as 2 a.m. on March 13th, a long stream of Edison trucks from all over the system, loaded with relief supplies, men and repair equipment were heading through the night to the stricken district.

At 12:41 a.m. the two main Big Creek 220,000-volt power lines, which were at that moment supplying most of the system load, were washed out as the flood reached their crossing of the Santa Clara River Valley. Los Angeles and most of Edison's metropolitan service territory was plunged into darkness, while Ventura and Santa Barbara were blacked out as a result of the inundation of vital transmission facilities at Saugus. Harried dispatchers called Long Beach Steam Plant to prepare them to meet the morning peak load demand only a few hours away.

Herculean efforts restored service to most areas before the morning peak began. Transmission Superintendent Charlie Heath and his crews built a temporary by-pass line around Saugus Substation even before the floodwaters had receded, enabling service to be restored to Ventura and Santa Barbara by 6 a.m. The then newly completed Vincent 220,000-volt line from Big Creek justified its expensive construction along an independent right of way as, loaded to capacity, it carried as much Big Creek energy as possible to Southern California. At Long Beach, Production Superintendent Andre ordered all nine units in Plants One and Two, (Plant Three had not yet been built) to run at full capacity and "into the

red" to meet the balance of the morning and evening peaks in Los Angeles and Edison's Metropolitan Division.

So successful was the emergency power supply effort that, had it not been for the morning's screaming headlines, few outside the Santa Clara Valley would have known of the disaster and its attendent electrical problems. To the people in the Valley, however, the dam failure and flood will never be forgotten. Two generations later, survivors still talk sadly or

Early in 1930 the steel foundation of the new Edison Building began to take shape.
EDISON COLLECTION.

The main lobby of the new Edison Building expressed the pride and confidence the Company felt despite the Depression.
EDISON COLLECTION.

The Fifth and Grand Building

The Fifth and Grand General Office Building of the Edison Company was an architectural monument from the moment it opened its doors on March 20, 1931. Years ahead of the time when most engineers thought it economically feasible, the Edison Company had produced the world's first all-electric building. Its lighting, air handling machinery, cafeteria ranges, mail tubes, clocks, elevators and all equipment were designed to operate electrically. Additionally, the heating and

cooling system was the first commercial application of the recently developed concept of the heat-pump, whereby the operation of a conventional air conditioning system is "reversed" to heat the air instead.

Insofar as building codes would permit, the new building was constructed with electrically operated equipment: jack-hammers, saws, welding machines, spray guns, hoists and so on. The building's steel skeleton was designed incorporating the most advanced seismic calculations yet performed to enable it to withstand the most severe of earthquakes. All of the earthquake bracing and special connections for resisting earthquake stresses were electrically welded, while the connections for supporting the live and dead loads in the remaining steelwork was both welded and riveted, because Los Angeles' Building Code did not then permit electric welding alone.

Architecturally, the building delighted the eye. Beautiful stonework and bronze fittings gave the main lobby a feeling of magnificent permanence. Four murals were executed by prominent artists of the day. In the main lobby, "Power" by Hugo Ballin symbolized the role of hydroelectric energy in mitigating the labors of humanity. "Transmission" and "Distribution," both by Barse Miller, ornamented the east wall over the elevator doors. The west wall of the elevator lobby displayed "White Coal" by Conrad Buff, a dramatic portrayal of the allegorical figures Light and Power, and their source in the High Sierras.

and Grand Avenue in downtown Los Angeles. A dance orchestra played soft music and baskets of flowers graced the principal offices as over 7000 people toured the beautiful structure.

A basic reason for the new building was the steady growth of the Edison Company through the 1920s. During that time more than 500,000 new customers in 360 cities and towns had been added. While 72 percent of the homes in the United States had electric service, 99 percent of those in Edison territory were so equipped. In the country at large, only 10 percent of the farms were electrified, but in Edison territory 90 percent were. This ever-increasing demand for electricity resulted in a growth in the number of employees. This caused Edison's former headquarters in the historic "Million Dollar Theatre" Building at Third and Broadway to bulge at the seams. The new building, however, provided 273,000 square feet of much-needed space.

angrily of the event, and scars on the landscape made by the water's passing, although softened, have not yet been erased.

At the cornerstone laying on June 5, 1930, President Miller had said: "The erection of this building and the laying of this cornerstone

In just a few months, the steel skeleton of the height limit building was rivalling the Los Angeles City Hall for dominance of the City's skyline.
EDISON COLLECTION.

The 1929 Annual Report of the Southern California Edison Company contained this key sentence: "The year just closed was the most prosperous in the history of your company ..." It went on to describe the many new industries that had settled in Edison territory. Los Angeles had become America's eighth largest city and the future looked rosy. Two years later, on March 20, 1931, the 35th Annual Stockholders Meeting was a gala affair, coinciding with the official opening of the Company's new $3 million headquarters building at Fifth Street

mark a milestone in the Company's history. In the construction of this building, the first consideration has been given to strength, durability and efficiency. The cornerstone, typical of these features, is not the usual hollow receptacle, but is a *solid block of granite*—stable, enduring, everlasting."

*The Fifth and Grand
Building at night.*
EDISON COLLECTION.

This confidence and pride had been fairly earned during the busy years of growth and prosperity in the "Roaring Twenties," but such triumphs were short-lived as the Great Depression of the 1930s settled down upon the United States. It was a difficult time of falling stock prices, mortgage foreclosures, bank failures and apple selling on street corners.

Early in the decade, the Edison Company suffered in rapid succession three serious blows to its management team. Within a span of 18 months, three chief executives died, each of whom had provided important leadership for the Company since its earliest days. The first to go was John Barnes Miller, who more than any other, had forged the modern Edison Company. As General Manager of the predecessor West Side Lighting Company in 1897, Miller participated in the organization of the Edison Electric Company and became its President in 1901. He continued as President of Southern California Edison until 1928, when the position of Chairman of the Board was created for him. Miller tirelessly directed the Company's fortunes virtually until the day of his death, April 14, 1932, at the age of 62.

168

Four months later, on August 24, 1932, Edison President Russell H. Ballard passed away suddenly at the comparatively young age of 57. Ballard, who had come to Edison in 1900, was very popular with the employees, and his loss, following so quickly upon that of John Miller, was keenly felt. Ballard was succeeded as President by George C. Ward, who served just one year before he, too, died at the age of 71 on September 11, 1933. An engineer who had gained distinction in Henry Huntington's organization, Ward was Executive Vice

President of Pacific Light and Power at the time of its merger with Edison in 1917. As Edison's Vice President of Construction, Ward had been the driving force behind the Big Creek and Long Beach Steam Plant projects in the Twenties.

The deaths of these three men shook the Company and closed an era. Fortunately, new leadership was available from within. On September 15, 1933, Harry J. Bauer was elected President and became Edison's principal officer as the position of Chairman of the Board was temporarily abolished. A lawyer by training, Bauer had to face difficult decisions to preserve employee security and to retain the sound financial condition of the Company. Edison was in better shape to weather the Depression than many companies, but there were deep-rooted problems to face.

The most urgent concern was how to reduce the number of employees to meet changed conditions. Because of major construction projects at Big Creek and Long Beach in the late 1920s, the Company had built up a large permanent workforce of engineers and skilled laborers. Thanks to a benefit program

construction forces from being laid off. When salaries were cut, those of senior management were reduced by the largest percentages.

The second measure that helped Edison through the Great Depression was the retiring of obsolete or inefficient equipment. The machinery inside the old Redondo Steam Plant was removed in 1934. The Azusa hydro station, with its obsolete two-phase generators, was sold to the City of Pasadena, who planned to build Morris Dam in San Gabriel Canyon. Even the historic old Mill Creek No. 1 hydro plant was modernized to make it more efficient. The San Joaquin and Eastern Railroad was abandoned and scrapped, as it was felt that future Big Creek construction could be adequately served by heavy trucks.

The third area of concern was over slumping sales of electricity. Not unsurprisingly, the Great Depression had caused a falling off in demand for energy all over the Pacific Southwest, and as the economy worsened, Edison worked hard to avoid an economic crisis caused by declining sales and the need to service the debt incurred in the great

considered the best in the industry, employee loyalty was high and turnover was very low. Bauer was determined that these men and women were not to be abandoned. He established as policy that the Company would keep as many as possible on the payroll, and reductions would be achieved through natural attrition. To spread the work, the six-day work week was reduced to five, which, except during World War Two, has been standard ever since. Although most new work was halted, enough projects were continued to keep Company

The Sales Department's office just off the main lobby of the new Edison Building, 1933.
EDISON COLLECTION.

John B. Miller at June 5, 1930 ceremony to dedicate the solid granite cornerstone of the new Edison Building at Fifth and Grand Streets.
EDISON COLLECTION.

The Company had long had a New Business Department whose function was to encourage additional ways of using electricity by housewives, farmers, business and industrial managers. In 1933, to take advantage of reduced electric rates, it was decided to spend a million dollars, more than twice any such previous amount, in an all-out campaign to familiarize the public with the advantages of electricity. Strategy was planned in cooperation with some 750 appliance dealers in Edison territory, and the Company's message was carried in newspaper advertisements, radio announcements, demonstrations in schools and homes, and in visits to factories and farms. New loads appeared in curious ways. During the Joe Louis–Max Baer championship fight, for example, Edison found that almost 30,000 kilowatts of demand was added to its lines as the public tuned in its radios.

As a result of the load-building campaign, millions of dollars worth of electrical appliances and devices were sold, stimulating the manufacturing sector and increasing the per-capita consumption of electricity. The net effect of these marketing efforts was to

Soup kitchens were a frequent sight during the Depression. This one was operated for the relief of victims of the 1933 Long Beach earthquake.
EDISON COLLECTION.

construction projects of the previous decade. Looming over this was the realization that by 1940, a tremendous amount of electricity from Hoover Dam would have to be absorbed, for which at the moment there seemed to be no market. Clearly, sales had to be stepped up, and it was very fortunate, therefore, that due to its highly efficient physical plant and to general economic conditions, the price of Edison electricity declined to new lows during the Thirties.

substantially improve the standard of living for most Southern Californians without raising the cost of living.

The fourth major internal problem dealt with by Bauer was the streamlining of the Company's capital structure. Advantage was taken of the sharp drop in interest rates during

Redondo Steam Plant's ancient reciprocating engines fell victim to a depression-era scrap drive. Dismantling had just begun when this 1935 photo was taken.
EDISON COLLECTION.

the late 1930s to retire old bond issues, replacing them with new issues bearing lower interest rates. This restructuring saved Edison over $2 million a year, which was passed on to customers in a further round of voluntary rate reductions.

Another victim of changing economics during the Depression was the historic San Joaquin and Eastern Railroad, whose rails were lifted in 1935.
PAUL THOMPSON COLLECTION.

During the 1930s economists, politicians and the general public vied with one another to find a basic cause for the Great Depression. Due in part to the spectacular collapse of Samuel Insull's utilities empire, and to the excesses engaged in during the promotion of certain holding companies, America's electric utilities became popular whipping boys. They were charged with bringing on hard times and ruining the economy through such devices as watered stock and empty holding companies. Although not immune from such attacks by

Selling Electricity

In the late 1930's, as the Depression waned, the Edison Company mounted a vigorous sales campaign to promote the use of all types of electrical devices. Rates lowest in the Company's history did much to stimulate sales.

Edison appliance technicians deliver a new electric range in 1941.
EDISON COLLECTION.

The Edison booth at San Bernardino's Orange Show, 1938.
EDISON COLLECTION.

Edison Home Economist Miss Carroll demonstrates the ice cube maker on a 1940 General Electric refrigerator.
EDISON COLLECTION.

Display installer Sumner Holland stands beside the Display Department's truck in 1929.
EDISON COLLECTION.

Edison Home Economists learn about a new product from a factory demonstrator, 1938.
EDISON COLLECTION.

Just what Growing Communities Need!

A billboard in Inglewood tells of Edison's electric range promotion in 1934.
EDISON COLLECTION.

173

"Busy Buttons" was the symbol of Edison service in the Twenties and Thirties.
EDISON COLLECTION.

The Thirties were a trying period for Edison, its employees and its leadership, just as they were for all Americans. Faced with debilitating economic problems, harassed by political controversy and stunned by unexpected natural disasters, Edison and its people awaited the return of good times. As early as 1934, Noel B. Hinson, Edison's Chief Engineer and the inventor of the modern statistical method for forecasting load growth for utilities, was predicting a significant turnaround in economic conditions and energy sales. Slowly the tide turned. An improving economic outlook after 1936, coupled with the continuing spectacular growth in Southern California's population, presaged a steady recovery in the last years of the decade. Before this most difficult of decades ended, however, nature had one last cruel trick to play.

Rain began to fall over Southern California on January 27, 1938. Day after day it continued with ominous persistency. By March 2nd, swollen rivers and creeks overflowed their banks and flooded wide areas of lowlands. The Santa Ana River turned away from its old outlet to the sea at Newport Beach and cut a new

Edison's Pump Engineers persuaded many of Southern California's oilfield operators to convert to electric pumping. In 1939, Huntington Beach sported a veritable forest of oil derricks.
EDISON COLLECTION.

embittered people, Edison was guilty of none of the sharp practices of which others in the industry had been accused. The passage of the Public Utilities Holding Company Act of 1935, which caused the neighboring Nevada-California Electric Corporation to completely restructure itself, had little effect upon Edison, but the message was clear: utilities were expected to conduct their affairs with exemplary conduct.

more northerly outfall in Huntington Beach. A rampaging Los Angeles River casually ripped out the concrete slabs that had been poured along its banks to channelize it and washed out bridges all along its length.

Total rainfall for the storm ranged from 12 inches at Eagle Rock to 27 inches at Lytle Creek. The greatest damage occurred to Edison's "Base Hydro Plants," the small, older facilities on Mill Creek, Santa Ana River, Lytle Creek and San Antonio Creek in the local

Santa Ana River No. 2 hydro plant was one of several base hydro plants damaged in the 1938 flood. Water crested over the top of the generator at rear.
<small>EDISON COLLECTION.</small>

mountains surrounding Southern California. A maximum of 15,500 kilowatts of generating capacity was put out of action by the storm. Most of the plants were only out for eight days but one, Ontario No. 2 at the mouth of San Antonio Canyon, was destroyed and subsequently abandoned. One employee,

William Hedlund, a relief operator at the Sierra Hydro Plant up in San Antonio Canyon, despite orders to evacuate, stayed too long at his post and was drowned.

At last the rains stopped and the sun came out. Repairs were made and service soon restored to all customers. With this last disaster, the 1930s, a vexing and uncertain period in history, waned. The Southern California Edison Company had weathered its most difficult decade.

A tower on one of the Big Creek lines near Castaic was damaged by the floods in the 1938 storm, but there was no interruption of service.
<small>EDISON COLLECTION.</small>

Hoover Dam in 1940.
COURTESY LOS ANGELES D.W.P.

Kilowatts from a Muddy River

Even during the darkest days of the Great Depression, a symbol of impending recovery was the great dam being built across the Colorado River in Boulder Canyon. Although a federal project, the Southern California Edison Company played an important part in bringing about the ultimate construction of the dam during the 1930s.

Edison's involvement with the muddy river extends back to 1902, when the first plan for a Colorado River hydroelectric plant was proposed. The great mining fever that swept the Western United States in the post-Civil War period did not ignore the Lower Colorado River Basin. Despite extremes of weather, periodic devastating floods, poor transportation and lack of suitable fuels, significant mining and milling activities grew up along the Colorado's banks and in the interior district tributary to the river.

In that era when steam engines were the ubiquitous prime movers of industry, fuel remained the single most important limiting factor to the region's mining activity. By the turn of the century, the electrical revolution was changing this, and as early as 1902 the Edison Electric Company investigated the potential for developing hydroelectric energy on the Colorado and selling it to nearby mining operations.

On May 10, 1902, Edison President John B. Miller signed an option "to utilize the waters of the Colorado River for the generation of power." The option was offered by a group of Los Angeles entrepreneurs. At that time Edison was interested in two damsites, one at Walapai Wash and the other in Boulder Canyon. On October 5th, when the river was at its lowest flow of the year, well-known local engineer J. B. Lippincott, representing Edison, and D. J. MacPherson, another prominent civil engineer, representing the lessors, set out on a 10-day trip to inspect the mines and damsites.

From the end of the railroad at Chloride, Arizona Territory, Lippincott and MacPherson took a stagecoach to White Hills, where a 14-foot wooden boat, previously ordered, had been

Boatman S. W. Alger, left, and engineer D. J. MacPherson with the boat in which they surveyed the Colorado in 1902. EDISON COLLECTION.

177

built and was waiting for them. The flat-bottomed, square-ended craft was hauled 30 miles to be launched at Walapai Wash at the lower end of the Grand Canyon. For seven days the expedition drifted downstream. By day, Lippincott and MacPherson took notes and photographs while boatman S. W. Alger of Chloride steered; by night the trio pulled up on sandy beaches to eat and sleep. They explored 193 miles of the Colorado, through Boulder, Black and Pyramid Canyons, past mines, mills, isolated ranches, and the Mojave Indian School. The voyage ended at Needles on October 15.

When they returned to Los Angeles, MacPherson and Lippincott prepared separate reports. That of MacPherson recommended a 30-foot rock crib dam in Boulder Canyon, with a 3,000 horsepower generator and an 80-mile transmission line, for an estimated cost of $365,000. "The conditions are such that there are few places in which electric power would work such a revolution as it will here," his report stated.

Lippincott's report was less enthusiastic. While noting that good damsites existed in Boulder and Black Canyons, and observing that MacPherson had filed notice appropriating water rights at the former site, he summed up the overall proposition by stating:

> "that ... the district in question ... is exceedingly remote from ordinary transportation facilities ... and as far as power consumption is concerned (there are) no towns. A power company to be successful would have to very liberally assist in the general development of the country before it would obtain substantial returns for its investment."

The greatest stumbling block to Edison undertaking this project in 1902 was one of technology. Although the Company and several of its predecessors had pioneered in long distance, high-voltage transmission of electricity, the distances involved with bringing Colorado River hydroelectric power to Los Angeles in 1902 were insurmountable, requiring the construction of power lines between 320 and 415 miles in length, which would have had to have been operated at voltages impossibly high for the technology of the era. The only other market for the power was in the mining industry of the region, already on the decline. Thus, Sinclair regretfully recommended to President Miller that the option be abandoned.

Despite this decision, interest grew in the Colorado River as a resource for irrigation water and electric generation. By 1910, the future of the Colorado River was being actively debated in engineering, agricultural and political forums. The need was clear: uncontrolled and unregulated, the river had limited value. The yearly spring runoff followed by rainless months made large

A view downstream of MacPherson's proposed damsite in Boulder Canyon, 1902. Considered and rejected as the location of Hoover Dam, this canyon is now flooded by the waters of Lake Mead.
EDISON COLLECTION.

In analyzing these two reports for President Miller, Henry Sinclair, then Edison's General Manager of Power Development, said that the best damsite appeared to be in Boulder Canyon, where a 40-foot high dam, presumably a rock-filled crib dam, could develop over 10,000 horsepower (over 7500 kw). Furthermore, Sinclair pointed out the possibility of building more than one dam upon the river.

irrigation or power developments uncertain and unprofitable. The undependable, silt-laden flow was not suitable for municipal water supplies. Dams were clearly called for, but who would build them and receive what benefit from them, and their very location, were to be the subject of countless arguments over the next 20 years.

After the merger with Henry Huntington's Pacific Light and Power Corporation in 1917, Edison acquired substantial new financial muscle to enable the undertaking of major new hydroelectric developments. This financial strength was first put to work expanding the Big Creek Project, but upon enactment of the Federal Water Power Act in 1920, the taming of the Colorado became financially feasible, as the Act made possible adequate long-term financing of hydroelectric projects. By now, advances in long-distance electric transmission, coupled with the burgeoning demand for electricity in the Southern California marketplace, made major power development of the Colorado River attractive and technically feasible.

In 1920, almost 800 miles of the river remained virtually unknown and unsurveyed. The Kinkaid Act of 1920 authorized the Secretary of the Interior to make a topographic and geological survey of the Colorado and Green Rivers. Under the terms of this act, Edison agreed to fund part of the survey and to provide men and material for the project.

Surveyors from Edison's Right of Way and Land Department pause to have their picture taken in Glen Canyon, December, 1921.
Edison Collection.

water-tight compartments in bow and stern ensured that they would float even if overturned. Two larger 36-foot "flat bottom tunnel stern punts" were built to carry the bulk of the surveyor's gear, and at least one 16-foot river skiff was also built.

For this difficult journey down the river it was necessary to use boats designed to withstand the wear and tear of shooting rapids, yet be light enough to portage around those rapids which could not be run past. In 1921, the Company placed an order with the Fellows and Stewart Shipbuilding Works on Terminal Island to construct four 18-foot kayak-like wooden boats, patterned after those designed by the Kolb brothers who had successfully run the river in 1911. The boats were named the *Grand*, *Glen*, *Marble* and *Boulder*. For shooting rapids,

Launching the tunnel stern punt near Lee's Ferry, Arizona, 1921. The Edison truck had carried the boat all the way from Los Angeles.
Edison Collection.

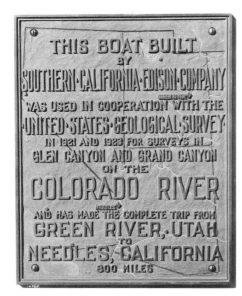

The "Marble," bearing the scars of its three year odyssey.
EDISON COLLECTION.

The Fellows and Stewart Shipbuilding Works on Mormon Island in San Pedro Harbor, about 1920.
COURTESY RICHARD J. FELLOWS.

The "Marble"

The Colorado River survey boat *Marble*, one of several built for the Edison Company's 1921-23 exploration of the river, survives today as a treasured relic of the Company's past. She was built by the skilled boatwrights of the Fellows and Stewart Shipbuilding Works on Mormon Island in old San Pedro Harbor. According to that firm's work order book, she was made of oak, spruce and cedar wood, fastened with brass screws and copper nails, and cost $176.06 for materials and $326.27 in labor.

With her sisters, the *Marble* was taken by flat bed truck from Los Angeles to Green River, Utah, a not inconsiderable feat given the poor roads of that era. After launching, the boats were buffeted and battered by rapids and rocks for several months as they made their way down to Lee's Ferry. *Marble* still shows the scars of this journey.

After resting for a year in a specially built boat house at the Edison base camp at Lee's Ferry, the *Marble* and her companions again tasted the muddy waters of the Colorado during the 1923 survey down to Needles. *Marble* was the pathfinder boat, seeking a safe course through the many rapids, and on one occasion had a hole punctured in her bottom. Later in the journey, near Havasu Creek, a sudden rainstorm upriver caused a flood to roar down without warning. When the waters receded, the surveyors found the *Marble* lodged among brush and boulders 21 feet above normal river level. She had to be recovered by block and tackle.

The second survey party disbanded upon reaching Needles on October 20, 1923, having taken three months to work downriver from Lee's Ferry. The *Grand* was donated to the Smithsonian Institution, while the *Marble*, *Glen* and *Boulder* were returned to Edison in Los Angeles. Survival of such relics is often fragile, but the *Marble* has been lucky. Placed on display in a picturesque log cabin on the grounds of the Huntington Lake Lodge, a summer resort then owned by Edison, the *Marble* was admired by many visitors until the Lodge closed its doors during the Depression. To save her from vandalism, the *Marble* was then moved down to Big Creek Powerhouse No. 1, where today she still can be seen.

277. So. Cal. Edison Co.
Order No. 37219 S.

(handwritten work order ledger)

1921
Aug 10 2 Boats 18' long 4'4" beam x 24" deep 1316 95000

232½ lbs. @ 8.00 232.50
34 " " 7.20 30.60
5 " " 7.00 4.38
32 " " 6.80 27.20
27½ " " 6.40 22.00
3½ " " 8.50 2.40
6½ " " 6.00 4.06
2¾ " " 4.00 1.25
5 " " 3.00 1.88
326.27 32627

Lumber
126 ft Oak @ 25 3150
106 ft 1¼" H.P. Oak @ 5 530
762 ft Spruce @ 9 6858
33⅓ ft Cedar @ 15 500 11038

Screws
... 4943
...
4 lb Putty 5½ gal Gray Paint 1285 1285

Labor 326.27 Material 17606 Total cost 50233

In September 1921, Edison and Geological Survey engineers began the first leg of their long journey down the Colorado from Green River, Utah, to Needles, California. This portion was grueling due to the many rapids encountered. As the tiny flotilla proceeded downstream, the boatmen steered their craft while the engineers tramped along the shore gathering scientific data. When canyon walls narrowed to the water's edge, the engineers climbed aboard, one astraddle the bow of each boat, one sitting at the stern.

When rapids were encountered, boatmen preferred to meet them stern first. Sighting downstream, they could avoid collisions with submerged rocks, and by rowing against the current, they reduced the mad rush of the river. A hemp lifeline was attached to the side of each boat from stem to stern and this was found to be of value a number of times when the boats turned over in making the trip through the rapids. In many cases, due to the low water of the season, there was not enough water to float the boats, or too many rocks were encountered, and it was necessary to haul the boats along the banks above the water level, an operation that required all hands.

In the early spring of 1922, the expedition halted at Lee's Ferry, and the boats taken from the river to avoid the dangerously high waters of the spring runoff. Not until 1923 did the survey party continue on its downstream journey through Boulder and Black Canyons to Needles.

After these surveys, Edison officials were highly optimistic about developing the Colorado. Over a five-year period, applications were filed with the Federal Power Commission

When the "Marble" wedged itself upon a rock while shooting a rapid in the Green River, its boatman had to be rescued by breeches bouy.
EDISON COLLECTION.

182 A quiet moment aboard the tunnel stern punt in a calm stretch of Glen Canyon.
EDISON COLLECTION.

for licenses to build dams and generating facilities at several locations: Glen Canyon, Diamond Creek, Boulder Canyon, Pyramid Canyon, and at Topock, below Needles.

During the next few years, in speeches, testimony to government bodies, newspaper interviews, and annual reports to stockholders, Edison stressed its willingness and ability to build dams and powerhouses on the Colorado.

But other forces were at work. Other agencies were eager to develop the Colorado, and other individuals had ideas on where the dam or dams should be located, who should build them and how they were to be financed. The controversy generated by these conflicting claims had to be overcome in order to develop the Colorado.

One conflict revolved around the growth of the "public power" movement. During the Twenties, proponents of "public power" viewed the hydroelectric potential of the Colorado River as the means whereby every investor-owned power company in the Pacific Southwest could be priced out of existence. For

this reason, some companies, although not Edison, viewed most Colorado River development proposals with deep suspicion.

The City of Los Angeles also had an interest in the Colorado. In the Twenties the City's engineers were actively engaged in making water and power filings on virtually every unappropriated watercourse in California. The City saw the river as a new supply of water for future needs and as a producer of electricity to pump water into Southern California and to

An Edison surveyor views a calm stretch of the river.
EDISON COLLECTION.

serve the energy needs of a growing population whose municipal utility was chronically power-short.

The federal government, too, was interested in the river. As early as 1918, Arthur Powell Davis, Director and Chief Engineer of the U.S. Bureau of Reclamation, presented a plan for a high dam in Boulder Canyon. In 1924, after the joint survey of the river, he recommended that the federal government build a dam in Boulder or Black Canyon. During the Twenties, while all these various disagreements were being ironed out, all applications for power development on the river, including Edison's, were held in abeyance. Solving these disputes took much patience.

Before any dam could be built, however, agreement had to be reached on the proper division of Colorado River water, which flowed through seven states. Beginning in 1919, the states sent representatives to meetings where these matters were discussed—but nothing was resolved. In 1922, Herbert Hoover, fresh from triumphs in Belgium and newly appointed as Secretary of Commerce, called the group

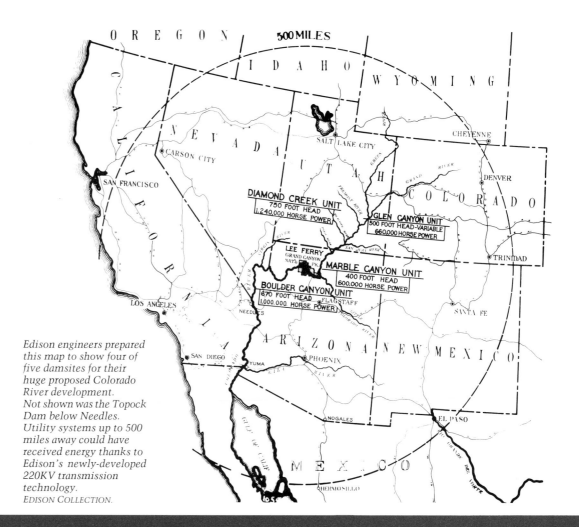

Edison engineers prepared this map to show four of five damsites for their huge proposed Colorado River development. Not shown was the Topock Dam below Needles. Utility systems up to 500 miles away could have received energy thanks to Edison's newly-developed 220KV transmission technology.
EDISON COLLECTION.

together at Santa Fe, New Mexico. Determined to find a solution this time, Hoover kept the representatives in session for 14 hours a day over a three-week span.

Finally, it was he who cut the Gordian knot. In his own neat handwriting, he penned the Colorado River Compact, which created an Upper Basin and a Lower Basin, the dividing line to be at Lee's Ferry. Originally, each area

was apportioned 7,500,000 acre-feet of water, with the right of the Lower Basin in any one year to add 1,000,000 acre feet, but in later years a treaty with Mexico changed this somewhat. Signed by the members of the commission on November 24, 1922, at Santa Fe, the Compact was presented to the legislatures of the Colorado River Basin states and to the United States Congress for ratification.

State and federal ratification of the Compact became enmeshed in the political controversy surrounding development of the river. For much of the decade, the proponents of public and investor-owned power tangled repeatedly. The State of Arizona compounded confusion by refusing to sign the Colorado River Compact and by filibustering against the ratification bills in Congress.

183

CALIFORNIA'S ELECTRICAL AGE IS HERE!

With energy from Hoover Dam soon to arrive, Edison's marketing programs began featuring the dam and the benefits it would bring to Southland energy users.
EDISON COLLECTION.

Finally, in December 1928 the Boulder Canyon Act, presented to Congress as the fourth Swing-Johnson Bill, was passed by Congress and signed into law by President Calvin Coolidge. Its main provisions approved the Colorado River Compact upon ratification by six of the seven states, and authorized construction of a multi-purpose dam in Boulder or Black Canyon and of the All American Canal into the Imperial Valley.

the conclusion to years of conflict by pointing out that the Boulder Canyon Project would "stimulate growth and prosperity in Southern California." After a decade of controversy, the stage was finally set for actual construction to begin. Despite the denial of its own Colorado River applications, and the surrender of all its filed water rights and applications upon the river, Edison and its predecessor, the Southern Sierras Power Company, were destined to play important roles in the construction story.

Before construction of the new dam could begin, however, the Boulder Canyon Act stipulated that the Secretary of the Interior must have firm contracts for the sale of power from the project in order to guarantee amortization of the project expense over a 50-year period. Friction developed once again between municipal power agencies and investor-owned companies as to which would generate and distribute the power and at what price. Ten agencies were interested in obtaining power. Two of them, Edison and the Los Angeles Bureau of Power and Light, at first sought to be the sole generators and distributors for Southern California.

Passage of the Boulder Canyon Act effectively doomed Edison's own applications for power projects upon the Colorado. Despite this, the Company enthusiastically supported the Bill in its final form, thanks to another compromise worked out by Secretary Hoover, whereby the federal government would build the dam but the public and investor-owned utilities would generate and distribute the electricity. This made government and utilities partners in the project. John Miller wrote enthusiastically of

Once again Herbert Hoover, by now President of the United States, and Interior Secretary Ray Lyman Wilbur patiently ironed out the difficulties. By a contract dated April 26, 1930, it was agreed that the Southern California Edison Company would generate for itself and other investor-owned electric utilities, and the Los Angeles Bureau of Power and Light would generate for the states, the municipal utilities and the Metropolitan Water District.

The contract of 1930 was a firm commitment on the part of Edison, Southern Sierras and the City of Los Angeles to find a market for the dam's tremendous power output. It is a tribute to the three Southern California utilities' faith in the future that the contract was made in the face of a substantial drop in demand for electricity due to the Great Depression. They displayed great courage in contracting for energy for which there was no apparent ready market, and which was priced above current market rates, especially as most of the Southwest's other public and investor-owned utilities refused to participate although given a chance. This contract, which apparently included a guarantee of a cash advance to the government to enable construction to begin, was the final necessary preliminary before work on the dam commenced.

In preliminary site studies of Boulder Canyon, geologists discovered an earthquake fault. The final choice, therefore, was Black Canyon, 13 miles down river. In 1930, Edison turned over to the government all of its survey data on the Black Canyon damsite. To checkrein the wild, turbulent Colorado effectively, it was decided to build the highest dam in the world—726 feet from bedrock to crest. The dam would create the world's biggest man-made lake, which could safely store the normal flow of the Colorado for two years and would trap 100,000 tons of silt. It would make possible a power plant capable of producing 5 billion kilowatt-hours of electricity a year.

The giant dam envisioned by engineers in 1930 became a reality in 1936. During the dedication ceremonies, by-pass valves were opened to create a spectacular cascade of water.
EDISON COLLECTION.

truck drivers and machinists to come to work on the Colorado River, many veterans of Edison's Big Creek Project, which had wound up in 1929, provided the nucleus of experience for the new Hoover Dam Project.

The logistics of the project were equally as complex as had been those for Big Creek. An entire new town, Boulder City, was erected on a sage-covered flat about 10 miles from the damsite. To carry the anticipated millions of tons of material to the damsite, in 1930, the Union Pacific Railroad built a 23-mile long spur from Las Vegas to Boulder City, and the Six Companies extended the railroad ten more miles to the damsite.

Of the many logistical problems encountered during construction, none was more important than arranging for a supply of electricity to the project. Nevada Power Company, the local utility in the area, had neither the facilities nor the capacity to serve the project load, and declined to participate. Edison, with the capacity to provide service, had already contracted to supply power for the Metropolitan Water District's Colorado River

186 Specifications and drawings for the dam were rushed to completion in the chief engineer's office of the Bureau of Reclamation in Denver. On April 20, 1931, construction contracts were awarded to the Six Companies, Inc. of San Francisco, a consortium composed of the Utah Construction Company; the Pacific Bridge Company; Henry J. Kaiser and W. A. Bechtel Company; MacDonald and Kahn Co., Ltd.; Morrison-Knudsen Co.; and J. F. Shea Company. The Six Companies' bid was $48,890,995.50—the largest labor contract

approved by the United States government up to that time. A huge sum for that era, the winning bid represented nearly one-twelfth of the entire federal budget for that Depression year of 1931.

In erecting the dam, the Six Companies profited from technical solutions worked out by Edison engineers at Big Creek a decade earlier. Furthermore, when the Six Companies issued calls for engineers, hard rock miners, skilled electricians, carpenters, railroad men,

Aqueduct Project, and deferred to the Southern Sierras Power Company, who was eager to serve the huge construction project.

On October 28, 1930, a contract was made between the government and Southern Sierras to deliver all electric energy needed for the Hoover Project, including domestic service to Boulder City. Eight months were allotted for construction of the necessary transmission lines and substation facilities. Three days after the signing of the contract, survey parties were in the field for location work, and within six weeks actual construction had begun. In a record-setting pace, crews built the 225-mile long, 132,000-volt line from San Bernardino to the damsite in only 225 days, despite having to cross some of the most inhospitable desert terrain in the world. Power deliveries began over the new line to Hoover Dam Substation, located on the rim of Black Canyon some 700 feet from the Nevada abutment of the dam, on June 25, 1931. During the nearly six years this service was provided, over 100 million kilowatt-hours were sold to the dam project, enabling this great engineering endeavor to go forward.

And go forward it did. Laboring on a round-the-clock schedule and enduring extremes of climate, the engineers, foremen and craftsmen got the Herculean job done. They dug four 50-foot diameter diversion tunnels, built cofferdams upstream and downstream to turn the Colorado from its course, excavated a cavernous foundation, poured an arch-gravity dam 60 stories tall, laid in two rows of penstocks on each side of the river, and built a powerhouse and a switchrack to connect with

On October 9, 1936, nearly a million residents of Los Angeles and neighboring communities filled downtown streets to view the first delivery of electricity from Hoover Dam. A golden key was pressed and great arc lights winked on to illuminate a parade.

transmission lines built by the principal energy purchasers. To complete this mighty task, the Six Companies' contract allowed seven years. The dam itself was finished in five.

There remained only to start generating power for those who had contracted for it. Commercial power production in the Hoover power plant was begun on October 26, 1936, when Unit N-2, the first of four Nevada-side

units then in the process of installation, was energized to serve the load of the Cities of Los Angeles, Pasadena, Glendale and Burbank. The power was delivered via the City of Los Angeles' new 266-mile long transmission line at a new world's record pressure of 287,000 volts, and earlier that month a tremendous parade illuminated by giant searchlights wound through the streets of Los Angeles.

In August 1937, Unit A-8 went into operation for the Nevada-California Electric Corporation, successor to the Southern Sierras Power Company, two years in advance of its previously contracted-for scheduled firm delivery date of 1940. Energy was delivered into the Electric Corporation's system at San Bernardino over the same 132,000-volt line built in 1930-31.

Working on Hoover Dam

From all over the country came workers
skilled in many trades to build the great dam
that would end flooding, irrigate farms, and
generate electricity for the people of the Southwest.

Preparing forms for pouring the concrete of the Nevada-side "stony gate".
EDISON COLLECTION.

The dam about three-fourths done, early 1935.
EDISON COLLECTION.

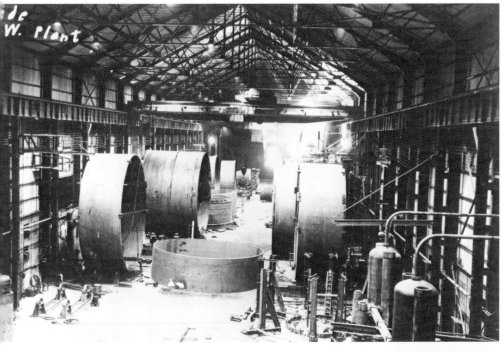

Hoover's penstocks were so large that subcontractor Babcock and Wilcox had to fabricate them directly at the site in a specially built factory.
WILLIAM J. YOUNG COLLECTION.

One of the legion of workers prepares the canyon walls for the dam abutment.
COURTESY UNION PACIFIC RAILROAD.

Three views of the installation of Unit A-5 in 1943.
EDISON COLLECTION.

During construction of the second Hoover line, an Edison lineman operates the "bull-wheel" used to tension cables as they are pulled through the towers.
EDISON COLLECTION.

In 1938, Units N-5 and N-6 were completed for the Metropolitan Water District of Southern California. Energy generated by these units was earmarked primarily for pumping water from Lake Havasu, behind Parker Dam, into and along the District's Colorado River Aqueduct. Over the years, energy from these units that was surplus to that needed for pumping by the MWD has been purchased by Edison and the City of Los Angeles.

Edison itself began receiving energy from Hoover Dam on June 19, 1939, a year in advance of its contractual deadline. This happened when Units A-6 and A-7 were energized and power was delivered via Edison's Boulder-Chino 220,000-volt line, which had been completed only a month earlier.

The Arizona Powerhouse, showing installation in 1943 of Unit No. A-5, leased to Edison.
EDISON COLLECTION.

Today, a half-century after it was built, the great Hoover Dam Project is a symbol of the Southwest. Not only is it a significant civil engineering landmark, it is a political landmark showing how patience and compromise can overcome divisive arguments. In the 1920s, Herbert Hoover labored to achieve agreement among conflicting claimants to harness the Colorado. In the 1930s, courage and faith was displayed by Southern California's utilities which, in the face of difficult economic times, created a market for power which enabled the dam to be built. In the 1980s, when the original power contracts were about to expire, the Western Area Power Administration demonstrated patience in working out a compromise agreement to fairly re-allocate Hoover Dam's electric generation resources to a swarm of competing entities.

191

A sightseeing boat gives an idea of the grand scaleof Hoover Dam.
EDISON COLLECTION.

Energy for Victory

When the *USS Arizona* was bombed at Pearl Harbor on December 7, 1941, Warrant Officer Edward Winter, on leave from his job as a mechanic at Big Creek, was one of those who died in the fiery holocaust. In the four years that followed, 899 Edison employees were called into uniform; 13 lost their lives. The 4,000 Edison employees who served on the home front also contributed to victory, by laboring long hours, using substitutes, keeping worn equipment running, buying war bonds,

donating blood, planting victory gardens and squeezing extra kilowatts out of steam and hydro plants.

World War Two was an "electric war," in which industry played a major role in bringing about victory. Electricity on the home front enabled factories to triple peacetime production, and it was this increase that was the great American secret weapon that wartime allied leaders welcomed, and enemy rulers feared. One of the

most highly developed industrial complexes in the country was located in Southern California. The Edison Company furnished electricity to such well-known concerns as the Douglas, Vultee and Northrup aircraft plants, Consolidated Steel, Craig, Fellows and Stewart and the Long Beach Naval Shipyards, as well as Kaiser Steel, Alcoa and Columbia Steel. These industries and more, such as oil refineries, tire plants, motor vehicle factories, ordnance works and numerous military bases and depots all over the region, placed an unprecedented demand upon the Company's generating resources, as electrical demand increased 94 percent between 1939 and 1944.

Long before Pearl Harbor, the outbreak of the war in Europe sent Edison planners to prepare for future load growth. A second 220,000-volt transmission line from Hoover Dam was completed in November, 1941, while work on Edison's Unit A-5 at the dam was speeded up. Preparations were made in other ways as well. Uniformed guards, including members of the California National Guard, were stationed on 24-hour duty at Big Creek's dams and powerhouses, at Hoover Dam and along the Company's high voltage transmission network. Employees were retrained, and temporary help hired, as the military began to drain away manpower.

Blackout Regulations

A brochure detailing blackout regulations was issued to all Edison customers early in the war.
EDISON COLLECTION.

Blacking Out With Drapes

Blackout draperies should be made quite full and permanently attached to top and sides of window frame, with at least a six inch overlap in center. An eighteen inch valance should be provided at top. Place snaps or buttons in center as shown to prevent accidental opening when brushed against.

Draperies produce a more pleasant atmosphere when faced on the room side with chintz or other decorative material.

Recommended materials are black or oxford gray cotton flannel, double nap or used in full drape of whatever thickness is necessary to insure full blackout; heavy sateen, double thickness or gathered full; black heavy twills; denims, jean cloth and duck cloth if of sufficient weight; velours and velvets, only if well lined.

PAINT is not recommended for blackout because it shuts out light in the daytime and because it tends to develop light leaks which may escape your attention. Black paint on glass is especially hazardous because uneven expansion and contraction occurs which frequently causes glass to break.

Roll-Down Shades

This type of roll-down blackout shade can be fastened permanently to the top of the window frame or hung by a cord as indicated in the sketches. Black or dark color heavy twills, denims, jean cloth or treated cloths not liable to crack or pin-hole when rolled, are suitable materials. Shades should overlap window opening by at least six inches each way.

Roll-down shades may be used inside or outside the window. Fasten a heavy wooden rod to bottom of shade to hold it in place when in use.

When not in use it can be rolled up by cords as shown, or fastened up by cloth ties, or rolled up and put in a closet.

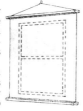

MOST blackout drapes. shades and screens are not a protection against flying glass, so if explosive bombs start falling proceed to the safest room in your house away from window areas. • • •

DON'T light cigarettes outdoors during a blackout. • • •

DRAPES need not be drab. Color and light help to remove fear.

Rigid Blackout Screens

These removable screens are of lightweight wood frames covered with opaque paper, cardboard, imitation leather or fabric. They fit snugly in place against the window frame and stack away neatly when not in use.

They should always be fastened above the window with flexible hangers (rings cut from an old inner tube, shoe laces or heavy twine) as shown. A friction type catch may be used at the bottom. This is to prevent the screen from being blown in under concussion of bombs and causing injury to people in the room.

Two ways of attaching screening materials to frames.

TAR OR ROOFING PAPERS are not recommended for home interior blackout use. Tar may run if subjected to heat, and damage wood, curtains, etc. • • •

FLASHLIGHTS for blackout use should be dimmed with a thickness of newspaper or cloth and never directed upward. Use them sparingly.

Decorative Blackout Screens

Removable screens may also be made using plywood or composition board which can then be covered with wallpaper or painted to match the color of the walls.

While these screens cost a bit more to make, they add considerably to the cheerfulness of the room.

If light plywood is used, it should be painted to help prevent warping.

These decorative removable panels can be fitted to glassed doors as well as windows.

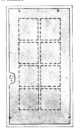

AS A SAFETY MEASURE, it is recommended that outdoor steps or stairways which are likely to be used in a blackout be painted with a strip of white paint two inches wide on the outer edge of each tread and two inches high on the upper edge of each riser. There are several luminous paints available for this purpose, but these are rather expensive and it has been found that ordinary white paint is quite satisfactory. • • •

FIRST AID KITS should include several triangle bandages, also some 2% copper sulphate solution (used in treatment of burns caused by phosphorus fire bombs).

Operator Bill Howardson monitors plant machinery and system electric demand in the control room at Long Beach Plant No. 2.
T. M. HOTCHKISS PHOTO.

Just after seven o'clock in the evening of Monday, February 23, 1942, the war was briefly brought to Edison's doorstep as shells from a Japanese submarine whistled in on the oil fields at Ellwood, near Santa Barbara. Little damage was done, one oil pump and some Edison transformers being the principal victims, but the blackout imposed during the attack resulted in several traffic accidents. This event did little to calm the war jitters felt all along coastal Southern California in the early months of the war.

Blackout and dimout regulations were imposed in coastal areas the day war was declared. Because of these lighting restrictions, consumption of electricity in Edison territory dropped three percent in the first year of the war. When in 1943 the Western Defense Command gave the Edison Company an award for its cooperation in complying with blackout regulations, the *Los Angeles Times* noted: "In the topsy-turvy world of war, the Southern California Edison Company yesterday received an award for keeping things dark."

After fear of Japanese coastal raids subsided, power demands began to climb. Soon, the power needs of wartime industries forced Edison employees to squeeze the maximum number of kilowatts from all existing generating stations. The Company had over one million kilowatts of installed generation capacity at the start of the war, some of it little utilized as an after effect of the Great Depression. Wartime power demand, however, soon absorbed this reserve margin, and construction of new units seemed to be the only answer.

Boilermen at Long Beach **195** *Plant No. 2 light off the gas burners as the plant "steams up" to carry load.*
EDISON COLLECTION.

In May 1942, however, at the suggestion of the Power Branch of the War Production Board, Edison joined with all other investor-owned and government-owned utilities in California, Southern Nevada and Arizona to form the Pacific Southwest Power Pool. Through interconnections, all utilities in the pool operated as one huge system for the duration of the war. Power-short utilities in one area were able to draw upon the reserve capacity available from others. In this way, Edison was able to defer adding a new unit at Big Creek Power House No. 3 by receiving surplus energy from Pacific Gas and Electric Company.

The output of Long Beach Steam Plant was handled in similar fashion. Much of the energy used in local war industries was produced at Long Beach, but wartime restrictions discouraged the burning of fuel oil. All of California's oil fields were being pumped to the maximum extent for the war effort. As a result of this much more gas was also being produced than could be consumed by domestic customers. The War Production Board therefore suggested to the Pacific Southwest Power Pool that Long Beach Steam Plant's 11

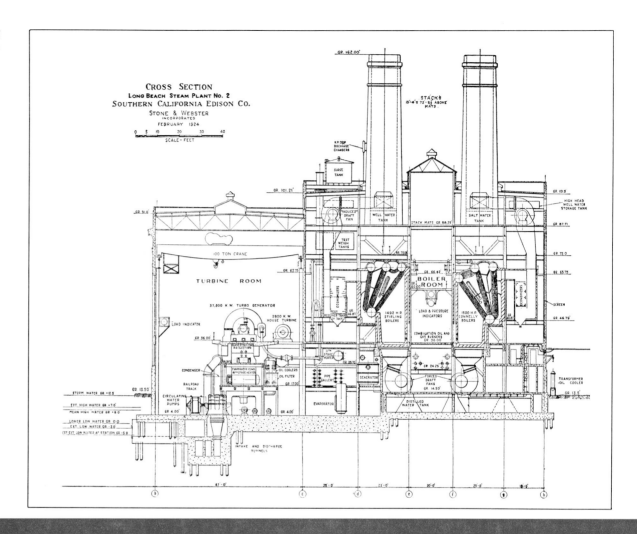

196 units be operated to full capacity using this surplus gas as fuel. That part of the plant's output not needed by Edison customers was supplied to San Diego Gas and Electric and the City of Los Angeles.

This logical and beneficial arrangement was interrupted on November 24, 1942, when the Procurement Division of the United States Treasury Department announced the "friendly seizure" of Units No. 7 and No. 8 at Long Beach. These two 35,000 kilowatt units, which

had been so rapidly built in 1924 to help alleviate the drought, were earmarked to be sent to Russia, our wartime ally, to fulfill Lend-Lease commitments. Edison, having the only major 50-cycle power system remaining in North America, had the only electrical equipment directly compatible with European power systems.

Immediately, Edison crews at Long Beach Steam Plant began to dismantle the two turbogenerators under the watchful eyes of

stone-faced Russian technicians. By February 1, crates containing the pieces were being loaded aboard a Russian freighter in San Pedro Harbor. The two exiles were destined for the Port of Vladivostok in Siberia, but as is typical of things connected with the Soviet Union, all knowledge of them, even as to whether or not they arrived safely, disappeared behind a veil of secrecy. To replace the "borrowed" Long Beach units, the government diverted a new General Electric 82,000-kilowatt machine to Edison, installation of which was completed in October of 1943.

Long Beach Plant No. 3's
massive boilers towered
over the boiler house
operators, who called this
the "Grand Canyon."
EDISON COLLECTION.

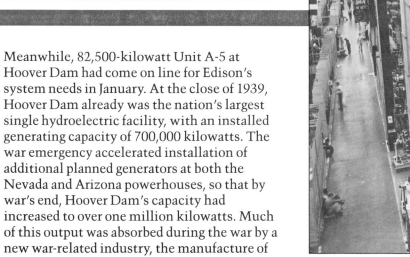

At Frank Ridley's service
station in Santa Monica,
Signal's Ethyl gas sold for
17.5 cents a gallon...if you
had a ration coupon.
EDISON COLLECTION.

197

Meanwhile, 82,500-kilowatt Unit A-5 at
Hoover Dam had come on line for Edison's
system needs in January. At the close of 1939,
Hoover Dam already was the nation's largest
single hydroelectric facility, with an installed
generating capacity of 700,000 kilowatts. The
war emergency accelerated installation of
additional planned generators at both the
Nevada and Arizona powerhouses, so that by
war's end, Hoover Dam's capacity had
increased to over one million kilowatts. Much
of this output was absorbed during the war by a
new war-related industry, the manufacture of

Edison also served
Douglas' Long Beach plant,
where the ubiquitous C-47,
military version of the
renowned DC-3, was
assembled.
COURTESY MCDONNELL
DOUGLAS CORPORATION.

Seize Edison Power Unit for Russia

U. S. Grabs Electric Generator

By International News Service
WASHINGTON, Nov. 24.
—The Treasury procurement division today took possession of a 35,000 kilowatt turbo-generator at the Long Beach steam plant of the Southern California Edison Co. under "a friendly seizure order' in order to expeditee its shipment to Russia.

Action also will be taken within the next month to acquire a second unit of the same size from the Long Beach station for delivery to Russia, it was stated.

Two turbo-generators at Long Beach Steam Plant were seized by the government and sent to Russia in the dark days of World War II. Taken because Edison's system frequency, 50 cycles, matched Russia's, the two units joined oil refineries, truck plants and machine tools as lend-lease aid to our war-time ally.
EDISON COLLECTION.

An employee at Long Beach had to sneak this photo of Unit 8 being dismantled prior to its shipment to Russia. Hard-eyed Russian security agents monitored every step and discouraged curiosity.
EDISON COLLECTION.

Two obsolete generating units at Borel provided 200 tons of cast iron, copper wire, steel and babbitt metal. Another 400 tons of cast iron tubes and headers came from the Long Beach Steam Station. At Florence Lake and the Mono-Bear area, salvagers found 300 tons of steel in the form of rails, flat cars and dump cars. A windfall of 800 tons of scrap iron came from the two incline hoists that once had operated between the old San Joaquin and Eastern Railroad and Powerhouses No. 3 and No. 8 at Big Creek.

During the war, the Company organized a force of security guards whose primary duty was to protect generators and transmission lines from possible sabotage. Among other assignments, this cadre replaced the California National Guardsmen who had been protecting Big Creek's dams since the outbreak of hostilities. While no deliberate incidents of sabotage are known to have occurred, some accidental damage was suffered by Edison facilities. In the early part of the war, Edison transmission lines were damaged by barrage balloons. When these pudgy gas bags broke loose from their

198 light metal. To produce magnesium for aircraft frames and incendiary bombs, the government's huge Basic Magnesium, Inc., plant near Las Vegas alone consumed as much electricity as did every customer on the Edison system.

Wartime salvage of materials was not a novelty because the Edison Company had been practicing this kind of industrial thrift all during the lean years of the Depression. Nevertheless, new amounts of scrap material

were collected from all over the system and stockpiled at the Edison warehouse in Alhambra to be offered for sale to dealers, manufacturers and other utility representatives.

Salvage included such items as rubber from gaskets and old automobile tires, copper wire from which the insulation had been removed, cast iron, steel and brass from worn-out equipment, and junk wooden poles that the Army found useful in building training equipment.

moorings, they frequently drifted across power lines trailing metal cables, resulting in a great shower of sparks and angry electric customers.

In another incident, a young Marine Corps pilot flew his trainer too close to a 220,000-volt line, breaking the ground wire and shorting out the line for several hours. The pilot survived unhurt although he had to endure much ribbing from his buddies. In a more tragic incident, a B-24 "Liberator" bomber crashed into Huntington Lake during a storm in 1943, killing all on board.

At the Alhambra General Store, a magnet was rigged upon a truck and driven around to pick up stray bits of scrap ferrous metal.
EDISON COLLECTION.

Peter H. Ducker, Edison's longtime Transportation Superintendent, headed the Company's wartime scrap drives. Rubber was one of the desired materials.
EDISON COLLECTION.

The four Edison engineers who worked on the Manhattan Project posed in the lobby of the Edison Building after the lifting of wartime restrictions on discussion of their work. The newspaper headline, "A-Bomb Space Ships Seen" seems prophetic.
EDISON COLLECTION.

services. To make up these shortages, the 40-hour work week that had been established during the Depression was temporarily extended to 44 hours. More importantly, the Company hired large numbers of women into what were then considered traditionally male jobs such as meter readers, laboratory aides, construction field clerks and substation operators. Many of these women stayed on after the war. In 1946, a customer who was

In March 1943, five skilled Edison engineers were quietly ordered to the University of California's Radiation Laboratory at Berkeley to work on a special project. Even their wives were not permitted to know what they were involved in doing. The secret was revealed in August 1945 by big headlines that described what had happened at Hiroshima and Nagasaki. These five men were part of a 60-man task force that had designed the electrical system for the Oak Ridge, Tennessee, plutonium-extracting facility, a vital

component of the super-secret Manhattan Project that had built the first atomic bombs.

For this and other wartime contributions, the Southern California Edison Company received a number of citations and awards, most importantly the Charles A. Coffin Award and the National Security Award.

As with all industries during the war, Edison had to face severe manpower shortages as many qualified employees went into the armed

about to move to another state bestowed her own award upon the Edison Company while acknowledging the unique contributions made by the female workers when she wrote:

"It seems strange to say goodbye to a corporation as if it were a friend, yet I can't help thanking you for your good services, even during the trying times of the war. And I wish someone would thank those nice lady meter readers who were so careful not to wake the baby!"

Progress in the Postwar Years

Southern California became the nation's fastest growing area at the end of World War Two.
JOSEPH O. FADLER PHOTO.

World War Two set off a new population explosion in California. Long a mecca for tourists and retired people, the Golden State now saw a tremendous influx of new residents and new industries. To the surprise of many, the industries that had settled in the region during the war did not shut down, but stayed and prospered. Thousands of military men and war workers liked what they had seen in California and returned to settle down and then encouraged relatives and friends to do the same. Today, Southern California is a dynamic

area that makes its industrial, financial, political, scientific and cultural weight felt all over the nation.

As people and businesses poured West, the Southern California Edison Company also expanded, working hard to keep up with a rising demand for electricity. Since 1945, it has added more customers than any other utility in the country. A significant milestone in this growth was achieved on April 12, 1951, when Edison's one millionth meter was placed in service. Reaching this figure required 65 years, but it took only 13 more years to pass the two millionth meter mark in 1964. The three millionth meter was connected 14 years after that, in 1978.

The first major event in Edison's postwar history was the conversion of its system frequency from 50- to 60-cycles. A cycle, or "Hertz" as it is known today, is the length of time required for the generation of one complete positive and negative wave of alternating current, and is usually given as "cycles per second." The frequency of a power system has little effect upon non-moving equipment such as radios, televisions, heaters or light bulbs, but does affect the performance of rotating equipment and electric motors. In the pioneering days of alternating current, system frequency was casually regarded. So-called "high frequency" generators, running at 133 cycles per second, were preferred for electric systems with loads exclusively from lighting. On the other hand, systems or private plants that powered motors, usually relied on 25-cycle generators, which delivered good power torque to the motors, but caused lights

Virtually all of the original A. C. plants built by Edison's predecessors in Southern California were built to this 50-cycle standard. Unfortunately, pressure from American electrical equipment manufacturers seeking protection from European competitors persuaded Congress to change the United States to a standard of 60-cycles, which ultimately resulted in the Edison Company

New residential tracts became a common sight in the Southland as the area's population continued to grow in the 1950s.
Joseph O. Fadler Photo.

The Dispatcher's Office in Alhambra, 1948. In the next 30 years, the Edison system, represented by the diagram on the wall, would grow many times larger.
Edison Collection.

to flicker. The fact that power systems run at different frequencies were not compatible made little difference until pioneer utility systems began to be consolidated. An international conference early determined that 50 cycles was an acceptable compromise between the power efficiency of low frequencies and the lack of flicker in higher frequencies, and 50 cycles per second was established as the international standard for commercial alternating current utility systems.

being out of step with most of the rest of the nation. In fact, the problem was originally of little importance, for manufacturers were willing to make motors to run on 50-cycle power, and frequency-changing devices, with some limitations, enabled power exchanges between systems of different frequencies.

Thus, Edison grew up as a 50-cycle system surrounded by 60-cycle neighbors; Southern Sierras Power, San Diego Consolidated Gas and Electric, L.A. Gas and Electric, San Joaquin

Light and Power, all used 60-cycle technology. In fact, even the Edison system was not uniform. Santa Barbara, long isolated from Edison's main system, was operated at 60 cycles until 1918, when it was connected to the Company's transmission lines, necessitating conversion to 50 cycles. Similarly, the system of the Mount Whitney Power and Electric Company was built to operate at 60 cycles, and when it was merged into Edison in 1920, Company engineers decided to retain that frequency. Large frequency changers at Vestal and Rector Substations in the San Joaquin Valley were used to connect the Mount Whitney system to Edison's 50-cycle Big Creek lines.

Except for that portion of the city supplied by L.A. Gas and Electric, Los Angeles had 50-cycle service. This was inherited by the Bureau of Power and Light when the City bought Edison's distribution system. In 1936, with the arrival of vast amounts of 60-cycle power from Hoover Dam imminent, the City converted, as did Pasadena, Burbank and Glendale. This left Edison as the last major 50-cycle utility in North America. Generating equipment and

Wayne Johnson (right) views welding equipment at Ford's Wilmington Assembly Plant, during the conversion to 60-cycle operation, 1947.
EDISON COLLECTION.

motors became costly and difficult to buy. Customers moving into the region complained that household appliances did not work right. Local dealers had to stock two types of clocks, record players, washing machines and refrigerators. As early as 1934 Edison seriously considered converting, too, but first because of the Depression, and then because of the war, deferred doing so.

A portable armature rewinding shop used during the frequency change.
EDISON COLLECTION.

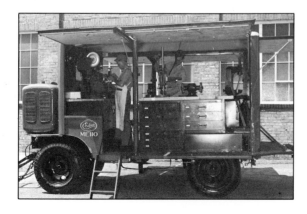

Early in 1945, however, with the war nearing a successful conclusion, top priority was given to plan the massive effort nicknamed "The Change-over." In July, the Railroad Commission authorized the project. Wayne N. Johnson became Edison's Frequency Change Manager. He established a temporary home for his 200 person staff in a creaking old wooden building on Boylston Street in Los Angeles that 20 years earlier had been the office of the Big Creek Project engineering staff.

Much of the work in preparation for the cutover at Bell Gardens and elsewhere involved the rewiring of industrial motors, pumps, heavy equipment and virtually all customer meters. The average householder was affected most directly through his electric clock. Establishing a procedure that was successfully used throughout the conversion project, the public was invited by mail, newspaper advertisements and direct contact, to bring their clocks to any convenient local "clock depot." There, Edison people offered each customer a choice of having his old clock rewired, or exchanging it for a new clock at a price of from $1.25 to $1.75, depending upon the model selected. Washing machines, refrigerators, electric timers on ranges, and record players, also affected by the cycle change, were adjusted or rebuilt by Edison crews canvassing neighborhoods in the weeks before the "cut over."

At exactly 10 o'clock in the morning of April 16, 1946, Wayne Johnson threw a switch at Laguna Bell Substation that cut in the new 60-cycle power. After this, and the other switch overs, sharp-eared customers could hear new sounds emanating from their electrical equipment: thumps, hums and assorted vibrations as machines speeded up slightly.

The frequency change touched virtually every aspect of Company operations. The public could exchange old clocks for new at special depots, like this one in Santa Barbara (below). Every meter on the system had to be rebuilt (left).
BOTH, EDISON COLLECTION.

Work on a "pilot survey" began the following January. A four and one-half square mile area in Bell Gardens, southeast of Los Angeles, was chosen to be the testing ground for changeover procedures before the entire system was converted. It was an area of 4,000 customers, easily isolated from the main Edison network, accessible to a 60-cycle power supply purchased from the City of Los Angeles' system, and it was not far from the Boylston Street headquarters.

The Bell Gardens pilot program was successful. Then the entire Edison system, except the San Joaquin Valley, which was already on 60 cycles, was divided into nine areas and the big job began. At the peak of the effort, 750 Edison employees and a similar number of contract employees were kept busy surveying, engineering, rewiring and canvassing. Nearly 2 million pieces of customer equipment were dealt with, from gigantic pumps and electric railway power conversion equipment, to record players and tiny clock motors.

Virtually all rotating devices on Edison's own system also had to be rewired or rebuilt. Generators, exciters, synchronous condensers, motor generator sets and over 700,000 meters were systematically dealt with by Edison crews. Long Beach Steam Plant's antique vertical turbines, Units 1, 2 and 3, too old and obsolete to justify the expense of rebuilding, provided the last source of energy to the rapidly shrinking 50-cycle service area. Not long after the job was done, they were scrapped.

The last cutover took place on October 26, 1948 at the La Fresa Substation when Edison Chairman of the Board Harry Bauer switched the remaining feeders to 60 cycles. The job had taken more than three years and had cost over $34 million, but the mission of better service for Edison customers had been accomplished.

In 1952, there occurred an action, which, although it drew little public reaction at the time, marked the beginning of a period of topsy-turvy economics caused by postwar inflation. Early in the year a rate case was filed calling for the first increase since 1921. This was only the second rate hike in the company's

history, and was caused, like the first one in 1921, by severe postwar inflation. Since 1921, on the other hand, Edison had consistently lowered the cost of electricity to reflect both the increased efficiency of its physical plant and the deflation of money caused by the Depression. The last of these voluntary rate reductions had been made as recently as 1946. Now, however, with a massive plant expansion taking place that had to be paid for at greatly inflated prices, rates had to go up. In the

exhibits filed with the Public Utilities Commission for this case, the Company held out as one example of the severe inflation it was experiencing that the cost of one barrel of fuel oil, which had cost only 80 cents in 1939, had more than doubled to $1.71 in 1952! Although most hoped that the rate increase would be temporary, it proved to be only the first as, especially after 1965, inflation grew much worse.

An appliance motor rewinding depot at the height of the frequency change, 1947.
Edison Collection.

Another major event in Edison's history came on New Year's Day of 1964, when the system of the California Electric Power Company was merged into Edison. "Calectric" as its employees nicknamed it, had grown out of the old Nevada-California Power Company and Southern Sierras Power Company systems.

Despite the loss of its important Imperial Valley service territory to the government-financed Imperial Irrigation District in 1943, Calectric still served a large area from Tonopah in Central Nevada to Palm Springs in Southern California. Unfortunately, most of this area was very sparsely settled, and the tremendous postwar population boom initially affected only a very small portion of the Calectric system. Nevertheless, as its load slowly increased after World War Two, Calectric constructed several new steam stations, including one at Highgrove which was the West's first completely outdoor steam plant.

Because Calectric and Edison had contiguous, often overlapping service areas in inland Southern California, there long had been duplication of facilities and functions between

Reconstruction of one of Eagle Rock Substation's synchronous condensers during the frequency change, 1947.
EDISON COLLECTION.

Edison Chairman Harry Bauer (second from right) prepares to throw a switch at La Fresa Substation to complete the final changeover to 60-cycle power, October 26, 1948.
EDISON COLLECTION.

the two companies. So, in 1963, when the population boom belatedly hit several of the traditional load centers on the Calectric system—including Palm Springs, Victorville, San Bernardino, Rialto and Riverside County—the two companies looked at a merger as a cost-effective way of improving service to their areas.

A close-up view of the fresh water unit on Catalina Island, 1964. Persistant drought fears persuaded Edison to try this technology, but the project was not successful.
EDISON COLLECTION.

The World War One-era former submarine diesel engine generators were moved into the Pebbly Beach Station when it was built in 1947.
COURTESY SANTA CATALINA ISLAND COMPANY.

Santa Catalina Island

Santa Catalina Island, long a popular vacation resort, lies 25 miles off the coast of Southern California. Twenty-one miles long and eight miles wide at its widest point, the island supports a small permanent population, concentrated mostly in the City of Avalon at its eastern end, but is inundated by thousands of tourists daily during the summer season.

The island was used primarily for cattle and sheep grazing until 1892, when it was purchased by the well-known Banning family of Wilmington. The Banning brothers attempted to develop the cove at Avalon as a summer resort, but this effort was only partially successful.

In 1919, chewing gum magnate William Wrigley, Jr. purchased Catalina Island and reinvigorated Avalon's popularity as a resort community. Wrigley's Santa Catalina Island Company made many needed improvements: in transportation to the island, in water supply to Avalon and in utilities service. Avalon had been getting electricity from a steam plant located in Falls Canyon on the outskirts of town. Twenty-year-old steam engines and belt-driven generators provided an uncertain service at best. Wrigley had them augmented by several diesel engine-driven generators salvaged from scrapped World War One submarines.

In 1947, the old Falls Canyon plant was replaced by a new facility built at Pebbly Beach, a mile east of Avalon. The old war surplus diesel engines were brought over to the new plant and additional engines were installed.

In 1954, the Avalon Public Service Company was formed to take over operation of the electric generating station, and of the propane gas receiving and metering facility that had been installed to serve Avalon. The City of Avalon, with its Electric Department that had been set up in 1913, owned and operated the electric, gas, fresh water and salt water distribution systems within its city limits. Ownership of the remainder of the island's electric system, as well as the fresh water wells and reservoirs, was retained by the Santa Catalina Island Company.

By 1960, it was apparent to all that this Byzantine arrangement of utility services was inadequate to cope with the growing tide of development upon the island. The Edison Company was approached about the possibility of purchasing the various systems. The voters within the City of Avalon decided by a wide margin in February of 1962 to sell their utility system, thus clearing the last hurdle blocking unification of Catalina's utilities.

Edison purchased the electric, gas and water systems on November 29, 1962, and immediately began overhauling and modernizing them. Today, self-reliant because of its isolation from the rest of the Edison system, The Catalina District nonetheless provides its customers with a service comparable to that on the mainland.

Pebbly Beach now boasts efficient new railroad locomotive-type diesel generators, and the water system, after a close brush with drought in the Seventies, has had its storage enlarged. As an echo from the Edison Company's earliest days, Catalina is the last place in Southern California where customers cook with Edison gas.

Avalon Harbor, back when the Great White Steamship was the only way to get to Catalina.
AUTHOR'S COLLECTION.

Edison's San Bernardino local office in 1948.
EDISON COLLECTION.

After a merger was agreed upon, employees of both companies worked to physically integrate the operations of both systems. This tremendous task was among the largest, most complex mergers of systems ever to take place in the electric utility industry, yet it was accomplished without a hitch by the time of Merger Day, January 1, 1964.

Even with these other important events, the big story in the three decades following the war remained the spectacular growth of Southern California's population. During this time the region endured the greatest mass migration in history, which for years exceeded a thousand people a week moving into the service territory of the Southern California Edison Company. To meet this unprecedented demand for energy, the Company undertook a dramatic expansion of its generating capacity from 1.2 million kilowatts in 1945 to 15.5 million kilowatts in 1983.

Between 1947 and 1960, the output of Big Creek's "Hardest Working Water in the World" was doubled. In 1951, Redinger Lake and Powerhouse No. 4 were completed on the San Joaquin River below Big Creek No. 3. Lake

207

Thomas A. Edison was built in the Vermillion Valley near Florence Lake in 1954 to provide still more water through Ward Tunnel to the upper plants along Big Creek. To make use of the fall of water through Ward Tunnel, Portal Powerhouse was built in 1956. In 1960, this major construction effort was capped by the completion of Mammoth Pool Dam and Powerhouse. At Big Creek Powerhouse No. 3, once famed as the "Electric Giant of the West," 32,000-kilowatt Unit No. 4 was added in 1948, and 36,000-kilowatt Unit No. 5 was installed in 1980.

Calectric's new San Bernardino General Office, completed in 1958. This building is now Edison's Eastern Division Office.
EDISON COLLECTION.

Big Creek was not ignored in postwar resource planning. Powerhouse No. 3 received a fourth unit in 1948.
EDISON COLLECTION.

A row of 220,000-volt transformers at Redondo Beach Steam Station, 1948.
EDISON COLLECTION.

An even greater and more significant expansion took place in steam generation resources. Until World War Two, both Edison and Calectric were predominantly hydro companies, with steam essentially used in standby service to meet peak demands or emergency situations. Following the war, however, new sites to construct large hydro plants adequate to meet most of Southern California's burgeoning demand for electricity simply were not available, so both companies were forced to rely most heavily upon steam plants. In 1946, this tremendous construction program got underway when work began on the new Redondo Beach Steam Station on the site of the former Pacific Light and Power plant. Over the next 27 years, ten new multiple-unit, oil and gas-fired power plants were built at coastal and inland sites in Southern California, seven by Edison and three by Calectric. An additional steam plant was built near Yuma jointly by Calectric and Arizona Public Service Company, to serve their respective loads along the lower Colorado River in California, Arizona and Baja California. Even the old Long Beach Steam Plant No. 2, built back in the Twenties, was extensively reconstructed using modern combined-cycle technology.

Calectric's Highgrove Steam Station pioneered outdoor power plant design in the West.
EDISON COLLECTION.

Even as this tremendous construction program was getting into full stride early in the 1950s, there were concerns for the future. Air pollution greatly worsened during this decade, drawing attention to both stationary and mobile emissions sources. There was a nagging concern, too, that petroleum fuels—oil and natural gas—were resources that might be limited in supply, and costly, by the end of the century. As a result, the Edison Company began exploring alternate methods of generating electricity for the future.

Long a community landmark, the twin stacks of PL&P's old Redondo Steam Plant, which had been abandoned in 1934, were toppled in 1946 to make way for Edison's new Redondo Beach Steam Station.
Edison Collection.

Edison's street lighting load increased in the postwar period as tract homes spread across Southern California.
Joseph O. Fadler Photo.

El Segundo Steam Station, 1964.
Joseph O. Fadler Photo.

During construction of the Huntington Beach Steam Station in 1957, a deep sea diver prepares to descend to the ocean floor to guide a section of cooling water conduit into place.
Joseph O. Fadler Photo.

What's in a Name?

What's in a name? Unlike many utility systems which simply number their facilities and power lines, Edison names its properties. These names can provide lessons in history or geography, can honor heroes of the past and can even provide unexpected humor or whimsy.

It was not always so. In its earliest years as a small utility in Los Angeles, Edison numbered its power plants and substations with no other distinction. Thus, Los Angeles No. 1 was the original steam plant at Second and Boylston Streets, L.A. No. 2 was a substation near Fourth Street, L.A. No. 3 was the big new steam plant over on Alhambra Avenue, and L.A. Nos. 4 through 9 were substations at various places. Even today certain old hydroelectric plants retain this terminology.

By 1905 Edison had begun using geographic names to designate its substations in order to reduce confusion. Thus, Alhambra Sub is in Alhambra, Baldwin Park Sub in Baldwin Park, on through the alphabet to Yorba Linda and Zuma. When communities grew large enough to have more than one substation, street names were often used, as for example,

Granada Sub in Alhambra, built on Granada Avenue. Sometimes the nearest street intersection inspired a name. Haveda Substation, for example, is near the corner of Hawthorne and Sepulveda Boulevards, and the former Westflor Sub was at Western and Florence Avenues.

Three Edison substations, Lighthipe, Barre, and Hinson, are named after prominent early company electrical engineers.

When a new 220,000-volt substation was being built in 1920 to connect the former Mount Whitney system to Edison's Big Creek lines, the name Richgrove was adopted after the nearest railroad siding several miles away. When construction materials were repeatedly delivered to the Richgrove railroad station rather than to the new electric substation, however, its name was changed to Vestal Substation, after Roman mythology's goddess of light.

Other substations describe the customers they serve. During World War Two, Fleet Sub provided electricity to the Long Beach Naval Base. Today, Paper Sub serves a paper plant in Fullerton, Space Sub serves one aerospace company, and Rocket Test another.

Sometimes whimsical puns may provide a name. When LaFresa Substation in Torrance was built, it was surrounded by miles of strawberry fields, which in Spanish are "Las Fresas." A substation in Redondo Beach that was the first to incorporate unitized portable components earned the name "El Porto," an adaption of the Spanish name for portable. Perhaps even more atrocious puns can be found in Desert Outpost Sub near Palm Springs and Oilrich Sub in the oil fields of Carson.

The merger with the California Electric Power Company caused many new names to appear and also forced the elimination of duplicates. Where duplication of names did arise, that facility with the fewest number of drawings had its name changed. Thus, Edison's Mill Creek Hydro Plants near Redlands retained that name, while CEP's Mill Creek Hydro Plant in Mono County was renamed "Lundy." Similarly, CEP's Highgrove Steam Plant kept its name, while Edison's Highgrove Substation became "Vista." Most appropriately, CEP's former San Bernardino Sub was renamed "Calectric" Sub adopting the popular nickname of the former company.

The tremendous postwar expansion of the Edison system required many hundreds of unique new names for substations and distribution circuits. The results have been interesting: Goldtown Sub near Mohave, with its Grubstake, Golden Queen and Discovery circuits; Murphy Substation has the Kilroy, Kilkenny, Mulligan, O'Malloy, O'Tool and Tipperary distribution lines; Tortilla Sub has the Poco, Frito, Patio, Peso and Burrito lines; and Orange Substation, in the City of Orange in Orange County, which has the Blue, Pink, Scarlet and Yellow 12,000-volt circuits.

When the once important milk producing district of Dairy Valley was in the process of being subdivided into today's Cerritos, an Edison planner who must have enjoyed crossword puzzles bestowed upon the area's new substation the name "Bovine," and upon its distribution circuits the names Brahma, Aberdeen, Durham, Longhorn, Hereford, Devon and Zebu. This author's favorite? Serving the Southern Pacific railroad yards in the City of Industry is Railroad Substation, with its Engine, Caboose, Gondola, Brakeman, Locomotive, Trestle and Cowcatcher circuits.

One decision that was taken was to adopt a steam plant fuel that was new to California although common elsewhere: coal. With large reserves of coal available in the West and with sophisticated new pollution-control technologies becoming available, many Western utilities began looking at this fuel at a time when Eastern power plants were abandoning it. Edison's first experience with coal was as a partner with Arizona Public Service Company in an expansion of its existing Four Corners Plant near Farmington, New Mexico. In 1968, ground was broken for the Mohave Generating Station at a site on the Colorado River near the southern tip of Nevada. Edison, as project manager for a consortium of Western utilities, prepared a design that drew international attention. A 275-mile long slurry pipeline, the world's longest, was built to bring coal from mines at Black Mesa, Arizona to the station, where it was burned to make steam to run two 750,000-kilowatt turbogenerators. This station, with its slurry line, dewatering equipment, giant boilers and turbines and most efficient pollution control equipment, was an incredible achievement for a maiden essay in coal plant design.

Despite these investments in coal plants, in the early post-war years nuclear energy was the technology that appeared most promising for the future. Harold Quinton, who had been elected to Edison's presidency in 1954, viewed with interest the early research into nuclear power plants. Despite several aspects of the technology that were non-traditional with conventional facilities, Quinton became convinced of atomic energy's potential benefits for utility operations.

Anatomy of a Power Plant

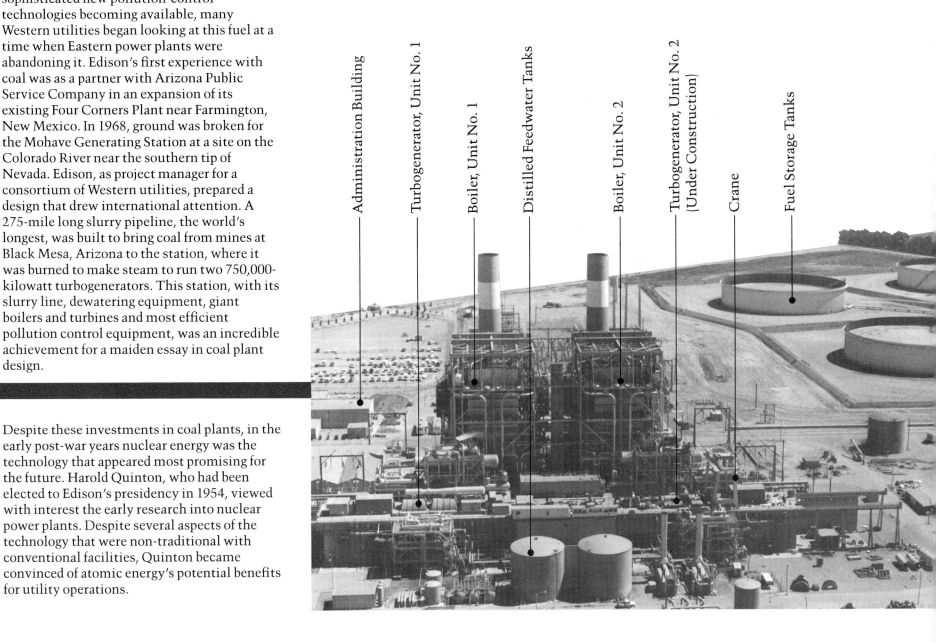

Administration Building

Turbogenerator, Unit No. 1

Boiler, Unit No. 1

Distilled Feedwater Tanks

Boiler, Unit No. 2

Turbogenerator, Unit No. 2 (Under Construction)

Crane

Fuel Storage Tanks

On July 12, 1957, the Southern California Edison Company became the nation's first investor-owned utility to generate electricity commercially from a non-military nuclear reactor, when its Santa Susana Experimental Station began operation. Built in conjunction with Atomics International's "Sodium Reactor Experiment," this 7500-kilowatt plant was built in a picturesque area of the Santa Susana Mountains near Chatsworth where, in the silent movie era, many Westerns had been filmed.

This little plant made more history when, on the night of November 12, 1957, the then-small Ventura County community of Moorpark became the first town in the world to receive its entire supply of electricity from a nuclear power plant. The switchover from conventional power to "atomic" electricity was conducted with split-second timing for benefit of a national television audience who viewed the event on Edward R. Murrow's popular "See It Now" series. By prearrangement with Moorpark's 1146 residents, the town went totally dark for a few seconds as it was disconnected from Edison's power grid, and then lights flashed back on again as electricity

Mohave Generating Station. The big tanks in the foreground are for storage of coal slurry received through the Black Mesa Pipeline.
EDISON COLLECTION.

A lineman at work, 1957.
JOSEPH O. FADLER PHOTO.

By 1970, most new residential tracts were built with underground electric cables.
EDISON COLLECTION.

212

arrived from the nuclear plant. Although conducted in a glare of publicity, this was a serious test that proved conclusively that nuclear reactors could successfully generate electricity to fulfill the widely fluctuating demands experienced upon commercial power systems. Two days later, the reactor and adjacent Edison generator were formally dedicated by Quinton and Lewis Strauss, Chairman of the Atomic Energy Commission. With great enthusiasm and high hopes, California's "Age of Atomic Energy" was launched.

In the euphoria of the moment, virtually everyone in the utility industry saw nuclear power in the same light as early pioneers had viewed hydro power: an apparently inexhaustible energy source which, although coming from plants that were expensive to construct, would cost the consumer much less than electricity from conventional steam turbines. Based upon this perception, many utilities, including Edison, prepared plans to build commercial-sized nuclear units and concurrently launched marketing programs to absorb this anticipated surplus of inexpensive energy.

Edison's 7500-kilowatt Santa Susana Experimental Station in 1957.
JOSEPH O. FADLER PHOTO.

In the 1960s, home economists in "Electric Living Centers" continued the Company's long-running electric appliance information program.
EDISON COLLECTION.

With CBS cameras poised on a nearby hillside to record the event, Moorpark in Ventura County receives electricity from the nearby Santa Susana nuclear plant, November 12, 1957.
EDISON COLLECTION.

The vigorous marketing program Edison had undertaken in the late 1930s had come to an abrupt halt during the war. It was slow to restart afterwards, as Edison struggled to cope with a rapidly growing population and electrical demand. By 1955, however, the Company had gained enough ground to begin a new advertising program with the slogan "Live Better Electrically." This was followed in 1958 by participation in the nationwide Medallion Home Program.

In 1963, the industry recognized the innovative new marketing programs the Edison Company had undertaken. At the Edison Electric Institute's National Convention in Atlantic City that year, the prestigious Thomas A. Edison Award, which formerly had been known as the Charles Coffin Award, was awarded to Southern California Edison. In a citation accompanying the award, recognition was made of the Company's successes with the Medallion Home Program, and of the "All Electric Building Program"—originated by SCE

The sophisticated electric ranges of the 1960s were a far cry from the first Hotpoint of 1915. *Edison Collection.*

Edison Chairman of the Board Harold Quinton (left) accepts the Thomas A. Edison Award in 1963. *Edison Collection.*

and subsequently adopted by other utilities as an industry-wide promotion. Harold Quinton, who had become the Company's Chairman of the Board in 1959, accepted the Award and stated on behalf of all Edison Company employees, "...it was the employees' imagination, initiative and efforts in execution which resulted in this recognition."

Based upon the success of its Santa Susana Experimental Station, and to fulfill the promise of inexpensive energy inherent in its marketing strategy, in 1963 the Edison Company began work on the San Onofre Nuclear Generating Station. A joint project of Edison (80 percent) and neighboring San Diego Gas and Electric Company (20 percent), San Onofre was built on the coast midway between Los Angeles and San Diego, on a site leased from the U.S. Marine Corps. In a five-year saga of modern construction, work progressed on what was then the nation's largest pressurized-water nuclear station. The huge reactor vessel arrived at Christmas 1966 after a journey by barge thousands of miles from Chattanooga, Tennessee, through the Panama Canal to the West Coast. The next year Edison really

launched into the nuclear age, when $27 million worth of uranium fuel was installed into the reactor, and start-up testing of the plant was completed. Dedication ceremonies at San Onofre on January 5, 1968, culminated almost 16 years of Edison's research and development into nuclear generation of energy. By the time San Onofre was in full production a few weeks later, international oil cartels had already taken the first actions that ultimately would lead to the petroleum shortages of five years later.

The most popular new appliance of the postwar era was the television. By 1956, evening TV watching caused significant surges in Edison load demand. *Edison Collection.*

Loading fuel at San Onofre. *Edison Collection.*

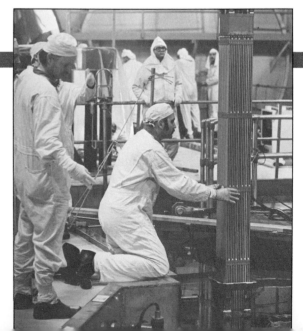

The volatile international situation held little meaning to the opponents of nuclear power, however. Rising on the tide of anti-war sentiment during the Vietnam War, these Twentieth Century Luddites grew strong enough to delay or halt new plant construction. Unable to build nuclear units at other proposed sites in Southern California, Edison concentrated upon additions at San Onofre. Ground was broken for Units Two and Three, aggregating 2.2 million kilowatts of capacity in 1972. Despite delays arising from the increasing complexity of licensing procedures and the need to obtain an unprecedented number of environmental and regulatory approvals in public hearings, San Onofre Unit Two went into operation in 1983, with Unit Three following a year later.

Nuclear power has demonstrated that it is a reliable generation technology, capable of producing energy in the tremendous quantities demanded by modern society. Compared with the air pollution problems of fossil-fueled power plants, nuclear power is clean, and its waste production easily manageable. In its first decade of operation, San Onofre Unit One

produced in complete safety more than 30 billion kilowatt-hours. Now, with its recent additions, the San Onofre Nuclear Generating Station will annually generate electric power equivalent to the energy produced by burning 25 to 30 million barrels of fuel oil, with concomitant reductions in air pollution. A product of the busy postwar years, San Onofre has proven to be a vital energy resource for complex times.

Refueling San Onofre Unit One's reactor in 1976.
EDISON COLLECTION.

San Onofre Unit One as built, 1968.
JOSEPH O. FADLER PHOTO.

San Onofre Units Two and Three under construction, 1979. Note remodled containment sphere on Unit One at top.
EDISON COLLECTION.

Edison's Family Tree

City of Avalon Electric Department 1913–1962

Santa Catalina Island Co. 1894–1962   [Electric generation and distribution facilities only]

Santa Barbara Street Railway Co. 1875–1896

Santa Barbara Consolidated Railway Co. 1896–1912

Santa Barbara and Suburban Railway Co. 1912–1929

Santa Barbara Electric Light Co. 1886–1901

United Electric, Gas and Power Co. 1900–1903

United Electric Gas and Power Company

Redlands Electric Light and Power Co. 1892–1902

SOUTHERN CALIFORNIA EDISON COMPANY

West Side Lighting Co.

INCANDESCENT & ARC LIGHTING AND ELECTRIC POWER.

Southern California Power Co. 1897–1899

West Side Lighting Co. 1896–1897

Edison Electric Co. of Los Angeles 1897–1902

Edison Electric Co. 1902–1909

Southern California Edison Co. 1909–present

Pasadena Electric Light and Power Co. 1888–1898

The Pasadena Electric Light and Power Company

Santa Ana Gas and Electric Co. 1891–1899

Visalia Electric Light & Gas Co. 1886–1890

Mt. Whitney Power Co. 1899–1903

Mt. Whitney Power and Electric Co. 1903–1920

Holt & Knupp 1886

Visalia Gas, Light and Heat Co. 1890–1905

Santa Ana Water Co. 1870–1901

VENTURA WATER, LIGHT AND POWER COMPANY

Ventura Land and Power Co. 1890–1897

Ventura Water, Light and Power Co.

Ventura County Power Co.

Mammoth Power Company Line No. 1 1905

San Gabriel Electric Co. 1897–1902

Kern River Co. 1897–1902

San Antonio Light and Power Company

San Antonio Light and Power Co. 1892–1902

Sierra Power Co. 1898–1902

C.R. Lloyd Highgrove Plant 1895–1896

San Bernardino Electric Co. 1895–1902

San Bernardino Gas and Electric Co.

Los Angeles Electric Co. 1882–1895

Los Angeles Gas and Electric Co. 1895–1904

Los Angeles Gas and Electric Co.

| 1870 | 1880 | 1890 | 1900 | 1910 | 1920 |

216 There are over 200 predecessors that were
amalgamated to create today's
Southern California Edison Company.
This abbreviated family tree presents
only those ancestor companies
which receive mention in this text.

Inyo Telephone Co. 1904–1911

Sierra Telephone Co. 1910–1954

Nevada-California Electric Corp. 1916–1936 (Holding)

Hillside Water Co. 1887–1936

NEVADA-CALIFORNIA ELECTRIC

Nevada Power, Mining and Milling Co. 1904–1907

Nevada-California Power Co. 1907–1936

The Nevada Power, Mining and Milling Co.

Pacific Power Co. 1910–1917

Southern Sierras Power Co. 1911–1936

Halton Power Co. 1905–1923

Avalon Public Service Co. 1954–1962

[Certain electric distribution facilities were sold to the City of Los Angeles Department of Water and Power in 1922 and 1939.]

SCE

Southern California Edison Company

[Certain former SCE electric distribution facilities outside the City of Los Angeles were resold to Southern California Edison Co. in 1939.]

| 1930 | 1940 | 1950 | 1960 | 1970 | 1980 |

219

Yuma Utilities Co. 1924–1936

Nevada-California Electric Corp. [Operating] 1936–1941

California Electric Power Co. 1941–1964

[Certain electric properties in the Imperial Valley were sold in 1943 to the Imperial Irrigation District. All electric properties in the Yuma area were sold to Arizona Edison Company in 1948. The telephone system of the Interstate Telegraph Co. was sold in 1954 to Continental Telephone Co. Ice plants in the Imperial Valley were abandoned by 1956.]

[Certain electric properties in Nevada were sold to Sierra Pacific Power Co. in 1969.]

Power of Mexico, S.A. 1917–1934

Industrial Electrica Mexicana, S.A. 1944–1960

[All electric properties in Baja California, Mexico, were sold to Comision Federal de Electricidad in 1960.]

Aluminum Highways

Major storms or other natural disasters can affect electric service, but interconnections, plus Edison's network of 500,000-volt lines, called the bulk power "backbone", helps minimize the chances of prolonged service interruptions.
EDISON COLLECTION.

Electric utility systems have long been interconnected in order to exchange large amounts of power either on a regular basis or in emergencies. As far back as 1918, a number of 66,000-volt transmission lines linked the Southern California Edison Company with its neighbors in order to share hydroelectric reserves to alleviate wartime shortages of fuel oil. As has been described in an earlier chapter, the drought of 1924 underscored the need for such "tielines," even as it caused them to be taxed to the limit. During that frantic summer,

66,000-volt hookups were made that established patterns for many future system interconnections. In fact, after normal water conditions returned, these interties enabled sales of excess hydroelectric capacity to other utilities who had no hydro plants of their own.

The amounts of energy exchanged in these early interties were comparatively small, in part because Edison's system operated at a frequency of 50 cycles, while surrounding utilities were at 60 cycles. Thus, connections

Kite safety programs began in the Thirties. Here, the lineman warns about the potential danger of a 66KV line in what is now Diamond Bar.
EDISON COLLECTION.

This frequency changer at Edison's Colton Substation was a major point of interconnection with Southern Sierras Power Company, prior to the frequency change.
EDISON COLLECTION.

Angeles Gas and Electric Corporation at L.A. No. 3 Substation, to the Los Angeles Bureau of Power and Light principally at Long Beach Steam Plant, and to the City of Pasadena's system. In addition, Southern Sierras was connected to L.A. Gas and Electric at the latter's Seal Beach Steam Plant and to San Diego at Rincon Substation in San Diego County.

The advent of very large amounts of energy from Hoover Dam and subsequently the start of World War Two caused these various interconnections to be raised in voltage and increased in number to tie together power systems throughout California, Southern Nevada and Arizona. The formation of the Pacific Southwest Power Pool as a wartime economy measure has already been mentioned. As pre-war reserves of excess generating capacity were absorbed by war industries, it was the Pool's close interconnections and integrated operation that enabled this tremendous wartime energy demand (which increased 94 percent between 1939 and 1944) to be met with the addition of only 25 percent in generation capacity.

required frequency changers, large rotating machines that somewhat limited interchange capacity. Nevertheless, by 1930, as a result of the drought or existing contracts, Edison was connected to the Southern Sierras Power Company at Colton Substation, with San Diego Consolidated Gas and Electric at Capistrano Substation (later moved to Chino), with the San Joaquin Light and Power Corporation at Kern River No. 1 hydro plant and at various other points, including Magunden and Vestal Substations. Locally, there were ties to Los

Despite this significant achievement, however, power exchanges were still limited by differences in frequency and voltage of tielines. As late as 1950, only Edison's tie to the Metropolitan Water District's Hoover Dam generation was at as high a pressure as 220,000 volts. All others were still at 138,000 volts or lower. These limitations were eliminated after Edison finished its conversion to 60 cycles in 1948 and as postwar energy demands extended construction of higher voltage transmission lines.

219

A junction tower on the 220KV line from Long Beach Steam Plant.
EDISON COLLECTION.

The Big Creek-Vincent 220KV line in the Antelope Valley. Building this line on a separate right of way was justified when failure of the St. Francis Dam washed out the original Big Creek lines and energy carried over this line was all that kept Southern California from being blacked out.
EDISON COLLECTION.

In the early days of high voltage transmission, one severe problem that had to be overcome before reliable long distance intertie lines could become a reality was that of unexpected fracturing of the cables themselves. Although not unknown before the advent of high voltage power lines, the problem became more serious as the diameter of the conductor cable increased and as the dependency of power systems upon distant generation resources grew.

It will be recalled that the first transmission line from Big Creek to Los Angeles was placed into service at a pressure of 150,000 volts in November 1913. This line, along with Southern Sierra Power's 89,000-volt Bishop Creek to San Bernardino "Tower Line," was the first major application of the new "aluminum cable, steel reinforced," or ACSR, conductor material. Only seven months after going into operation, the Big Creek line was plagued by the first of a long series of unexplained breaks in the power cables. After the conversion of these lines to 220,000-volt service in May 1923, by which time the Big Creek Plants had become Edison's major generating resource and the transmission

220 *The crew responsible for maintaining the Kern River 75KV lines back in 1914.*
EDISON COLLECTION.

lines their vital link to Southern California, these mysterious breaks began to cause major concern.

George Stockbridge, Edison's Superintendent of Transmission, took it upon himself to solve this problem. He personally conducted a series of exhausting investigations of the areas where cable failures were greatest, spending many uncomfortable days and nights standing in towers in all types of weather. On March 14, 1925, Stockbridge discovered that the

George Stockbridge investigating snow loading on a wire of the Vincent 220KV line at Tejon Summit. He is holding a 12-inch ruler.
EDISON COLLECTION.

Performing hot maintenance on the Eagle-Bell 220KV line in 1935.
EDISON COLLECTION.

Installing an early style Stockbridge Vibration Damper on one of the Big Creek lines, about 1930.
EDISON COLLECTION.

aluminum wire strands of the power cables were crystalizing and breaking at the point where they were clamped to the insulators, due to wind- and weather-induced vibration, much in the same fashion as a wire coat-hanger can be broken by constantly bending it back and forth.

Within two months of his discovery of the cause of the wire breaks, Stockbridge had designed a vibration damper to mitigate the problem. First placed on Edison's Eagle-Bell 220,000 volt lines then under construction, they were soon retrofitted on the Big Creek lines and proved to virtually eliminate the problem. Originally assembled at Edison's Alhambra General Store, but later licensed to hardware manufacturers world-wide under the generic name of "the Stockbridge Vibration Damper," these devices are today used on high voltage power lines everywhere around the world. This major technical innovation removed one significant obstacle to the reliable operation of regional transmission networks.

After World War Two, electric system planners dreamed of linking the tremendous thermal generating resources that had been built in California since the war with the vast hydroelectric resources of the Pacific Northwest. Such an interconnection would be of great benefit to both regions. In 1959, the federally owned Bonneville Power Administration (BPA) made overtures to California utilities concerning the possibility of purchasing surplus energy from its Columbia River hydro plants.

Changing an insulator string on the Eagle-Bell line in 1947. Note that plastic hardhats have just been introduced.
EDISON COLLECTION.

Stringing wire on the Mira Loma-Lugo 500,000-volt line in Cajon Pass, 1979.
EDISON COLLECTION.

Preparing to pull through some more cable.
EDISON COLLECTION.

The big "bull wheel" tensioning devices for 500KV line construction were much larger than their 220KV ancestors used in the building of the Hoover Dam lines (see Chapter 11).
EDISON COLLECTION.

Stringing Wire

(Excerpted from the *Edison News*, November 23, 1979)

"Even before the sun had popped above the horizon the Edison team was gearing up for the day's action—to begin the stringing of conductor cables along a 40-mile stretch of the

new Lugo-Mira Loma 500,000 volt line. In the easy slang of the construction crews the task is called 'stringing wire,' but the simple-sounding chore is in fact an enormous job.

"For months the Transmission Construction Field Force has been busy assembling the 125 foot tall steel towers that would support the 'conductors' or power cables. Perched on hilltops, striding across valleys, the two parallel lines of towers march down rugged Cajon Pass into bustling Southern California. Today the Edison team would string six lines of electrical transmission cable weighing nearly 120 tons through a series of 10 towers spanning a distance of over 15,500 feet, nearly 3 miles.

"A company chopper roared over a nearby ridge. Its job was to string a rope through pulleys suspended from the insulators on each tower, a separate rope for each of the 3 phases and one for each of the two "skylines". Like threading a needle, the chopper guided the rope through each tower's pulley, eventually connecting all ten. Then, using the rope's end as a connecting point, cable would be run through each of the towers, carefully pulling it through so as not to overstress the towers.

"Finally the heavy aluminum cable with the steel wire core has been pulled through each tower, correctly tensioned and ready to be tied off. Now the tower climbers move in. Like trapeze artists, immune to dizzying heights, they complete the essential "tie-offs" and make final adjustments.

"Before sundown three more miles of 500,000 volt tower line will be added to Edison's growing network, built by crews of rugged individualists using specially designed equipment, that versatile helicopter and know-how."

three extra-high voltage lines between the Pacific Northwest and Southern California.

Each of these lines represented a major advance in electric transmission technology. Two were designed to carry alternating current (A.C.) at 500,000 volts, while the third line would carry direct current (D.C.) at 800,000 volts. In the early 1960s there were no such lines yet in operation; Edison engineers, working with their counterparts from the Los Angeles Department of Water and Power and other participating utilities, established most of the parameters for tower, insulator and switchgear designs.

The finished product, the Lugo-Mira Loma 500,000-volt transmission line descending Cajon Pass into Southern California.
T. M. HOTCHKISS PHOTO.

This inquiry led to extensive negotiations between investor-owned utilities, government-owned utilities and various agencies of the federal government. Jack Horton, who had just succeeded Harold Quinton as Edison's President, represented the Company in these negotiations, assisted by William R. Gould and Howard Allen. Following the passage of necessary legislation by Congress, a complex series of contracts was prepared. These agreements enabled the various utilities involved to begin work on the construction of

223

Working over 150 feet above the desert floor, an Edison crew assembles a tower for the Vincent-Lugo line.
ARTHUR ADAMS PHOTO.

Dramatic construction view of the building of the Vincent-Lugo 500,000-volt transmission line, part of Edison's bulk power "backbone."
ARTHUR ADAMS PHOTO.

A substation maintenance man stands beside one of the new 500KV air circuit breakers at Vincent Substation.
EDISON COLLECTION.

The two 500,000 volt A.C. lines of the Pacific Intertie reach 1000 miles from the Columbia River to the Mojave Desert, traversing some of the most rugged terrain in the world. Their construction was a modern saga of achievement in the face of problems not limited to harsh topography, bad weather and shortages of equipment and supplies. Construction forces of the Southern California Edison Company successfully accomplished the formidable task of crossing the rugged Tehachapi Mountains in winter, despite heavy snow and gale force winds. Seventeen of the towers were constructed using helicopters exclusively to transport workmen and materials to each site. Helicopters also assisted in the stringing of the aluminum cables each tower supported. The first of the A.C. lines was completed in November 1967, and the second was energized in 1968. Immediately, large amounts of electricity began passing over the aluminum "highway" between the Pacific Northwest and Southwest.

These high-voltage lines, which eventually extended clear across Edison territory eastward towards New Mexico, presented a challenge to

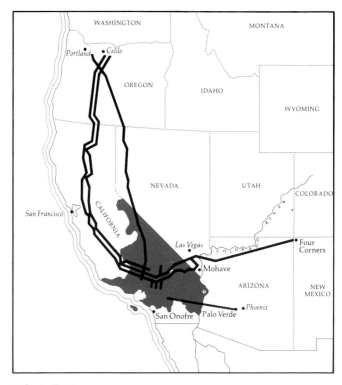

■ *Service Territory*
— *Extra-High Voltage (EHV) Transmission Lines*

the engineers and field crews of Edison's Transmission Division. Forty years earlier, the utility world had been amazed by the Company's conversion of the Big Creek 150,000-volt lines to the new 220,000-volt technology while the lines remained energized. Now Edison took the equally significant decision to maintain the new 500,000-volt system while it, too, was "hot." While the lines were still under construction, Engineers John Eckman and C. A. Stel put together a team to design new tools, hardware and procedures so

this work could be done safely. Successful beyond original expectations, Edison's innovative "Hotline Maintenance Program" has since been imitated by many other utilities.

The 800,000-volt direct-current transmission line of the Pacific Intertie, a joint project of Edison and the Los Angeles Department of Water and Power, was also a significant step forward in modern electric transmission technology. When the 846-mile long line went into service in May 1970, it was the highest

capacity, longest-distance D.C. line in the world, as well as the first extra-high voltage D.C. transmission line ever constructed in the United States.

The decision to construct one of the Pacific Intertie lines as a high-voltage direct-current transmission line was a daring step. Although converting alternating current to D.C. requires complex facilities, this expense is offset in very long lines by the much lower cost of tower construction. More importantly, it was seen that use of direct current would provide superior operating characteristics by ameliorating many of the problems of electric system stability and synchronism associated with long distance A.C. lines.

Today, the Pacific Intertie is an important link in a network of extra-high voltage transmission lines that interconnect utilities in 14 Western states, British Columbia and Alberta. Other lines of various voltages circle to the east, then northwards through Utah, Idaho, Wyoming, and Montana and westward to the Pacific Northwest. Recognizing that a need existed for regional coordination of the growing system of

Western "bulk power" lines, the Edison Company participated in the formation, in August 1967, of the Western Systems Coordinating Council (WSCC). Building on the idea of the wartime Pacific Southwest Power Pool, WSCC coordinates the construction of new extra-high voltage transmission lines and integrates operation of generation resources so that all are utilized most efficiently for the benefit of all the West's utility customers. Thanks to WSCC's planning and coordination efforts, on any given day, under normal

Edison Company linemen use a "shepherd's hook" tool to install a 500,000-volt insulator on Pacific Intertie tower.
ARTHUR ADAMS PHOTO.

Massive thyristors at Sylmar Converter Station change direct current back to alternating current.
COURTESY LOS ANGELES D.W.P.

225

It Makes Sense to Them

Conversations around the Edison Company, whether they be between members of a line crew, generation plant personnel or a group of engineers, are studded with a colorful jargon that is crusty and to the point, and not always printable. Confusing to the outsider and newcomer, this vernacular of equipment nicknames, descriptions of engineering concepts and colloquialisms is a verbal shorthand used to replace complicated technical terms.

A line crew will have a "tailboard" (job discussion) before starting work to discuss in detail what is to be accomplished. A typical conversation between a lineman and a groundman might sound like this:

"We've got to hang this bug back there on the property line and we'll need the old man, two redheads, two blankets and the vaseline. We also need two snakes and a nose bag. Don't forget to mount the cathead on the truck." Translated this would mean, "We are going to install this transformer on the rear property line and we will need a transformer A-frame, two temporary by-pass jumpers, two rubber insulation protective blankets and the connector grease. We also need two rubber insulation protective line coverings and a material bag. Don't forget to install the capstan winch drum on the truck."

One tower of Edison's growing network of 500KV lines stands sentinel in Cajon Pass in the winter of 1973.
T. M. HOTCHKISS PHOTO.

This Calectric line truck from 1955 carried all of the tools and gear spread out before it. Everything has a special nickname in the lineman's jargon.
EDISON COLLECTION.

The D. C. line and the Sylmar Converter Station suffered severe damage as a result of the 1971 earthquake, but power service continued over the relatively undamaged A. C. network.
COURTESY LOS ANGELES D.W.P.

Furious winds from a winter storm toppled nine towers of the 500KV A. C. Pacific Intertie line near Tracy, California, on December 22, 1982, causing brief power outages all over the state.
COURTESY PACIFIC GAS AND ELECTRIC COMPANY.

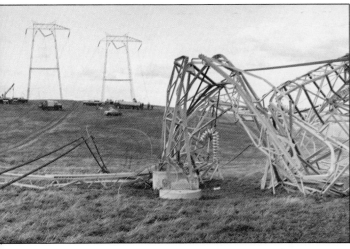

successfully coped with every disturbance that has occurred, including several considerably more severe than the one that caused the infamous Northeast Blackout in November 1965.

The first big test of WSCC's integrated bulk power system planning came early in 1971. Late in January, severe ice storms hit the Pacific Northwest. Extreme cold weather placed the highest demand ever recorded upon the power systems of that region, at a time of year when their tremendous hydroelectric generating capacity was at its lowest ebb. Utilizing the Pacific Intertie, the Edison Company and other California utilities generated electricity and sent it to the power-short Northwest. Even when a storm toppled towers on the A.C. lines, the undamaged D.C. line, on a separate right-of-way a hundred miles to the east, continued carrying the vital flow of power northward.

Just a few weeks later, only days after the damaged A.C. towers in the Northwest had been repaired, the great Sylmar Earthquake struck Southern California. The February 9,

The most significant test of WSCC's work came on December 22, 1982. At 4:29 p.m., major energy deliveries from Bonneville Dam to California's utilities were interrupted when cyclonic winds from an arctic storm downed nine towers on both of the 500,000-volt A.C. Pacific Intertie lines, near Tracy, California. In order to prevent a major blackout from cascading through the West, Edison temporarily severed connections with most neighboring utilities and also briefly interrupted power to scattered blocks of its own customers.

By firing standby units at its own plants, and by purchasing power from other Western utilities as system interconnections were restored on the surviving undamaged WSCC interties, Edison was able to resume service to most of its customers within an hour. With order restored on its own system, Edison then began supplying energy to its northern neighbor, Pacific Gas and Electric Company, whose system was especially hard hit by the storm. This was the worst system disturbance to threaten California's utilities since WSCC was formed. Although the problem was widespread

circumstances, Western utility systems operate in parallel, resulting in a unified system where available generation is shared with any who need it.

Most importantly, the WSCC has made significant progress in its efforts to assure the reliability of the interconnected bulk power systems, in order to prevent the "cascading effect" that has upon occasion resulted in widespread power failures in other regions of the nation. Consequently, the system has

1971, temblor extensively damaged the 800,000-volt D.C. line's terminal substation at Sylmar. Power flowing over the virtually undamaged 500,000-volt A.C. intertie lines helped the systems of Edison and City of Los Angeles to remain stable during the critical minutes following the quake. Because damage to the Sylmar Converter Station was so extensive, the D.C. line remained out of service for a year, but the A.C. lines maintained the essential exchanges of energy for the WSCC network.

and severe, service was quickly restored to virtually all customers, including not just Edison's, but those of other affected utilities, thanks to the Bulk Power Network and WSCC's emergency planning.

The Edison Company is proud of its role in creating these aluminum "highways" for the exchange of energy throughout the West, a reflection of the Western tradition of being a good neighbor.

Edison's Wind Energy Center near Palm Springs, in 1981. COURTESY LOS ANGELES TIMES.

The Alternative Energies

Throughout its history, the Southern California Edison Company has perceived its role to be that of provider of a reliable supply of electric energy in any amount, at any time, to its customers. Since its earliest days, and especially during the period of rapid growth following World War Two, economies of scale in the construction of new facilities benefitted Edison's consumers by helping to hold down rates and offset the effects of inflation, while at the same time adding the new capacity needed to serve a growing demand for electric power.

Since 1970, however, a great change in social and economic values has taken place, which has resulted in a tremendous impact upon the operations and business philosophy of the Company. The emergence of environmental awareness, the prolonged public debate over nuclear power, the petroleum fuel shortages of the mid-Seventies, and the international political and economic instability that resulted, all helped to bring about a corporate and a public awareness of the need for greater environmental protection, as well as to conserve national energy resources and to manage existing electrical loads more wisely.

It comes as a surprise to many to learn that Edison's concern over the environment pre-dates by decades the "eco-movement" of the Seventies. Back in 1947, before the word "smog" even had been invented, Edison became the first utility in the nation to begin a program of smoke abatement and air pollution control. Early in those postwar years, the dismantling of the region's once-great electric rail rapid transit network and its replacement with the automobile, coupled with the rapid population increases and industrial expansion in the "South Coast Air Basin," caused a great increase in that brownish, eye-stinging air pollution that came to be known as smog.

The conditions that caused smog were not at first understood. Power plants and other oil-burning industries, rather than gasoline and diesel engined vehicles, were believed to be the primary culprits for the type of air pollution then predominant. In 1947, the first smoke abatement laws and county "smog" ordinances

were passed, which were aimed at oil-burning facilities. The Company had begun its big postwar steam plant construction program, and these new plants primarily would burn oil, because natural gas was available to Edison only on a short-term, interruptible basis. Thus, Edison voluntarily began a research effort directed at reducing visible emissions and sulfur dioxide, using laboratory-scale techniques.

Using information in part obtained from Edison power plants, noted authority Dr. A. J. Haagen-Smit of CalTech identified the conditions that caused photochemical smog. He also discovered that motor vehicles were the primary source of pollutants. Nonetheless, county agencies found it too politically sensitive to go after the automobile. Instead, in 1955, with the smog problem becoming critical in Los Angeles, the Air Pollution Control

Unit No. 3 at Alamitos Generating Station, showing the experimental bag filter house built in the early 1960s.
EDISON COLLECTION.

District threatened to issue no further permits for power plant operation. Fortunately, the clear need to maintain electric services forestalled that action.

In June 1956, Dr. Haagen-Smit was retained by the Edison Company to conduct full-scale research into smog abatement. This was the pioneer effort in the industry. Based at Edison's El Segundo Steam Station, Dr. Haagen-Smit with the assistance of Company engineers developed pollution control technologies that since have been adopted nationwide, including two-stage combustion boilers (1957), electrostatic precipitators for oil (1956), and coal (1963), and bag filterhouses (1957). At this time, the team also developed the catalytic converter, which, while not used on power plants, has since seen wide use in automobiles.

Dr. Haagen-Smit retired in 1963. Six years later, using techniques and tools not available earlier, Edison researchers working with a consultant

The Ellwood Energy Support Facility near Santa Barbara houses a gas-turbine unit and features an aesthetic low-profile design.
EDISON COLLECTION.

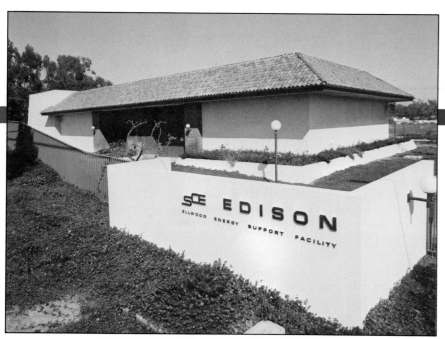

230

developed the "off-stoichiometric combustion boiler," which proved to be the most successful technology to date in reducing air pollution resulting from burning oil. An important, if short-term, step was also taken by chemically lowering the sulfur and ash content of the oil fuels burned. As a result of these efforts, in 1982, the South Coast Air Quality Management District estimated that Edison power plants produced less than 2 percent of the smog-forming air pollutants created in the air basin they monitor.

Edison crews install new Dreyfus-designed 220KV towers in El Segundo.
EDISON COLLECTION.

Perhaps the aspect of electric system aesthetics of greatest interest to the individual is the undergrounding of new and existing distribution lines. Although Edison had operated in an underground distribution network in downtown Los Angeles before 1900, overhead technology was preferred wherever permitted, because of the high cost of underground installations and the comparative unreliability of underground cable technology. By 1963, however, development of new cables utilizing "space-age" insulating materials, and Edison's acceptance of a safe pad-mounted transformer design, enabled extensive undergrounding of new construction sites to begin. The cost of underground service installations was further reduced by the invention of aluminum cables with cross-linked polyethylene insulation. To supplement this effort, in 1965, Edison, working with local community leaders, commenced a long-range program to place underground many miles of existing overhead distribution lines.

Other environmental efforts in which Edison has been involved include the operation of a fish hatchery at Big Creek, with its attendant

While air pollution has been of prime concern since World War Two, Edison men and women have worked to solve other environmentally-related problems as well. Aesthetic treatment of facilities dated back to the early 1920s, when substations were designed to harmonize

architecturally with their neighborhoods, but received new impetus in the Seventies with the use of landscaping to augment distinctive architecture. Land beneath Company transmission lines has been made available for other uses, primarily farming and recreation. The towers themselves have been redesigned for greater eye-appeal. In 1968, nationally known industrial designer, the late Henry Dreyfuss, worked with Edison engineers to produce the nation's first aesthetic transmission tower design, examples of which were first installed in El Segundo.

responsibility to restock certain reservoirs, and a tree farm and seedling planting program carried out in conjunction with Company-owned forest lands near Shaver Lake. Marine studies begun in 1954 have harmonized the existence of the Company's coastal power plants with the marine ecology. Today, a staff of geologists, botanists, biologists, and archaeologists investigate in advance of major facilities construction, to minimize interference with ecosystems and to prevent possible damage to sites of pre-historic human habitation.

The 1968 removal of distribution poles from Euclid Avenue in Ontario done as part of Edison's undergrounding program.
JOSEPH O. FADLER PHOTO.

In the early 1970s, as new power plants became more difficult to construct because of environmental concerns and regulatory delays, the Edison Company became the first major utility in the nation to discontinue all promotional advertising and replace it with conservation messages aimed at reducing the overall consumption of electricity. This move at first surprised the industry and drew skepticism from many environmentalists, but it was soon seen to be a firm commitment based upon sound business judgement. If Southern California's population continued to grow, albeit at a slower rate of increase, yet few new power plants could be constructed because of conditions beyond the Company's control, then the most realistic course was to reduce per-capita consumption of energy. In the short term, this conservation effort would delay the need for new generating capacity and forestall possible energy shortages, while in the long run such practices would conserve dwindling fuel resources.

While the message of "Make Every Kilowatt Count" was spreading through Southern California, another concept was being expressed, especially to large industrial power consumers. Called "load management," the term simply referred to the practice of shifting the demand for electricity away from those hours of the day when electric power is used most. By spreading the use of electricity more evenly throughout the day, the need to build new generating units is deferred. Small early power systems frequently practiced this technique, but it had become unnecessary when huge new power plants were built in the Twenties.

There was yet another reason for these conservation and load management programs. In 1970, about 80 percent of Edison's electricity was generated by burning oil. During the tumultuous decade of the Seventies, because of the actions of the O.P.E.C. cartel, the price of imported fuel oils increased over *twelve hundred percent*, from $2.46 per barrel in 1970 to $32.16 in 1980! At the same time, the

Edison marine biologists review the growth of lobsters grown under the mariculture program.
Edison Collection.

By the time the California Public Utilities Commission ordered other utilities in the state to develop conservation programs, Edison's voluntary effort had proven successful enough to serve as a role model. More to the point, when the Arab Oil Embargo of 1973 caused a serious fuel shortage throughout the nation, the Edison Company weathered the crisis better than many utilities, in part because of its ongoing conservation efforts.

inflation rate in the United States' economy surged ahead into double digits. These external factors, over which Edison had no control, inexorably drove up the cost of electricity in a spiral without precedent in the history of the industry. Fortunately, most Edison customers, residential and industrial alike, saw conservation and load management techniques as a way to mitigate the impact of energy cost increases.

The 1970s proved to be an unpleasant decade for both the Edison Company and its customers, but there were positive results from the turmoil of those years. Thanks to comprehensive conservation and load management programs that were well received by utility customers, in part to changing economic conditions, and in part to increased availability of natural gas and purchased power, by 1982 Edison had reduced its use of oil fuel to the point where only 4 percent of its energy was derived from that source. Furthermore, insofar as the Company's new plant construction was essentially limited to completing San Onofre Units Nos. 2 and 3, the building of which required just over ten years because of various regulatory delays, the commitment to conservation and load management programs by all classes of customers helped Southern California to weather the period without service capacity shortages.

During the Seventies, these efforts were augmented by an intensification of the Edison Company's ongoing research and development program to find alternative methods of generating electricity in the large quantities required by Southern California's large population. On October 17, 1980, just less than a decade after the nation's utilities had been surprised by Edison's adoption of conservation programs, Chairman of the Board William R. Gould stunned them with an announcement of another major policy shift:

Keeping drier lint traps clean is but one of many easy conservation steps that can be taken at home.
EDISON COLLECTION.

"As a result of some significant successes in a number of research and development areas", Mr. Gould stated, "the Company now believes that some forms of power generation which a few years ago were speculative or unproven have progressed to the point that they can be aggressively developed and relied upon to provide a significant part of the electricity to supply the additional needs of our customers later this decade."

Each individual's energy conservation efforts are important steps toward national energy independence. This helps to reduce consumption of costly imported fuel oil until alternative generation technologies can be developed.
EDISON COLLECTION.

The Bendix-Schachle wind turbine in 1983.
EDISON COLLECTION.

As a result of this, Gould announced that, of the new generation capacity to be added by 1990, one-third, about 1.9 million kilowatts, would be from plants using so-called alternate and renewable technologies. Mr. Gould added that these technologies included wind power, geothermal, solar, fuel cells, cogeneration and hydroelectric generation, and noted that nuclear power and coal would still provide a substantial part of the balance of new energy requirements.

Cogeneration, the utilization of a single fuel to produce both process steam and electricity, is a concept that dates back to the early days of the utility industry, when some private industrial power plants occasionally put power into utility grids. It will be recalled how, during the drought of 1924, some of these private plants, although long unused, were reactivated to help meet the energy shortfall. It was not long afterward, however, that in many parts of the country, such facilities were rendered obsolete by the reliability, availability, and very low cost of utility-supplied energy. This not-withstanding, on February 17, 1967, a modern version of the cogeneration concept reappeared

on the Edison system, when a facility to produce 12,000-kilowatts of electricity concurrently with making steam for paper recycling was built at the Garden State Paper Company in Pomona. Since 1980, additional cogeneration plants have been built in conjunction with paper manufacturing, milk processing, oil refining, landfill gas recovery, cement and chemical production, and even with the heating and cooling of classrooms and residential condominiums.

This boiler at the Garden State Paper Company was Edison's first industrial cogeneration installation in modern times. It produces up to 80,000 pounds of steam per hour from waste heat exhausted from an adjacent 12,000-kilowatt gas-turbine generator.
EDISON COLLECTION.

The wind has been harnessed as a motive power for at least two thousand years. The use of wind turbines to generate power had been proposed many times in the electric era, but despite several small installations on the East Coast, as late as 1970, no serious consideration was given to applying wind generation to commercial power grids. Late in 1975, however, the Edison Company identified the Beaumont Pass-Palm Springs areas as a potential wind resource area, having enough days of winds of sufficient velocity to make large-scale generation feasible. Edison and the United States Department of Energy (DOE) jointly monitored wind speeds in the area from 1976 until 1978, at which time Edison, satisfied with the resulting data, established a wind energy center adjacent to its Devers Substation, eight miles north of Palm Springs.

Utilizing a design developed by inventor Charles Schachle, the nation's largest experimental wind turbine ever to be connected to a commercial power system went into operation in December 1980. The 165-foot high, horizontal axis, three-bladed turbine was initially rated at 3,000 kilowatts. After

The original 500-kilowatt Darrieus vertical-axis wind turbine dominates this 1981 view of the Wind Energy Center.
ARTHUR ADAMS PHOTO.

but smaller, and with control and braking design improvements, was placed into service. These tests indicated that wind turbines producing up to 1,000 kilowatts could be commercially feasible, depending upon reliability of the wind.

A second part of the Edison Company's wind resource development plans called for the encouragement of private entrepreneurs to participate in joint Wind Park projects. In these parks, it was proposed that the developer would

One important modification to the Schachle wind turbine was the installation of new blades in 1982.
EDISON COLLECTION.

modification to overcome design flaws, the unit was rerated to generate 1,300 kilowatts in a 30-mile-per-hour wind. Early in 1981, a second wind turbine, of the distinctive appearing Darrieus vertical axis "egg-beater" design, was constructed alongside the earlier unit. This 500-kilowatt machine seemed promising, but on April 3, 1981, destroyed itself during acceptance testing, when overspeed relays and an automatic braking system malfunctioned. Subsequently, a third wind turbine generator, similar to the second unit

own and finance construction of the wind turbines, with Edison providing technical support, interconnection services and other non-financial help as needed. Edison also guaranteed to purchase the full output of each Wind Park at prices that proved to be competitive. The first "wind farm" was built near Tehachapi late in 1981. The Wind Park concept proved so successful that Edison planned to achieve a significant portion of its 1990 wind generation capacity using this concept.

235

The Wind Farmers

Remote, windy Tehachapi Pass, once home to cattle ranchers, saw a new type of farmer in the early 1980s, the "wind farmer" who generated electricity from the heavy winds which blow through the area. Tall towers with multi-bladed propellers or eggbeater-like vanes began to dot the remote hilltops around the pass as a new generation of farmer-entrepreneur, in partnership with the Southern California Edison Company, utilized this modern version of an ancient technology.

Spawned in part by the Edison Company's strong commitment to develop alternative and renewable generation resources, in part by provisions of the Public Utility Regulatory Policies Act of 1978, and in part by passage of state and federal tax credits, the development of so-called "wind farms" proceeded to the point where by mid-1983, Edison had more than 20,000 kilowatts of wind turbine generation capacity in operation and contracts in place for more than 200,000 kilowatts of additional capacity from "wind farms" depending upon wind conditions.

In a novel departure from past industry practices, Edison does not itself own all of this capacity, but rather, in many cases purchases the output of wind turbine generators owned by others. The wind farmers are individual entrepreneurs or groups of investors who put up the money to erect the turbines while Edison provided technical support and power interconnection services. These small power producers, as the wind farmers are officially named, have demonstrated that even in our complex modern society, there is room for individuals with creativity.

236

"Blue Max" (modified Merkham) horizontal axis 50-kilowatt wind turbine at American Wind Energy Systems facility.
EDISON COLLECTION.

The Transpower Wind Farm.
EDISON COLLECTION.

In the 1960s, it was assumed that all cost-effective hydroelectric generation sites in California had been developed, or protected from development by environmental regulations. Hydro power, once Edison's most important resource, was thought to have been relegated to an ever-diminishing "back seat" as energy demands climbed. In an apparent confirmation of this belief, by 1980 hydro generation accounted for only 6 percent of total energy production, despite the fact that the 916,000 kilowatts of owned capacity available was the greatest in the Company's history. As fuel prices rose, however, small hydro development and even so-called "micro hydro" projects once again became cost effective. Some new hydro capacity was gained from a turbine reconstruction program which began in December of 1981, where each of the Big Creek units was rebuilt to improve its efficiency. The first micro hydro project involved placing a small turbine at the lower end of the Metropolitan Water District pipeline supplying the City of La Habra with domestic water. This having proven successful, experimental units involving special low-cost designs were installed in the Avalon water system on Catalina Island, and in the fish water release

Wind turbines at the Zond "Victory Garden" near Tehachapi, 1983.
EDISON COLLECTION.

A micro-hydro installation: this 30 kilowatt generator was added to existing pipes in the Avalon water system operated by Edison.
EDISON COLLECTION.

system at Shaver Lake; others, aggregating 90,000 kilowatts of additional capacity, were contracted for installation by 1990.

Even large hydro was found not to be dead after all. Work began in 1983 on the Balsam Meadows Plant at Big Creek, where 200,000 kilowatts of energy would be developed from the water flowing from Huntington Lake to Shaver Lake through an existing tunnel system. Interestingly, this was on the sites of old Big Creek Plants No. 5 and No. 6, proposed in the master plan of the Twenties.

A 25-kilowatt Jay Carter horizontal axis wind turbine near Tehachapi.
EDISON COLLECTION.

A fifth unit, of 38,000 kilowatts capacity, was added to Big Creek Plant No. 3 in 1981.
Edison Collection.

Edison's interest in geothermal energy production dates back to 1964, when the purchase of the California Electric Power Company brought potential geothermal resource areas into Edison service territory for the first time. Historically, however, Calectric's predecessor, the Southern Sierras Power Company, had thought enough of the technology to have one of its engineers survey potential sites back in 1924 and 1925. As a result, three geothermal steam wells were drilled in 1927 near Niland at the edge of the Salton Sea, but the project proved unsuccessful. In 1962, Calectric began examining the possibility of building a 15,000-kilowatt geothermal plant at Casa Diablo, near Mammoth. Edison continued this investigation after the merger, and expanded it to include test wells drilled near Mono Lake.

The area where Edison's first geothermal generation was to appear was far to the south, however, at Brawley. In July 1978, Edison and the Union Oil Company entered into an agreement to design, construct and operate an experimental 10,000-kilowatt geothermal plant at a site two miles north of Brawley, where

Just prior to the merger with Edison, Calectric began exploring the feasibility of generating power from geothermal steam at Casa Diablo, near Mammoth, California. Edison continued research at this site until the late 1970s.
Edison Collection.

unsuccessful oil drilling had disclosed instead the existence of hot geothermal brines. Union was to drill the wells, recover the steam and reinject the waste brines, while Edison was to operate the power plant. Successful utilization of this resource required the invention of separation techniques to remove chemical brines and other impurities from the geothermal steam. The Brawley plant began operation in July 1980. No previous geothermal plant anywhere had been faced with the potential for corrosion such as was

Edison drilled another exploration well for geothermal steam on the shore of Mono Lake in 1968.
Arthur Adams Photo.

encountered at Brawley, and the successful solution of this problem opened up new prospects for geothermal development. Building upon this technology, a second 10,000-kilowatt unit was dedicated near Niland, in January 1983, at a site not far from where Southern Sierras had drilled its wells back in 1927.

Although a comparatively inefficient technology existed in the Nineteenth Century to convert coal to gas, it was quickly abandoned following the introduction of low-cost natural gas. The petroleum fuel shortages of the 1970s rekindled interest, however, as utilities saw it as a way to derive a clean burning fuel from the nation's abundant coal reserves. Success of a pilot plant late in the decade led Edison and Texaco, Inc. to form a partnership to build a full-scale facility. In December 1981, construction began at a site next to Edison's existing Cool Water Generating Station near Daggett, of the nation's first commercial coal gasification plant and combined-cycle generating station. At this plant, the manufactured gas is burned in jet engine-like gas turbine generators to produce the first

output of electricity; then the exhaust heat from the turbines is cycled through special "waste heat recovery boilers" which, as in a conventional steam plant, produce steam to operate another turbogenerator, producing a second output of energy. Although not completed at the time this book went to press, the Cool Water Project has drawn world-wide interest.

The Brawley Geothermal **239**
Plant, 1981.
EDISON COLLECTION.

Highly saline geothermal fluids are run through complex piping to extract steam to generate 10,000 kilowatts of electricity at the Brawley Geothermal Plant.
EDISON COLLECTION.

Drilling in Hell's Kitchen

H. N. Siegfried was an engineer with the Southern Sierras Power Company whose responsibilities included development of new markets and new generation resources. In 1925, he submitted a series of reports to the Power Company's management that summarized his investigations into a revolutionary concept, that of tapping naturally occurring steam zones to generate electricity. Siegfried knew of the pioneering work in geothermal power development already done in Larderello, Italy, and was also aware that some consideration was being given to a similar project at The Geysers in Sonoma County, California.

As a result of Siegfried's reports and field work, the Southern Sierras Power Company decided to further explore this new technology. The engineer was made president of the Frontier Development Company, a subsidiary created specifically to drill geothermal wells at Mullet Island, an extinct volcano whose cone, sometimes an island, at others a peninsula, rose above the fluctuating waters of the Salton Sea near Niland.

Captain Charles Davis, owner of Mullet Island, had built upon it a home he called "Hell's Kitchen." When the Southern Sierras Power Company's engineers and drillers arrived to begin work, they learned why that name had been chosen. Braving summertime temperatures hovering around 120° F., enduring plagues of mosquitoes and scorpions, and making do with only the most primitive of facilities, the crews drilled a test well and then another deeper well. In October 1927, Well No. 2 produced steam in such quantity as to cause a blowout similar to an oilwell "gusher" before it became plugged up. A third well also produced steam and corrosive brines.

Therein lay the problem. Steam was there to be sure, but so were brines, corrosive beyond

the ability of then available metallurgy to deal with. Such corrosion would quickly destroy steam turbines and so the decision was reluctantly made to abandon the Mullet Island Project, the first serious attempt by an American utility company to develop geothermal power. It is appropriate that today, just a couple of miles away from the Mullet Island site, lies Southern California Edison's Niland Geothermal Project.

Other unique energy generation methods that the Edison Company has investigated as part of its research and development program include biomass or "trash power," fuel cells, methanol fuels, solar salt ponds, solar parabolic dish and trough generation and solar photovoltaic technologies. Although not all may prove commercially feasible, the widespread attention drawn to them by Edison's research work is causing improvements to be made that are making them more cost effective as time passes.

One technology whose time has come is that of solar-thermal generation. Long scoffed at as unrealistic, a solar thermal plant utilizing tracking mirrors to focus the sunlight came to be looked at seriously in the mid-1970s. The Edison Company, in partnership with the Los Angeles Department of Water and Power and the U.S. Department of Energy, started construction of a 10,000-kilowatt plant near the Cool Water Generating Station in September of 1979.

Edison engineers viewing an experimental solar trough.
Edison Collection.

The plant, named "Solar One" because it was the nation's first commercial solar-thermal power plant, produced its first energy in April 1982. In operation, Solar One uses more than 1800 computer-controlled tracking mirrors to reflect and concentrate sunlight onto a 300-foot high central receiver and boiler tower, where steam is produced that generates electricity as in a conventional plant. An innovative thermal storage system allows up to 7,000 kilowatts of limited energy production to take place after sunset, or on cloudy days. So successful was

A photovoltaic panel on the roof of Edison's Rosemead building has provided valuable data on the weather resistance of panel design.
Edison Collection.

Solar One's 1,818 heliostats continuously track the sun and are controlled by this computer.
JOSEPH O. FADLER PHOTO.

The receiver (boiler) glows brilliantly during aceptance tests at Solar One in April, 1982.
EDISON COLLECTION.

Solar One under construction, 1981.
EDISON COLLECTION.

Solar One that late in 1982 Edison began design work on a larger commercial unit nicknamed "Solar 100," planned to go into service by 1990.

The depth and success of the Edison Company's commitment to alternative and renewable generation resources can be measured by the fact that, at the end of 1982, only two years after the policy was announced, the Company already utilized a combination of eight primary resources to produce

electricity—oil, gas, wind, geothermal, coal, nuclear, solar and water—more than any other electric utility in the world. Whether old standbys such as hydro, or newcomers like solar, these technologies offer a promise of adequate energy in the years ahead.

A significant public recognition of the Edison Company's commitment to alternative and renewable generation technologies came on

August 18, 1981. On that day, Edison became the first corporation ever to win the prestigious "John and Alice Tyler Ecology-Energy Award." Endowed by John Tyler, the late Chairman of the Farmers Insurance Group, and his wife, Alice, the Tyler Prize had previously been awarded only to individuals. The prize

Mr. Gould also cited other examples of the Company's involvement in environmental research, clearly demonstrating how Edison had been concerned about the environment long before such care became fashionable as a movement.

Another award symbolized the impact the Company's efforts have had upon the utility industry in general. On June 8, 1983, it was announced that Southern California Edison had been given the prestigious Thomas A. Edison Award for 1982. Originally endowed back in 1922 by retiring General Electric Chairman Charles A. Coffin, a long-time associate of Thomas Edison, the medal was to honor "distinguished contributions to the development of electric light and power for the convenience of the public." Named the Charles Coffin Medal at first, recipients were chosen by the National Electric Light Association, the forerunner of today's Edison Electric Institute, a nationwide association of investor-owned utility companies and manufacturers. In 1947, the one-hundredth anniversary of the birth of Thomas Edison, the medal was renamed in honor of the great pioneer.

At the Solar House in Montebello, California, Edison technicians experimented with various residential solar and conservation technologies.
EDISON COLLECTION.

selection committee for 1981 was so impressed by the scope and depth of the Edison Company's concern about the environment, however, that they took the unprecedented step of designating a corporate recipient.

During ceremonies accepting the Tyler Prize, Edison Chairman William R. Gould pointed out that one of the earlier Prize-winners, the late Dr. A. J. Haagen-Smit, had conducted some of his pioneering smog research in facilities and with funds provided by the Edison Company.

This author believes it appropriate that the Southern California Edison Company has won this award more often than any other utility in the nation. Edison was the first recipient of the medal in 1922, and won it again in 1944, 1963, and in 1982, clearly demonstrating that its peers, too, believe Edison to be a company of creativity and innovation.

In accepting the Edison Medal, Chairman William Gould offered an observation which well summarizes the history of the Company and its predecessors over the past century:

"This recognition is the result of the dedication and productivity of Edison employees I am proud to express appreciation for your efforts in helping Southern California Edison meet today's complex challenges. In our technological society, electricity is as basic a commodity of life as food or water, and the Company remains committed to providing an adequate and reliable supply for its customers. I am confident that, utilizing a long and proud employee tradition of innovation and creativity, the Edison Company will continue to live up to its long-time motto of 'Good Service, Square Dealing and Courteous Treatment'."

The new Rosemead General Office was completed in 1971.
JOSEPH O. FADLER PHOTO.

245

The Southern California Edison Company has won the prestigious Thomas A. Edison Award more times than any other utility. The gold medals signifying the 1982 award (left) and the 1963 award (center) are displayed next to the Charles A. Coffin Medal won in 1922. The 1944 Award was not a medal due to wartime shortages.
JOSEPH O. FADLER PHOTO.

Combined construction force for gas system and underground electric system of the Edison Electric Company, about 1909.
EDISON COLLECTION.

Bibliography

For reasons of space, it was not possible to include a complete bibliography of all sources consulted by the author. Any serious researcher desiring such information is invited to contact the author by writing to him in care of the publisher: Interurban Press, P. O. Box 6444, Glendale, California, 91205.

For further reading, the following books are recommended:

Anderson, David N., and Beverly A. Hall, editors. *Geothermal Exploration in the First Quarter Century*. Geothermal Resources Council Special Report No. 3. No place or publisher noted, 1973.

Bush, Elsie R. *The Big Creek Album: Yesterday and Today*. Coarsegold, California: Dale L. and Elsie R. Bush, (1982).

Coleman, Charles M. *P. G. and E. of California, The Centennial Story of Pacific Gas and Electric Company, 1852-1952.* New York: McGraw-Hill, 1952.

Glenn, Myron. *Sierra Nevada Interlude: A Pictorial Reminiscence of 57 Years in the Sierra.* Big Creek, Calif.: Myron W. Glenn, 1975.

Gorowitz, Bernard, editor-in-chief. *A Century of Progress, the General Electric Story.* Schenectady: Hall of History Foundation, 1981.

Hammond, John Winthrop. *Men and Volts: the Story of General Electric.* New York: Lippincott, 1941.

Johnston, Hank. *The Railroad That Lighted Southern California.* Los Angeles: Trans-Anglo Books, 1966.

Kennedy, Samuel M. *Winning the Public.* Second edition. New York: McGraw-Hill, 1921.

Lofberg, Lila, and David Malcolmson. *Sierra Outpost.* New York: Duell, Sloan and Pearce, 1941.

Outland, Charles. *Man-Made Disaster, The Story of St. Francis Dam.* Revised edition. Glendale, Calif.: The Arthur H. Clark Company, 1977.

Peterman, L. S. *Ventura County Kilowatts, A Story of Electric Generation.* Brochure reprinting article from Ventura County Historical Society *Quarterly*, May and August, 1959. Ventura: Ventura County Historical Society, 1959.

Redinger, David H. *The Story of Big Creek.* Second edition. Los Angeles: Angelus Press, 1952.

Redinger, Edith I. *The Other Half.* Santa Barbara: Privately Printed, 1977.

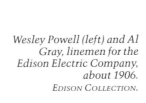

Southern Sierras' storekeeper G.F. Grunwald in his office, 1915.
EDISON COLLECTION.

Wesley Powell (left) and Al Gray, linemen for the Edison Electric Company, about 1906.
EDISON COLLECTION.

Local staff at the Long Beach office, about 1908.
Edison Collection.

Index

I Thank You